Sarah & the Senator

Sarah &

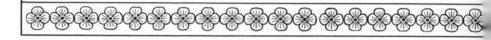

the Senator

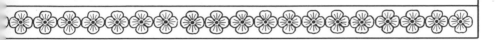

by ROBERT H.
KRONINGER

Howell-North · Berkeley, California
1964

Printed and bound in the United States of America.
Library of Congress Catalogue Card No. 64-7522

Published by Howell-North Books
1050 Parker Street, Berkeley, California 94710

2001.10

INTRODUCTION

Portions of the narrative which follows were submitted to several friends and associates while it was still in preparation. They invariably asked three questions, the first two of which were fortunately advanced before reading the manuscript, the last after learning something of the people and events with which it is concerned. The answers to these questions are offered by way of introduction in anticipation of possible similar queries by others.

The first question asked was "What is it about?"

It is about a number of uncommon people who lived in San Francisco in the 1880's and the effect of the litigation they inspired: Civil suits ranging from divorce to libel and slander; criminal prosecutions ranging from adultery, perjury, and larceny to murder; and all this accompanied by myriad contempt of court citations and *habeas corpus* writs. These actions plagued both state and federal courts for nearly ten years. They were responsible for at least 14 appeals to California's highest court and nine proceedings in the federal circuit court. Three times they found their way to the Supreme Court of the United States.

Jurisprudence eschews superlatives or absolutes and so I will only say further that the peculiar conjunction of time, place, and persons provided the formula for a series of events which, if not unique in America's history, were fortunately rarely duplicated.

The second question was, "Why did you write it?" This legitimate if inelegant query comes mainly because my previous literary efforts have been limited to occasional technical legal writings.

This book is the product of several years' effort to appease my own curiosity. Few law students complete their training without exposure to one or more of the judicial decisions which were the effluence of the Sharon litigation. My introduction came in that way, and after admission to the bar I continued

5

to encounter various segments of that fertile dispute. Each new discovery amplified my curiosity about the people who precipitated such a broad spectrum of legal jousts.

Judicial opinions rarely give full exposition to the background of the litigation, however, and a collection of the twenty-odd published court decisions provided only a skeleton. It was necessary to go to the trial records themselves, and to other contemporary sources, mainly newspapers, to begin to give form to the actors and the events. They proved to be real people, if unusual and sometimes bizarre, capable of humor, anger, sorrow, hate and all of the emotions which shape the destinies of the rest of us.

Trial records are not to be confused with judicial decisions which are preserved in the law books for use as legal precedent. The stenographic record of testimony and court proceedings on which the decisions are based is transcribed only when a decision is appealed. Since so many of the actions reported in this book were appealed, thousands of pages of trial records were transcribed and often printed. The great 1906 fire destroyed those kept in San Francisco and it seemed it might be necessary to search out Supreme Court records in Sacramento to determine what had been said in the presence of the judges whose decisions in these cases are now legal history. The diligence of the staff of the Alameda County Law Library brought to light printed copies of the trial records which had been received and preserved in my own back yard, so to speak, the Courthouse in Oakland.

This book is written in the hope that others will be as interested in the people and events involved in these cases as I have been. The litigation which they spawned was worthy of them. They presented to the courts a wide variety of novel factual and legal problems, a number of which had never before been confronted. While few were of large scope, the courts' solutions to many of them still color and some yet control the law of the subjects with which they dealt.

They were difficult cases for the courts. A legal adage holds that hard cases make bad law. But adages are only sometimes

true and though such unique contests as the Sharon affair
sometimes induce awkward judicial postures, it is a tribute to
the stability of American jurisprudence that it has been able
to accommodate itself to them. I hope that the occasional legal
discussions will also be found of interest.

The third and last question, asked after reading the manuscript was, "How much of this is true?"

All of it is true. All of the actors existed. Each said everything he is quoted as having said, none is represented to have
said or done anything that was not done or said, nor are motives
surmised or supplied. Every act and every statement is supported by contemporary records. The only license taken has
been sometimes to omit the usual distracting symbols for dele-
tions within quotations; but no such omissions have been permitted to change the sense of what was said.

All of the events depicted in this book are supported by
contemporary documents. For making them available, I thank
the Alameda County Law Library, the Alameda Free Library,
the Bancroft Library at the University of California, the Oakland Public Library, the San Francisco Public Library and the
archives of the Supreme Court of the State of California.

Footnotes are inserted occasionally, at the risk of irritating
those who have no interest in them but who find their eyes
drawn irresistibly to the bottom of the page. To those of a
strong will and lack of interest in legal citations or expositions I
suggest that they be ignored. Nothing useful to the narrative
will thereby be lost.

ROBERT HENRY KRONINGER

Berkeley, California

July, 1964

How small
of all
That human hearts endure,
That part which laws and
Kings can cause or cure.

Samuel Johnson

TABLE OF CONTENTS

Chapter

9

LIST OF ILLUSTRATIONS

CHRONOLOGY AND CITATIONS OF MAIN CASES

The events of this story center around two main cases based on actions brought in the state and federal courts respectively. Participants in these cases probably found the many actions based on the same subject matter quite confusing. The public which followed their progress through the journals of the time certainly must have been bewildered. The reader of today may find them easier to follow with the aid of a simple chronology.

Sarah's divorce action was brought in the courts of California and referred to as *Sharon* v. *Sharon,* and progressed over a seven-year period as follows:

November 1, 1883: Complaint filed in Superior Court.

March 10, 1884: Trial begins.

December 24, 1884: Judge Sullivan renders his decision.

June 29-December 31, 1885: California Supreme Court considers motions to stay proceedings and to dismiss appeal. (67 Cal. 185, 215, 220 [7 Pac. 456, 635]; 68 Cal. 326 [9 Pac. 187]).

January 31, 1888: State Supreme Court decision on appeal from the judgment. (75 Cal. 1 [16 Pac. 345]).

July 17, 1889: Decision on appeal from order denying new trial. (79 Cal. 633 [22 Pac. 26]).

June 10, 1890: Decision on appeal from cost and alimony order. (84 Cal. 424 [23 Pac. 1100]).

The Senator brought suit in United States federal court asking that Sarah be enjoined from using the marriage contract as a basis for action against him. This action was entitled *Sharon* v. *Hill.*

October 3, 1883: Suit filed.

March 3, 1884: Demurrer. (20 Fed. 1)

October 16, 1884: Plea in abatement. (22 Fed. 28)

March 9, 1884: Same. (23 Fed. 353)

December 26, 1885: Circuit Court Decision. (26 Fed. 337)

September 3, 1888: Revivor petition granted. (36 Fed. 337)

In addition to these main cases there were the host of ancillary actions which arose out of circumstances pertaining to the main cases. Some were trivial, others important. A number of these cases have provided "landmark" legal precedents for generations of lawyers and judges in the succeeding years. If the reader bears in mind the distinction between the two main cases and the ancillary cases there should be little confusion as to these satellites to the primary action. A final group of cases referred to in the text and footnotes would be the citations used to support lawyers' arguments and judges' decisions. These are previous decisions which may seem to provide precedent for the new decision requested or rendered.

For those unacquainted with the lawyer's tools, the case references — e.g. "75 Cal. 1" — should be read as "volume 75 at page 1 of *California Reports*." "Pac." refers to *Pacific Reporter,* "Fed." to *Federal Reporter, and* "U.S." to the *United States Supreme Court Reports*. Each of these is a series of volumes collecting the decisions of the respective courts. These books may be found in any courthouse law library or well-equipped law office.

THE LEGAL TALENT IN THE SHARON CASES

Sarah's Attorneys:

George Washington Tyler
Tyler's son
Colonel George Flournoy

Walter H. Levy
David S. Terry
W. T. Baggett

The Senator's Attorneys:

William H. L. Barnes
O. P. Evans
Henry C. Hyde
William Stewart
Henry I. Kowalsky

Frank G. Newlands
William F. Herrin
S. M. Wilson
J. P. Hoge
John Currey

The Judges:

Superior Judge J. F. Sullivan
Superior Judge W. H. Levy
Superior Judge Shafter
Chief Justice Morrison, California Supreme Court
Associate Justice McKee, California Supreme Court
Associate Justice McFarland, California Supreme Court
Associate Justice McKinstry, California Supreme Court
Associate Justice Thornton, California Supreme Court
Associate Justice Ross, California Supreme Court
Associate Justice Sharpstein, California Supreme Court
Associate Justice Paterson, California Supreme Court
United States District Judge Lorenzo Sawyer
United States Judge Hoffman
Examiner S. G. Houghton
United States District Judge Matthew P. Deady
Associate Justice Stephen J. Field,
    United States Supreme Court
Chief Justice Fuller, United States Supreme Court

Chapter I THRUST AND PARRY

N SATURDAY, September 8, 1883, former United States Senator William
Sharon's accustomed afternoon repose
was interrupted by his arrest on a charge of adultery. The
incident was remarkable in a number of ways, most of which
were obvious, but one of which was singularly unaccountable
to the thousands who read of it at their Sunday breakfast
tables.

Such a charge always has prurient values, of course, and
when the culprit is a prominent political figure, general interest
is further aroused. Senator Sharon was, additionally, a multi-
millionaire. His arrest took place in his comfortable apartment
in the San Francisco Palace Hotel, one of many properties
owned by him. It was not surprising, therefore, that not only
the San Francisco newspapers, but those throughout the United
States — with the aid of the new nationwide wire service —
should industriously turn to the task of edifying their readers

The most peculiar aspect of the case was the fact that only
a married person could be guilty of adultery under the law,
while the Senator claimed, and was generally believed, to be
a widower.

William Sharon was approaching his sixty-fifth year at the
time of his arrest. He had studied law in the office of Edward
M. Stanton, later Lincoln's Secretary of War, but was not happy
in a brief law practice. When in early 1849, news of the California gold discovery reached Ohio, he put all his funds in
supplies and merchandise and joined a wagon train headed
westward. Trading in merchandise and land with a vigor and
sagacity later to be much admired, within ten years he was
worth a quarter of a million dollars and owned a fair amount of

San Francisco property. But, while credited with courage and imagination, he had been too cautious to become directly involved in the gold and silver mining speculations which could, in a matter of days, make a man a millionaire or a pauper. His fortune was therefore modest by San Francisco standards of the period.

Among San Francisco's more dramatic financial operators was William C. Ralston, a banker who through a mutual friend became Sharon's companion and confidant. Sharon, with a boldness inspired by Ralston's counsel, joined the throng daily engaged in the wild stock speculations of the period. But in 1864, with ore production diminishing, he lost almost everything he had gained. That blow proved to be no disaster, however, but catapulted Sharon into the most relentlessly acquisitive career in the West.

Ralston with Darius Ogden Mills, another gold immigrant, had established a highly successful banking operation which, in 1864, evolved into the Bank of California, the largest bank west of the Mississippi. The bankruptcies and mine closings which ruined Sharon also alarmed Ralston and Mills. Their bank held a great many promissory notes secured by mining stocks and properties. If the mines failed, the notes would not be paid and the security would become worthless. Ralston hit upon the idea of putting William Sharon in charge of a branch of the bank in Virginia, Nevada, in the heart of the mining country, to keep operations under close scrutiny. Sharon was pleased to accept the employment.

In the next ten years, largely through his shrewdness and unrelenting perseverence, old mine shafts were extended and new ones developed with money advanced from the bank, with the result that a number of new multi-million dollar ore strikes were made. It was not alone the bank which benefited from the new bonanza.

By 1870 Sharon was known as King of the Comstock. Within ten years after his arrival in Nevada, he and his two partners had made profits of ten million dollars from their joint mine operations, four million of which went to Sharon. He later estimated that during one 15-month period his personal income from a particular mine was $500,000 a month.

As his position became more secure he built a railroad which thereafter controlled the flow of supplies and ore between Virginia City and Reno, the nearest point on the Central Pacific link of the young transcontinental rail line. At its peak the railroad paid him two thousand dollars a day. He boasted that, with subsidies, the line had not cost him "one cent" to build. He further consolidated his position by building sawmills, roads, flumes, and tramways in the mining area, all of which proved profitable.

Having amassed a great fortune, Sharon, like many another wealthy man, turned his thoughts to possible political fame. In 1874 he bought the Virginia City *Territorial Enterprise*, one of Nevada's principal newspapers. In 1875 the state legislature was pleased to select him as United States Senator from Nevada. He continued to devote most of his time and attention to the West throughout his six-year term, and was unsuccessful in seeking reelection in 1881. He left a barely perceptible mark on the Senate. Toward the end of his term he felt constrained to make one of his rare utterances from the Senate floor, expressing indignation at the comment his absences had inspired and explaining that he was a busy man.

While Sharon was in Nevada consolidating his position, his more impetuous friend, Ralston, had been attempting to make San Francisco a self-sufficient city, devoting large amounts of money to a number of grand promotions, including the manufacture of watches, tobacco products, furniture, and carriages, a woolen mill and a street railway. He had also undertaken the construction of two large luxury hotels, the Palace and the Grand, to be built on Market Street, the city's main street, and across from each other on New Montgomery Street.

These altruistically inspired but financially dubious ventures were enough to make his situation precarious, notwithstanding the cornucopia which was spilling gold and silver down the slopes of the Sierra in an apparently endless stream; but the optimistic and expansive Ralston was, at the same time, building for himself a $300,000 town house, and, for week-end entertainment, a million-dollar mansion at Belmont, a few miles south of San Francisco.

Even so, the mining and banking operations and their auxiliaries might have carried him through; but Ralston, in early 1875, independently undertook to gain control of a speculative mine which he felt was promising. At the peak of his buying, the anticipated new ore deposit proved illusory, and in a matter of hours the value of the stock fell by two hundred and fifty dollars a share. He had borrowed heavily from his Bank of California (sometimes forgetting the usual amenities) to buy stock. The bank immediately closed its doors, with liabilities of thirty million and cash on hand of thirty thousand. Ralston resigned the next day at a hastily called meeting of the directors. He walked from the bank building to San Francisco's north beach, where his body was found floating in the bay later the same day.

In the financial panic which followed Senator Sharon generously accepted all of Ralston's obligations — and assets — and immediately set about settling with the dead man's creditors, offering to pay them a few cents on the dollar as an alternative to receiving nothing in the event of bankruptcy. It would be difficult to say how the Senator came out on balance. Some of Ralston's unhappy creditors later sued him, claiming that he had misrepresented the extent of Ralston's insolvency in order to induce them to take much less by way of settlement than was reasonable. At all events, when the Palace Hotel had its grand opening two months after Ralston's death, the Senator was its new owner. By the time his amatory difficulties arrived, he was also the owner of the Grand Hotel, the West Coast Furniture Company, and Ralston's mansion at Belmont, and was worth an estimated twenty to thirty million dollars.

In the same year, 1875, the Senator's wife died. Loath to give up the pleasures of feminine companionship, the Senator, by his own later account, began employing young women on a monthly salary, requiring only that they make themselves readily available and that they be discreet.

Throughout his life he was described by contemporaries as a man of much nervous energy, who made cautious but quick judgments which he thereafter boldly and tenaciously maintained, apparently never countenancing the possibility that he could be defeated in any encounter, conversational, financial, legal or amatory. He had intense gray eyes set well in a thin-lipped impassive face surmounted by an increasingly unencumbered dome-like forehead. He generally dominated conversation, drawing frequently on apt quotations from poetry and the Bible and was a witty if not brilliant raconteur.

Though he cared little for elegance, and nothing for food, he occasionally entertained visiting nobility and other such international figures as former President Grant, at Belmont. But after his wife's death in 1875 he had kept an apartment at the Palace Hotel, avoiding loneliness with a succession of young female companions.

✓   ✓   ✓

Immediately on his arrest, the former Senator posted $5,000 bond and the same day took a train for a previously planned trip to the East, leaving his attorney to probe the charge and to have the case delayed.

The adultery charge had been brought on the complaint of a William M. Neilson, and alleged open and notorious adultery with Miss Gertie Dietz. The Senator was intimately acquainted with Miss Dietz, the intimacy having recently become complicated by the birth of a child. The questions which his attorney had been charged with answering were: Who was Neilson? What was his interest in pressing the charge against the Senator? How was it claimed that the widowed Senator had the marital status legally essential to commission of adultery?

As matters developed, the Senator had not needed to employ counsel to obtain the answers to these questions; with the help of the press, he himself evoked the answers at long range. A week after his arrest, San Francisco newspapers reported an interview by a Chicago newsman with the Senator. He branded the charge as a lie, declaring, "I am a pretty old fish and that kind of bait won't catch me."

This inspired his accuser, Neilson, to hold an indignant meeting with the press. "Now that the millionaire Senator has had his say, let me answer for the lone, fatherless and motherless woman and I shall be happy to answer any question you

may ask." He confirmed the surmise that this "motherless
woman" was not Miss Dietz but the young woman who, he
said, was the lawful wife of the Senator, the former Miss Sarah
Althea Hill.

The Senator and Miss Hill had been married privately in
1880, Neilson told eager reporters, but the Senator had pledged
her to keep the marriage secret for a period of two years. The
reason was that the Senator had wanted time in which to settle
his problems with Gertie Dietz. Neilson said that the former
Miss Hill now wished to assert her status as Mrs. Sharon, but did
not wish a divorce, hence the charge of adultery, which would
bring the marriage into issue. He had seen a marriage contract
signed by Miss Hill and by the Senator, Neilson claimed, as
well as a number of letters from the Senator in which he saluted
her as "My Dear Wife."

Three days later the newspapers carried a letter "to the
public," signed by "Mrs. William Sharon, née Sarah Althea
Hill," corroborating Neilson's assertions. Neilson was not an
attorney but a recent arrival from Australia of vague background and profession, and "Mrs. Sharon" explained his selec-
tion as her champion, saying, "I had been trained by Mr.
Sharon to believe that he could buy all the lawyers in this city,
and I sorely needed an advisor when I selected Mr. Neilson."

The Senator returned to San Francisco from the East three
weeks later and told the large group of reporters who met his
train that the whole incident was merely the result of a black-
mailing conspiracy between an adventurer (Neilson) and a
crazy woman (Sarah).

The papers had in the meantime been recalling that Miss
Hill, "well known in society circles of this city," had a month
or more earlier been rumored by "the tea-table tattlers of fashionable hotels" to be secretly married to the Senator. The day
after the Senator's return, San Francisco papers carried a long
letter which had been solicited from a prominent citizen of
Miss Hill's birthplace, Cape Girardeau, Missouri, appeasing
some of the curiosity which had arisen concerning her background.

The correspondent, who described himself as a family friend, declared that Sarah was "related to some of the best families in the country" and came from good stock, listing a number of her distinguished forebears. Her father, a prominent attorney, and her mother, daughter of a wealthy lumber dealer, had both died in her early childhood. She and her brother, Morgan, had been raised by their "slack-reined" maternal grandparents with the aid of a governess. Sarah completed her education at a local convent, and, noted throughout the area for her great beauty and volatile temperament, she grew to womanhood in much her own way. She was not popular among her girl companions, being something of an intriguer. But "her name was never tarnished with scandal," despite the fact that she had many suitors and many conquests. Once she was reportedly engaged to three young men at the same time, all of whom she ruled imperiously.

At the peak of her popularity, as suddenly as she did most things, she determined to leave home. Some said the abrupt decision resulted from the loss of a young man for whom she had felt genuine affection, but whom she had been unable to resist treating as overbearingly as the others. Her grandmother was already living in San Francisco and in late 1870, having arrived at or close to legal majority, Sarah claimed the modest but adequate estate left by her parents and headed for California.

The Missouri correspondent did not state Sarah's age, but said that if she was twenty-seven years old at the time of her asserted marriage in 1880, as reported by the newspapers, her many courtships before leaving Missouri ten years earlier had been even more precocious than had been generally surmised. (Various sources gave her age at the time of the litigation at from twenty-nine to thirty-three.) The correspondent closed by saying that Missouri friends had been sorry, but not surprised, to hear of Sarah's involvement in the fiasco taking place in California.

Little more was known of Sarah's life since her arrival in San Francisco. Within a few months newspaper readers throughout the country would know more of her private life than some of them cared to learn.

Chapter II PROLOGUE TO ACTION

HREE days after his return to San Francisco, while the adultery charge was yet pending, the Senator, through William H. L. Barnes, his attorney, filed a civil suit against Sarah in the United States Circuit Court in San Francisco, entitling it *"Sharon* v. *Hill,"* alleging that he was not and never had been married to her, that any marriage contract was a forgery, and that he was being greatly harassed by Sarah's pretense that such a document existed. He requested the court to prohibit any claim by Sarah to be his wife or to assert the validity of any contract. With more friends in the national government than at the state level, the Senator urged the federal court to take jurisdiction of the case because of diversity of domicile, declaring that, while Sarah was a resident of California, he was a resident of Nevada.

The newspapers gave the federal suit much space the next day, but it was to drop from public consciousness for over a year, quietly pursuing an ultimately fatal course surpassing even the flamboyant proceedings which were to precede and long overshadow it.

✓   ✓   ✓

George Washington Tyler, the attorney hired by Sarah as special prosecutor, and Barnes, the Senator's defense counsel, had their first confrontation a few days before the adultery trial was scheduled to begin.

Tyler asked the judge to postpone the adultery trial, pleading Neilson's temporary absence. It was a trivial beginning to a contest which was to be waged on many legal battlefields with ever accelerating bitterness, demanding the full atten-

22

tion and the utmost skill and ingenuity of both attorneys; both were eventually to be scarred by the conflict, and one would see his career in ruins before it was ended. Neither attorney was prescient, but it is doubtful that either would have been deterred by foreknowledge of the paths into which the contest would lead them.

Trivial or not, Tyler's request for a postponement provided both attorneys with a vehicle for the splenetic contention which would mark the Sharon litigation to its end.

Tyler had been among the earliest to yield to the lure of gold, arriving in California by ship on July 5, 1849. For a time he dabbled in local politics, gold prospecting and law, then returned to the East (having come from Vermont) to take a law degree at Cambridge, and to find a wife. After achieving both goals, he was again drawn to California shortly before the Civil War, this time to stay.

One of his early appearances as a public figure was predictive of the boldness and unorthodoxy for which he was to become well known. As the Civil War began, Tyler, a strong Unionist, called a public meeting "to form a Union Club" in the most belligerently pro-southern district of California's central valley farmlands. He had barely opened the well attended meeting when a voice from the audience urged his lynching. The meeting quickly disintegrated into a riot, as Tyler expected. And, as he also expected, newspapers throughout the state indignantly reported and editorialized on the sorry fact that a Unionist could not safely speak in public, thus solidifying previously indifferent sentiment for the Union.

Physically, Tyler had stern, strong features, steel blue eyes capable of registering benevolence or outrage instantly on the slightest provocation, and a wide thin-lipped mouth. He was addressed as "Judge," having briefly served on the bench, but he had been in private law practice in San Francisco, specializing in criminal cases, for almost twenty years at the time of the Sharon case. He was then in his early fifties and in robust good health, except for a slight limp caused by a gunshot wound in his left heel acquired in an early political discussion.

William H. L. Barnes was a relative late-comer to California. Born in New York and educated at Yale, he entered law practice in New York with Joseph H. Choate, later Ambassador to the Court of St. James. After brief Civil War service Barnes went to California, where he was soon recognized as a leader of the bar, gaining a reputation for being quick, diligent, and perceptive, a man well grounded in the law.

He also enjoyed great popularity socially and as a civic leader, being by avocation a linguist, artist, lecturer, and actor. Some thought him a dilettante; he was noted for always taking champagne with his meals, and the chef at the Palace Hotel, once having been asked to rank the sophistication of various local lights, had described Barnes as an "intelligent" diner. He was known as "General," and if his friends were vague as to how he came by the rank they were happy so to honor him nonetheless. San Francisco adjudged him a gentleman and a scholar.

✓   ✓   ✓

Barnes, for the Senator, objected to the postponement. "The story of this accusation," he told the police judge, "has travelled as far as the electric wires extend, and the *Associated Press* teems with every fact and circumstance, real or imaginary, that belongs to it. The defendant is naturally impatient, irritated, and presses to be heard."

Tyler was well known to enjoy supporting his legal arguments with apt, if not quite faithful literary quotations, and after some pungent but irrelevant ridicule of the Senator's federal injunction suit, he said "There is a poet who once said that all proud flesh is subject to irritation." The Senator no doubt thought he ought to be treated differently from ordinary mortals, he declaimed, "but I have not that conception of the rule."

Tyler won a delay for an additional week, though not necessarily because of his poetic allusions.

On the date finally set for the trial, the police court was crowded long before it convened, and the courtroom doors were closed against the clamor in the corridor. The trial opened with the kind of confusion, enmity and tangential flailing which were to characterize its successors for several years. The judge had not yet made himself comfortable at the bench when Neilson shouted that the opposition had made countless threats and bribe offers and that it was impossible to proceed with the case because the police had refused to subpoena Gertie Dietz as a witness. Denials and counter charges were promptly hurled by the Senator's cohort.

The judge quelled an incipient riot by ordering that the case proceed. To general consternation, Tyler, as special prosecutor, then requested that the case be dismissed on the ground that there had been a technical error in the wording of the complaint.

"We waive all technicalities," Barnes shouted in reply, "and will waive anything and everything if the case will only go on. Bring up your marriage contract. Produce it."

The shouting contest was instantly revived, Barnes appealing to the judge to quiet Neilson "or let me lash him. The way he talks," said Barnes, "would make one think that the alleged adultery had been committed on him." When the wrangle threatened to erupt in physical violence, Tyler, *sotto voce,* offered to bet on Neilson.

When order was restored the judge agreed with Tyler that the charge had not been properly framed and required dismissal. The large audience was disappointed at not seeing Gertie or Sarah, who had not attended, and at being deprived of the titillation the trial would have afforded. But there was consolation in the fact, reported by the press, that "the proceedings throughout were marked by great bitterness, and at times it seemed as though personal encounters would result."

The affair was not long out of the papers; four days later Neilson, with bruises on his face, head and neck, swore out an alias complaint against two unknown assailants who, he said, attempted to kill him as he left his home that morning. He was confident they were in the hire of the opposition.

Speculation by City Hall loungers as to the reason for the dismissal of the criminal charge was brought to an end a few days later on November 1. Tyler, on behalf of Sarah, filed in the San Francisco Superior Court, California's court of general trial jurisdiction, a suit against the Senator for divorce. She alleged a marriage based on a written agreement, and charged the Senator with willful desertion and adultery with nine named women, including Gertie Dietz. Sarah and Tyler had decided to put the marriage directly in issue in a civil case, where a mere preponderance of the evidence would suffice. This would avoid the risk of having the issue decided against her in a criminal trial, where a favorable decision (the Senator's conviction) would depend on proof beyond a reasonable doubt. Moreover, their chief witness, Gertie Dietz, was apparently as unwilling as she was essential to the criminal case.

Barnes immediately demanded on behalf of the Senator the privilege of inspecting the document on which Sarah based her claim of marriage. Sarah was ordered to produce it in court at 11:30 on the morning of November 8. Interest in the dispute was immediately revived.

✓   ✓   ✓

San Francisco's criminal courts were still sitting in the "old" City Hall, a former downtown theater which had been converted with much cost and corruption many years past. Though the principals and many of the witnesses would often find themselves in that building in the coming years, the divorce case itself would be tried in the "new" City Hall, where the civil departments of the courts were housed along with most city and county departments.

Some distance removed from the commercial district, the new building was, with the possible exception of the Palace Hotel, the most ambitious yet attempted in San Francisco. Its cornerstone had been laid in 1872 and additions and embellishments were still being added as the trial commenced. Its many wings, both constructed and contemplated, inspired local wits to express a fear that it might fly away. Its massive dome had not yet been constructed, but great Corinthian pilasters surrounded the building, giving it an impressive if squat appearance. It would still be under construction when it collapsed in the earthquake and fire of 1906, but in 1883 it was already a mark of San Francisco's new stability and sophistication.

San Francisco's development had been unprecedented in its speed and scope. By the time of the Senator's arrest in 1883 there were a quarter of a million people, though the city was barely thirty-five years removed from virtual oblivion: The lower arm of the vise which imprisoned the Sacramento and San Joaquin River waters in San Francisco Bay, releasing them twice daily through the narrow Golden Gate with the consent of the Pacific Ocean tides, had been abandoned by the Hudson's Bay Company in 1846, leaving fewer than three hundred inhabitants.

Within months after the announcement of discovery of gold in the foothills in 1848, men were pouring through the Gate by sea, and by land over the Sierra Nevada in what seemed two endless streams. Many headed directly for the diggings, but some who had come by ship stopped off temporarily or permanently at the point of debarkation, while others who, like the Senator, had come overland, drifted on down the rivers to the Bay.

The ships which brought the gold seekers came to anchor in San Francisco Bay. Many were immediately abandoned by their crews who joined the scramble up the flanks of the Sierra. Some of these multi-masted floating derelicts, which came to resemble a forest grown out in the Bay, were used as lodging for a time. But a tent and wooden shack town was soon under way, with unceasing construction never meeting demand.

Frequent fires — three in one early year alone — destroyed all or most of the town. Each time tents were pitched again and framing of new buildings started while predecessors' charred remains still smouldered.

In 1850 there were ten brawling lawless men to every woman in San Francisco. At the time of the Senator's arrest, men still outnumbered women by more than two to one despite the staggering rise in total population. The imbalance of the sexes made its mark in a number of ways, some of which were as would be expected. Some would still be reflected in the San Francisco of a hundred years later.

A few of the sudden millionaires had been unable to resist the temptation to compete with each other in the construction of Victorian mansions, opulently furnished from all parts of the world. But, with relatively few families, San Francisco in the 1880's had far fewer private homes than any other city of comparable size. Instead, it boasted more luxury hotels, first quality restaurants and bawdy houses per capita than any other city in North America.

There had also developed an institution quite peculiar to San Francisco. While called boarding houses — a later generation might call them residence hotels — they were developed to meet the demand of the many single men, and men who had left their families in the more fastidious East, who were amassing great wealth and who wanted the comforts of a fine home without its burdens. These boarding houses were lavishly constructed, many costing hundreds of thousands of dollars to build and furnish. Their operators searched as far as Europe to find master chefs to head their kitchen staffs.

Most of the city's social life by 1883 centered in its hotels, restaurants and boarding houses — and in the bordellos. The Vigilance Committee had become superfluous, the popularity of duelling had waned, and, if inconceivable vices were still reportedly practiced in Chinatown, that was a world apart.

During the fickle years of mine discovery and exploitation, wealth and poverty had often been separated by days or even hours. But by the 1880's relative levels of affluence had become sufficiently secure among the San Franciscans to permit social stratification of the City. San Francisco was by then well established on the schedules of touring nobility and of luminaries of the opera, theater and lecture hall. Oscar Wilde, on his lecture tour of the previous year, had prostrated the ladies and bored the gentlemen in about the same degree as in any other American metropolis.

Though not all of its streets were yet cobblestoned, San Francisco was the cultural, as well as the financial and shipping center of the West.

✒   ✒   ✒

The "Law and Motion" department of the superior court convened the morning of November 8, 1883, to take up its regular calendar of procedural and other technical questions in

pending cases. Late in the morning, an elderly attorney, sedu-
lously occupied in elucidating his views on an abstruse point of
law, became vaguely conscious that the theretofore empty
courtroom was gradually beginning to fill. As the hour of 11:30
approached the spectators became increasingly restless.

Their boredom and impatience were finally dispelled and
the old attorney's unwonted gallery explained when Sarah
entered, beautiful, in a black silk dress "well fitted to her slight
figure," and a long mantle and high crowned hat with rolling
brim, but no veil to hide "a complexion described by poets and
idealized by painters," according to the *Chronicle* reporter.

In her small retinue were William Neilson and a girl named
Nellie Brackett, identified by the press as a "former acquaintance of ex-Senator Sharon," but whose loyalties would become
increasingly difficult to follow in the ensuing months. Soon
George Tyler, Sarah's attorney, as well as the Senator with his
attorneys and private investigators, arrived and took seats inside the bar at the counsel tables with an air which said plainly,
"Everybody must give way for us. This is a millionaire's case."
At the stroke of 11:30 the judge courteously interrupted the
aged advocate and the clerk called out, "Sharon versus Sharon."

Tyler immediately came to his feet and commenced the proceedings by explaining to the judge that though he had asked
her to do so, Sarah had refused to turn over the marriage contract for inspection by the Senator. Tyler said she wished
instead to make a statement to the court.

Sarah quickly glided to the bench and demurely told the
judge she would give up the contract for examination if he
ordered her to, but that she regarded it as the only protection
of her honor and did not wish either Barnes or the Senator to
handle it, unless the judge would be personally responsible for
the contract's safety. Barnes complained that Sarah was taking
undue liberties in assuming a place on the bench with the
judge, and asked how he could inspect the contract without
handling it.

Sarah rejoined that the Senator already knew the contents
of the contract as well as she did, whereupon he arose and
shouted, "It's a damnable lie, the damnedest ever uttered on

earth." The judge demanded order, the bailiff seated the Senator, and Sarah gravely repeated her plea, adding that the Senator had driven her from her home and that she had no funds with which to defend herself.

At length she reluctantly handed the judge an envelope which he tore open, exposing for the first time in public the paper which might be the key to many millions of dollars and which was to propel more litigation and misery, and arouse more widespread interest, than any document of its character in history.

Written on both sides of a single sheet of note paper, it read:

"In the City and County of San Francisco, State of California, on the 25th day of August, A.D. 1880, I, Sarah Althea Hill, of the City and County of San Francisco, State of California, age 27 years, do here, in the presence of Almighty God, take Senator William Sharon, of the State of Nevada, to be my lawful and wedded husband, and do here acknowledge and declare myself to be the wife of Senator William Sharon, of the State of Nevada.

"/s/ Sarah Althea Hill

"August 25th, 1880, San Francisco, Cal.

"I agree not to make known the contents of this paper or its existence for two years unless Mr. Sharon himself see fit to make it known.

"/s/ S. A. Hill

"In the City and County of San Francisco, State of California, on the 25th day of August, A.D. 1880, I, Senator William Sharon, of the State of Nevada, age 60 years, do here, in the presence of Almighty God, take Sarah Althea Hill, of the City of San Francisco, Cal., to be my lawful and wedded wife & do here acknowledge myself to be the husband of Sarah Althea Hill.

"/s/ Wm. Sharon, Nevada

"Aug. 25, 1880"

The judge, victim to a weakness suffered by most men in the presence of the beautiful Sarah, gently told her the contract would be subject to inspection only in her presence, and in court. With his repeated assurance, Sarah permitted the judge to initial it for identification and hand it to the clerk, who took it to the defense counsel table.

Barnes grasped it eagerly, glanced at it, and passed it on to the Senator with a smile.

"It's a forgery, the whole thing is a forgery," said the Senator, and Barnes echoed the judgment.

"Don't you dare to repeat that here again before the Court," said Tyler, incensed. "I think it is outrageous that a man would stand up here in a court of justice and before your Honor, who is to try the case, pronounce it a forgery without being under oath."

The Senator and Tyler traded insults, and the judge sought to restore order by threatening to commit both of them for contempt of court. The Senator continued to mutter and exchange glares with Tyler; and the judge, to forestall further trouble, ordered the bailiff to remove the Senator from the courtroom. The contract was then examined for a half hour. Barnes remarked that it was not very satisfactory without his client being there, but an effort by the Senator to reenter was repulsed by the bailiff.

Gradually, as they had entered, the parties, their retinue and the satisfied spectators left the courtroom. The old attorney who had started the court day came forward, picked up the threads of his argument, and resumed the pleading of his case to an again deserted courtroom.

The contract was kept overnight by the court, to be photographed and deposited in the City Hall safe. The next day, at the time set for its return to Sarah, the courtroom was again crowded, largely with city employees and attorneys seeking a glimpse of Sarah. They were presented with an unexpected minor drama when the judge announced that inexplicably the safe could not be opened. It was immediately rumored that there had been tampering, and Sarah began to sob. Several young attorneys promptly offered to kick the safe in. A lock-

smith soon opened it with ease and the relieved judge benignly
handed the contract to Sarah, who thanked him with a mag-
nanimous smile and left.

The cause of at least a part of Sarah's anxiety was revealed,
and much speculation aroused that afternoon, when, a few
minutes after she left court, a policeman entered with a subpoena directing the production of the contract at a Grand Jury
session to be held that afternoon. "So ended the prologue of
what promises to be one of the most interesting society dramas
of the day," said the *Chronicle*.

Senator William Sharon appeared dapper and determined when he faced
the photographer for this portrait. — *Bancroft Library*.

Sarah Althea, about midway in the course of the litigation with Senator Sharon. — *Bancroft Library.*

Chapter III   PRETRIAL SKIRMISHES

HE GRAND JURY sat throughout the second week of November but its sessions were by law secret, so newspapers had to be content with speculation and with reporting traffic in and out of its chambers. As both Sarah and the Senator had been subpoenaed, as well as many of their friends, it was understood the marriage was some way in issue. The press expressed the view that, while outnumbered, there was more order in the ranks of Sarah's small army than in that called into the field by the Senator's hired investigators.

For several days the case lay dormant, so far as the general public was concerned. The major news was that Black Bart, poet laureate of stage coach bandits and scourge of Wells Fargo operations, had been captured in Stockton, "for which stockholders will be thankful." It was reported from time to time that efforts were being made, with indifferent success, to take the depositions of various witnesses in preparation for the divorce trial. The Senator, as expected, had filed an answer to Sarah's divorce suit denying all of its material allegations and charging that, in fact, the marriage contract had been forged within the last two months.

The case was soon back in the headlines, with Tyler, Sarah's attorney, asking the superior court to discharge the Grand Jury for exceeding its powers. He claimed the jury was planning to indict Sarah for filing a false divorce suit; but, he complained, the law prohibited a perjury prosecution while the very case in question was still pending, and here the issues in the contemplated perjury prosecution and in the divorce suit would be the same, namely: Was there a valid marriage? For good measure, Tyler asserted that the members of the Grand Jury had been lavishly entertained by the Senator, thus precipitating a

33

lively argument, much enjoyed by the large audience. This subsided only when the judge ruled that Tyler's request was pre-
mature, as one could only speculate on what the Grand Jury
might decide to do.

The next day Tyler wrote a letter to the Grand Jury, charging that the Senator claimed to control nine of its members
and that some of them had in fact been bought. He closed the
letter by describing the Senator as a financial and erotic giant
but an intellectual and moral pygmy. The jury complained to
the judge, who ordered Tyler immediately brought into court
to face a contempt charge.

By the following day San Francisco newspapers were collecting all of each day's separate threads of the dispute under
one banner, generally captioned "THE SHARON SCANDAL."
They reported that evidence was being taken in Tyler's contempt hearing, that depositions were still being taken in connection with the divorce trial, but most sensationally — though
not unexpectedly — that the Grand Jury had returned indictments against Sarah and Neilson charging them each with
forgery, conspiracy, and perjury.

All these events occurred on Saturday, a relatively slow
court day. Sunday, Neilson attempted to make a speech from
the City Hall steps, painting a picture of corruption and conspiracy in high places. When he was recognized, he drew a
large crowd and a number of rotten eggs.

The following week opened with Tyler arguing for his deliverance from the contempt citation. He asserted first that he
could not be guilty of "contempt of *court*" as the Grand Jury
was not a court. "This point failed to impress the court," the
Chronicle reported next morning, "notwithstanding his comparison of the Grand Jury to the biannual administration of
physic which New England mothers were accustomed to give
their children, which, although cleansing in its effects, was
gotten rid of as soon as possible."

He next argued that his letter had not been contemptuous,
containing nothing one might not read in church. The judge observed that such an assertion was disrespectful of the Sabbath.

Tyler last pleaded the truth of his assertions, with a dramatic close that greatly pleased the audience. The members

of this Grand Jury, he said, were marked figures at whom the deliberate, unwavering finger of scorn would become implacably pointed.

The judge was less moved than the audience, and found Tyler in contempt, imposing a fine of $500, to be served in jail at the rate of one day for every two dollars if unpaid. Tyler asked if he could pay two weeks worth of fine so that he might remain at liberty through Thanksgiving, but the judge, having declared a recess, was on his way to chambers and did not acknowledge the query.

Tyler promptly left the courtroom and evaded the bailiff long enough to make a hasty trip to the Supreme Court chambers, located nearby, where he obtained a writ of *habeas corpus*.

The Supreme Court (California's highest and then its only appellate court) now felt the impact of the Sharon dispute for the first, but far from the last, time when Tyler's writ was called for hearing a few days later. The courtroom overflowed with the transiently curious as well as the loyal fans who had by now taken to following the various facets of the case from court to court. The legal arguments were substantially as made earlier, but presented with more circumspection. The crowd was disappointed when the Supreme Court calmly took the matter under submission.

Some days later the Court announced its decision that grand juries were as much entitled as courts to the protection afforded by the law of contempt, and upheld Tyler's five hundred dollar fine.*

---

* *Matter of Tyler*, 64 Cal. 434 (1 Pac. 884): Contempt of court is an ancient device, almost as old as the courts. It was contrived by judges themselves, and was evolved for the purpose of enforcing orderly conduct of court proceedings through threat of punishment. Thus contempt is a curiosity of the law, a civil-criminal hybrid.

Sophists have claimed that the concept of punishment for contempt of court evolved from an otherwise irreconcilable conflict between an ideal and a fact: Judges should be above reproach, but, being human, the ideal can be achieved only by assuring that no one reproaches them. In most common law jurisdictions legislative bodies have now recognized the value of the concept by enacting statutes which embody it. The courts generally still retain their inherent power of holding a person in contempt. This case was one of first impression in California, and has stood as an accepted authority on protection of grand juries ever since.

As the year 1883 ended and the divorce trial date drew closer, the attorneys' offices were increasingly crowded as they took depositions of potential witnesses. The accelerating tempo was matched by the gusto of the attorneys, the bitterness of the parties, and the distress of witnesses. The opposing armies were frequently in court to have a recalcitrant witness ordered to answer questions or to complain of the alleged misconduct of the opposition. Sarah became sufficiently outraged at Barnes' demeanor during one deposition that she used the telephone, a newly introduced means of communication, to tell him what she thought of him. At his direction the telephone company subsequently promised never again to connect her line with his.

Reporters, at Barnes' invitation and over Tyler's strenuous objection, were in attendance at some of the depositions, and their subsequent accounts, often verbatim and lengthy, gave the public a preview of the kind of forces which were massing for the coming battle.

The most sensational pre-trial disclosure came early in the deposition of one Frederick C. Burchard; it was also the most ephemeral, however, and he was soon to be styled "Poor Freddie" by the press. A foppish young man from the East, he had been in San Francisco for a time during the spring of 1881 and was brought back by the Senator's minions to tell of his brief acquaintance with Sarah.

At the taking of his deposition he said he had been introduced to Sarah one evening in the spring of 1881 at the Palace Hotel as she was promenading with the Senator. Under Barnes' guidance Freddie related that shortly thereafter he accepted an invitation to accompany her to the Senator's country mansion at Belmont with another couple, the Senator not making the trip. On that visit to Belmont, in late April or early May, 1881, he said he had become engaged to marry Sarah, though the engagement was broken a week later.

The significance of his testimony was obvious and was reflected in the reaction of the large press corps in attendance. At a time when Sarah claimed to have been six months married to the Senator, Freddie now claimed that she had accepted his proposal of marriage. Newspapers were on the street with reports of his testimony within an hour of this revelation.

Tyler was visibly surprised and indignant. Barnes, who had expected the alarm of the vanquished, uneasily gave Freddie into Tyler's care for cross-examination. His discomfort increased as Tyler's dissection of Freddie progressed.

The initial impact of Tyler's wrath, in the form of questions about his background, was sufficient to drive from Freddie's mind the date of his birth, his present age, and when and where he received his last formal education.

"Is there any defect of your memory that you are aware of, Sir?" Tyler finally asked.

Freddie said there was not, but when Tyler asked him to detail the circumstances of the betrothal Freddie could not remember. Why? Because she was not the first woman in his life, "so why should I remember Miss Hill more than the others?"

Well, asked Tyler, what words did he use?

The same silly language always used on such occasions, said Freddie. Tyler pressed him and Freddie protested, "It is ridiculous to have to tell it."

"It is a ridiculous story, in my judgment, you have come here to tell us," said Tyler. "I want you to go through all that minutely. That is the day of all others that you ought to remember. You became engaged to this lady."

Barnes attempted to rescue Freddie by interposing trifling objections, but Tyler pressed forward each time. With much effort he gained the admission from Freddie that no intimacies had ever passed between them, that Sarah's maid or other friends were present on every occasion when he was with her with the exception of the few minutes at Belmont when he proposed and she accepted. Neither had ever confided anything of their previous lives to the other, with the exception of a number of lies he admitted having told her. One of these was a tale to the effect that his former wife was a famous actress with whom he had spent most of his life touring Europe.

Tyler then asked Freddie what caused the claimed engagement to be broken. He answered that he had heard derogatory

things about Sarah and suspected that she was interested in
him for money. This provided Tyler with one of the pleasures
that trial attorneys dream of but rarely have the privilege to
enjoy. He thrust a hand into his files and, like a cavalier un-
sheathing his sword, brought out a piece of paper. He handed
the document to Freddie and asked what it might be. It was,
Freddie admitted, a letter he had written to Sarah about a
week after he broke the engagement. Tyler then read it into
the record. It was a long letter, and Tyler's reading did it justice. Freddie had written in part:

> Allie [Sarah's soubriquet]: Forgive me for ad-
> dressing you. It is for the last time. I have writ-
> ten this immediately after leaving your room, a
> man and gentleman that would lay down his life
> for you. God knows, if I did not love you as I do,
> I never could have stood such harsh, cruel words
> as I have stood from you.
>
> Oh, Allie, if you only knew what I would give
> for your friendship. I would be your slave, serv-
> ant, wait at your commands. I have counted the
> hours, minutes, when I thought I could only see
> you again. If I can add one jot to your welfare or
> happiness, I am always at your service. I shall
> never visit you unless you wish it. All I ask in re-
> turn is that you will think kindly of poor Fred,
> who will be very lonesome, and were he not a
> man and thought he might some day be of use to
> you, would end his life right here and now.
>
> Good bye, Allie, and may these lines kindle a
> little friendship in your kind heart that others
> have tried to steel against me.
>
> Always your friend and slave.
>
> Fred C. Burchard

Having ejaculated the last half dozen words of the letter
like a series of oaths, Tyler raised his eyes from the letter to
Freddie and asked, "How can you reconcile your statements
with that letter?"

Freddie sat glumly silent for a time, but under Tyler's prodding, admitted that it appeared inconsistent with his testimony. Tyler went back over each phrase of the letter. What were Sarah's "harsh, cruel words," of which he wrote? She had accused him of deceiving her about his wealth, Freddie said. But hadn't she just loaned him two hundred dollars to pay his debts? Yes. And hadn't he testified that he never made any representations to her about his financial condition? Yes.

After an uneasy pause, Freddie said that perhaps the breaking of the engagement had been by mutual consent. He had not meant to imply that it had been by his action alone. He now remembered that the letter had been inspired by regret over the breach and in an attempt at reconciliation. After still further questioning, he decided that perhaps it was Sarah who had broken the engagement.

Tyler turned to other matters for a moment. Freddie had almost recovered his composure when Tyler thrust another letter at him. In it Freddie had said "I will not press my attentions on a lady where they are not returned." and promised that Sarah would not be annoyed by him again. Asked by Tyler how he could explain that letter, he said it had been inspired by Sarah's failure to reply to his earlier letter. Was that the only explanation he could give? asked Tyler incredulously. Freddie said it was.

Most of those who heard or read accounts of Freddie's testimony felt that he had been vanquished. All that remained was to carry him ignominiously from the field of battle. But Tyler, like most war horses, relished the experience too much to give up the chase even when the enemy was in full rout.

He kept Freddie answering questions in Barnes' office for nearly a week. Newspapers which had earlier described Freddie as "too, too utter" (an echo of San Francisco's exposure to Oscar Wilde during his recent speaking tour) soon reported that he was beginning to wilt. His affectation of bored contempt and his habit of constantly stroking his well-waxed mustache with "delicately tapered fingers" became increasingly nervous. As the examination ground on, his boredom gave way to alternating anger, confusion, and fear. But if Freddie had lost all pleasure in the deposition the public had not. Newspaper circulation was up sharply throughout the week. Everyone, with the exception of Barnes and Freddie, was enjoying the entertainment sufficiently that they were happy to see Tyler prolong it, even at the expense of relevance. Tyler expressed interest in the reason for Freddie's abrupt appearance in California at the time he met Sarah.

Freddie said he had come West for his health, for lameness.

"Q: Lame?

"A: Yes.

"Q: What was the matter?

"A: That is my business.

"Q: I want to know what you were lame from.

"(Barnes): Don't tell him.

"A: I will not tell you.

"Q: I will try and see that you answer it. You refuse to answer what you were lame from?

"(Barnes): I object and ask the Notary to stop this.

"(Notary): I do not think that question is relevant.

"(Tyler): I want to know from you what you were lame from.

"A: I will not tell you.

"(Tyler): The Notary has no power to pass on the questions.

"(Barnes): He has a perfect right to pass on the questions.

"(Tyler): He has no right and you know better.

"(The Notary): What is the Notary Public for?

"(Tyler): If you live long enough you will know more about it. All the Notary Public has to do is take down the testimony and the objections and the court passes on them. You are a very nice young man to say that he should not tell."

After a great deal more argument Freddie yielded. "If you want to know very bad, and I request the newspapers not to publish it to the world, it was from indiscretion with women."

Tyler choked on an explosive laugh and Barnes laconically said to the stenographer, "Put down the laugh." The newspapers faithfully reported Freddie's request, but also reported his lameness.

Freddie's deposition threatened to outlast the impending trial itself but its long overdue end was inadvertently precipitated by Sarah herself. She had attended most of the deposition sessions and allowed her mobile features to shower holiday smiles upon the crowd of attorneys and reporters. She even favored Freddie with a few bright and seemingly forgiving glances from time to time, the papers reported. But at one point she became so incensed by his testimony that she ran from the room. She was back shortly, heralded by much noise from the corridor, with a policeman and a crowd of supporters. To the merriment of everyone else, Freddie was placed under arrest for perjury. A few days later the charge was dismissed on the ground that it was improper while a person's testimony was still being taken. Thereupon, to everyone's relief, Freddie hastily departed, never to return.

The newspapers felt that little additional entertainment could have been anticipated from perpetuation of Freddie's ordeal. Tyler was at home with an ulcerated tooth, at first reported broken in the heat of questioning Freddie, and it was speculated that Barnes, who could not be found for several days, had countered with a rheumatic finger joint. "The proceedings could not be expected to partake of that highly scientific character imparted when George W. Tyler and General Barnes measure their rapiers of wit and sarcasm or indulge in rhetorical flights of adjective-laden eloquence interspersed with dramatic illustrations," reported the *Chronicle*. "The heavy legal batteries which have been firing blank charges at each other have temporarily exhausted their chests of wind ammunition, invective cannister and grapeshot wit."

The new year of 1884 was ushered in with Tyler attempting to take the Senator's deposition. At the same time legal arguments on the indictments against Sarah and Neilson were progressing from day to day. Tyler persisted in his contention that the whole purpose of the indictments had been to embarrass and intimidate Sarah in the divorce case. He repeated his earlier charge that the Senator had, as was apparently now conceded, communicated with a number of the grand jurors privately and had been present during a part of the jury's deliberations.

At Tyler's urging the judge called the grand jurors into
court to inquire whether they had been improperly influenced.
After several days of argument over whether a grand jury
should be required to divulge its secret proceedings, the judge
remained uncertain and it was agreed that the question should
be submitted to the state Supreme Court as a test case. After
first solemnly asking counsel if the suit was bona fide, and
being as solemnly assured that it was, the Supreme Court accepted the case the following day. Following argument and
deliberation the court decided that grand jurors need not divulge the process by which the indictments were returned,
even though jury misconduct was alleged.*

The Sarah-Neilson indictment continued to draw much better than any of the other "entertainments," as the press was
calling the cases. It played almost daily to a packed courtroom,
although generally the show consisted largely of legal argument between Tyler, who had not been dissuaded by the ad-
verse Supreme Court decision, and the district attorney. Even
the arrival of John L. Sullivan by overland railroad did nothing
to reduce the daily audience. Tyler's attack on the indictments
was entering its seventh week when the judge confided that he
was heartily sick of the whole matter. Shrewdly interpreting
this as an invitation to stop talking and let the judge decide
the case, Tyler subsided. The judge promptly dismissed the
indictments on the ground that some of the grand jurors were
prejudiced against Sarah and Neilson over matters having

---

* *Ex Parte Sontag*, 64 Cal. 525 (2 Pac. 402). The case was again one of
first impression. Tyler argued that as the criminal law provided that
indictments which have been returned through irregularity in the proceedings should be dismissed, a defendant must be permitted to prove that
the proceedings were improper. Since grand jury sessions are secret, he
reasoned, the only way to prove irregularity would be by questioning the
grand jurors themselves, they being the only persons present. The Supreme Court credited Tyler with much ingenuity in presenting his argument, but held that while perhaps seemingly paradoxical, it occurred not
infrequently in the law that though one might have a right, it could not
be exercised for want of a remedy. The court concluded that the sanctity
of their deliberations required that grand jurors should not be compelled
to divulge the manner in which they arrive at indictments. The case
stands yet as the basic authority on the subject.

nothing to do with the indictments, and that Senator Sharon had privately made accusations calculated to influence the jurors. Neilson demanded the privilege of being tried on at least one count. The judge obliged by letting one count against him stand.

Tyler, in odd moments, was finding time further to protest his own contempt citation. He attempted another appeal to the Supreme Court while with much agility dodging the sheriff, who wanted to execute the order by taking him to jail. Eventually Tyler was compelled to pay the fine.*

Both legal contingents were being distracted again by Neilson's independent frolics. He had been charged with disturbing the peace as a result of his speech on the City Hall steps. Though Tyler succeeded in having the original charge dismissed, Neilson was immediately charged once more with disturbing the peace, causing an unlawful assemblage, and traducing a police officer. The officer in question, I. W. Lees, Captain of Detectives, was destined to play an ambiguous role throughout the divorce litigation. The increasingly titillated public was beginning to compare the affair with a family of rabbits.

While these matters were occupying the attorneys' days, their evenings were still devoted to taking depositions. This routine was occasionally broken by pilgrimages to court to get a ruling on disputed questions. In the course of these Tyler generously told Barnes that he intended to impart to him a good bit of legal lore before the case was concluded. Barnes thanked him, expressing regret that Tyler himself never seemed able to profit by instruction.

The deposition of C. D. Cushman, an elderly former employee of the Senator, aroused almost as much interest as had Freddie. At Tyler's invitation, Cushman testified that over the years he had become intimately acquainted with the Senator's signature and handwriting, having paid out hundreds of thousands of dollars based on that signature. Cushman was then

---

* *Tyler* v. *Connolly*, 65 Cal. 28 (2 Pac. 414). Another landmark case in the development of the law of contempt, in which the court held that a contempt order was not appealable. This remains the law today.

shown the marriage contract and a number of letters in which Sarah was addressed as "Dear Wife." He declared positively that the letters and the signature on the contract were in the genuine handwriting of the Senator.

Barnes apparently intended to surpass Tyler's performance with Freddie. He launched a meandering, largely irrelevant cross-examination, asking the elderly witness about misdeeds with various chambermaids, all of which Cushman denied indignantly. Late that night after more than nine continuous hours of answering questions, the witness timidly remarked on the time. "If I can get a message to my wife, I'll tell her I'm safe and will turn up . . ."

"Tomorrow," snapped one of the attorneys grimly.

The interruption inspired adjournment negotiations which soon degenerated into an abusive exchange among the attorneys. Barnes said he didn't care how long the deposition took. All tacitly agreed they had had enough for the evening, however, and hastily gathered their effects. The witness, wearily pushing himself out of his chair, asked Tyler if Barnes' questions had been fair. Tyler, coloring, seemed to choke on his attempted answer. As Barnes strolled out he urged Tyler to "try and look pleasant."

ʃ   ʃ   ʃ

In the weeks preceding the divorce trial the principals had little time for, and the press paid no attention to, the suit the Senator had brought in the federal court to have Sarah enjoined from using the marriage contract. Tyler did take the time to file a demurrer in that action, contending that federal court had no business taking the case, since marriage and divorce were controlled by state law. Judge Lorenzo Sawyer, for the United States Circuit Court in San Francisco, rejected Tyler's motion a few days before the divorce trial was to begin.* He held that if the Senator was not granted the privilege of suing to stifle an allegedly spurious marriage contract, Sarah could wait until his lips were sealed by death before putting

---

* *Sharon* v. *Hill*, 20 Fed. 1.

forth her claim to his millions, leaving no one to dispute her fraud, "if fraud there be." Apparently the federal court was not willing to acknowledge the existence of the divorce trial which was about to begin, and in which the question of fraud would be very hotly disputed.

Chapter IV THE DIVORCE TRIAL BEGINS

HE LEAD article in all of the San Francisco Bay area newspapers on March 10, 1884 proclaimed that the famous, notorious, scandalous or entertaining (depending on the reading audience to whom they catered) Sharon versus Sharon divorce trial was at long last begun. Judge J. F. Sullivan's courtroom in the new City Hall was, as expected, filled beyond its capacity. Choice seats had been reserved for city officials, and functionaries abandoned their offices in other parts of the building to join the throng of avid plebeians in dedicating the historic occasion.

Sarah was more minutely described than ever before. The next morning's *Chronicle* said, "Sarah Althea looked as demure, innocent and sweet as the arts of the toilet could make her. Her costume was black silk over which she wore a brocaded velvet dolman faced with black fur around a throat which, if the truth must be told, is no longer as round and full as it no doubt was not many years ago. The face is shapely and oval. The features are regular; the mouth is well cut; the lips are rather full and are the most expressive feature. They look resolute but betray also that their owner has a temper. The nose also looks spirited. It is cast on the Roman model. The eyes lack the expression of trustfulness. Their color is gray-blue and sometimes a little brown. Their movement is quick, the lids full and well creased. The whole face betrays intense nervousness, quickness of perception and mirrors faithfully all that is going on within her mind. Her hair is auburn and, if it is not false, is of luxuriant growth, above the forehead devoted to curls and ringlets which fall in profusion. In the back the tresses are gathered into a Grecian knot, and on the top they are covered by a bonnet trimmed with jet passementerie and what appear to be butterflies with yellow dotted wings."

Readers were equally edified on the Senator's appearance. "Small in stature but erect in carriage, small in waist but certainly stiff in the backbone, he is apparently the least remarkable man in the courtroom. He is clad in sober broadcloth, black necktie. His face conveys the idea of mildness. The features are motionless and a smile is apparently a stranger to them. The forehead is round, full and even. Under it are two piercing brown eyes, which look out inquisitively over a nose which tells nothing, not even Greek or Roman descent. The mouth recedes, for the lips are thin, while the chin is rather sharp and protruding, perhaps more than it was in the ex-Senator's youth, for the increase of years, though it has added to his store of wealth, seems to have taken from his adipose tissue. Mr. Sharon is in fighting trim bodily as well as legally. For with him and his attorneys there came a three-bushel-basketful of books, papers, diaries and other manuscripts."

The newspapers called Sarah's attorneys "too well known to require description." They were led by the flamboyant George Washington Tyler and his son and also included Colonel George Flournoy and Walter H. Levy, who was to become a judge long before the case was finally concluded. On the second day of the trial they were joined by David S. Terry, former Chief Justice of the California Supreme Court. He was better known for having resigned that exalted office in 1859 in order to fight a duel with, and kill, United States Senator David C. Broderick. Terry's entry into the case was deservedly given no prominence at the time, but was to prove the first step toward ultimate disaster.

On the Senator's side only Barnes and O. P. Evans appeared. They were to take on recruits as the trial progressed, ultimately fielding a larger if not louder team than Sarah's. But Tyler and Barnes were to dominate and direct not only the long trial that was finally beginning, with its scores of witnesses marshalled on the opposing sides, but the years of appeals whose magnitude they could not then suspect, as well as the myriad ancillary proceedings which had already begun to plague and distract them, but at whose ultimate variety and consequences they would have been appalled.

However well known they were, the *Chronicle* felt it should be stated that Tyler had cut neither hair nor beard for months past, perhaps being too busy for such niceties, and looked unusually grim, "while Mr. Barnes is not only shaved but honors the occasion with a suit which he never before wore in any courtroom."

Most of the first day of the divorce trial was devoted to the attorneys' opening statements, in which they told Judge Sullivan what they intended to prove and how they intended to prove it. The closing years of the nineteenth century were the *magni anni* for courtroom oratory in America, and Tyler and Barnes were among the best rhetors of San Francisco. Spectators were duly appreciative, as each spoke for almost half of the opening day of the trial with no visible lessening of audience interest.

Barnes was not given opportunity to perform to best advantage. Tyler interrupted the flow of words and the thread of thought with frequent objections. The tactic was an old one and honored with frequent application, but after Barnes had struck back at his tormentor several times, Judge Sullivan remarked that both were taking rather wide latitude and mildly admonished them.

At the conclusion of the opening statements there was still time for the taking of some testimony on the opening day. To the surprise of everyone not privy to Sarah's case the first witness called by Tyler was Mrs. Martha Wilson, a dressmaker who had done work for Sarah for some years. Tyler launched his first attack without preliminaries. Did she ever have a conversation with Sarah about a marriage? he asked the witness. Barnes was out of his chair immediately with the first of the countless objections which would punctuate and enliven the trial for the next six months.

The question, of course, called for self-serving hearsay. Unless the situation fell within one or another of the fairly numerous but strictly applied exceptions to the hearsay rule — the rule of law which excludes repetition of statements made

In the City and County of San Francisco State of California in the 25th day of
August A.D. 1880 — I Sarah Althea Hill of
the city and county of San Francisco State
of California — age 27 years — Do here in the
presence of almighty God take Senator
William Sharon of the State of Nevada
to be my lawful and wedded husband —
and do here acknowledge and declair
myself to be the wife of Senator William Sharon
of the State of Nevada —

                                    Sarah Althea Hill

                    August 25th 1880 San Francisco Cal
I agree not to make known the contents
of this paper or its existence for two years unless
Mr Sharon himself sees fit to make it known — S. A. Hill

                            In the city and Coun-
ty of San Francisco State of California in the 25th
day of August A.D. 1880 — I Senator William Sharon
of the State of Nevada — age 60 years — Do here in

the presence of almighty God Take Sarah althea
Hill of the city of San Francisco — cal — to be my
lawful and wedded wife — I do here acknowledge myself to be the husband of Sarah althea Hill =

S. Sharon   Nevada

                    Aug 25 1880

Above and on the previous page is the Marriage Contract, subject of
determined vigilance on the part of Sarah, acrimonious dispute among the
attorneys, and minute examination by a parade of handwriting "experts."
Ultimately it was destroyed by fire, but not until it had been duly photographed for court records. — *Bancroft Library*.

outside of court — the objection should be sustained and the question rejected. Barnes, however, found himself entangled in the liberality of his own pleadings and learned to his great chagrin that he would be fighting the war on more fronts than he had anticipated.

Judge Sullivan needed no assistance from Tyler to remind Barnes that in denying the claims made in Sarah's complaint he had not only charged that the marriage contract was a forgery but had alleged that it had been fabricated within the last sixty days. So, the judge pointed out, Barnes had though perhaps unintentionally put in issue the question of whether the contract was a recent forgery. He therefore ruled that Sarah was entitled to show that the contract had been discussed with others in the more remote past. This opened a field for which Barnes had not prepared and which he would require some time to meet. He sank back in his chair reflectively.

With Barnes' objection overruled, Mrs. Wilson testified that one October day in 1880 Sarah had told her that Senator Sharon was furnishing an apartment for her at the Grand Hotel. Mrs. Wilson had remonstrated, telling Sarah that a young lady should not accept such gifts from a man. This remark, said Mrs. Wilson, moved Sarah to draw a piece of paper from her bosom, saying that perhaps it would clarify her status. It proved less edifying than Sarah hoped, as Mrs. Wilson was illiterate. Fortuitously, a friend of Mrs. Wilson, Mrs. Vesta Snow, happened by, the witness said. To satisfy herself that Sarah was not jesting, she asked her friend to read the document to her.

"Produce it!" interrupted Barnes, still smarting from the recent calamity.

At Tyler's urging Sarah reached deep in her bosom and brought out a cloth bag from which she extracted a tattered sheet, which the court clerk marked "Plaintiff's Exhibit Number One." Tyler showed Mrs. Wilson the marriage contract, which she recognized as the same paper. She and Mrs. Snow had seen the contract again a year later without Sarah's knowledge, she said in conclusion.

The witness and her testimony, as well as the judge's ruling, had obviously surprised Barnes. He launched his cross-examination with a few tentative probings, measuring the adversary while collecting his thoughts. He concluded that his most effective point of attack lay in Mrs. Wilson's illiteracy and her identification of the contract.

How, if she could not read and could not tell what it said, was she able to identify the paper in court as the same one she had seen in 1880 and in 1881? he asked.

Well, the first time she saw the paper it was clean, and now it was creased, soiled and discolored, she replied.

Barnes' spirits rose, and he pressed on.

"Q: In other words, you have seen one clean paper, and one dirty paper. Do you mean to say any more than that?

"A: No, sir.

"Q: How do you know it is the same paper?

"A: I know it is the same paper, because it is the same paper as read to me then.

"Q: How do you know it the same paper?

"A: Because I identify it."

Illiterate or not, Mrs. Wilson was closely paraphrasing Shakespeare: "I have no other but a woman's reason — I think him so, because I think him so."

At length, however, she was able to make clear that she intended to say that the paper she saw in 1880 was clean, that the paper read to her in 1881 was the same paper but had become soiled, and that the paper shown her in court was the same soiled paper she had seen in 1881, hence the chain of identity between the paper of 1880 and Plaintiff's Exhibit One. With that, Barnes gave up the witness.

Mrs. Vesta Snow, Mrs. Wilson's lector, was the second witness called. She supported in every detail the testimony of Mrs. Wilson concerning the two readings of the marriage agreement. Mrs. Snow, unlike Mrs. Wilson, had never done any work for Sarah, had had no interest in Sarah's activities since their single meeting in 1880, and had known nothing of the litigation until approached by Mrs. Wilson a week ago, she said. Her manner on the witness stand was neither equivocal nor contentious and Barnes was unable to shake her on cross-examination. The spectators, who had discounted Mrs. Wilson as both obtuse and partisan, were visibly impressed as Mrs. Snow left the witness stand.

With the conclusion of her testimony, Judge Sullivan announced the first day's adjournment and retired to chambers. The bailiff's gavel echoed the declaration, as Barnes grumbled that the case was moving too slowly. Tyler amiably promised to provide sufficient entertainment to satisfy the most sanguinary demands.

Chapter V   SARAH TESTIFIES

N THE morning of Sarah's expected ascension to the witness stand the courtroom was filled earlier than was even usual for the now famous case, a large number of girls and young women being in the audience. The marked disparity in the manner of dress of the various feminine groups observed around the courtroom, from modest to garish, suggested to sophisticated reporters an equally great disparity in their usual pursuits and degree of chastity. This conclusion was to be tested and its soundness verified in a short while.

Sarah arrived a few minutes late that morning, and Tyler apologized to the judge with a grimace which, it was assumed, he fancied to be a suppliant smile. When Sarah did appear, said the *Chronicle,* she "floated toward the witness stand and stillness fell upon the room." Her face was flushed and her manner a little nervous.

Tyler stood throughout the examination, his face contorted into the most gentle and soothing expression of which it was capable. The defense platoon moved its table and chairs to a point directly facing and no more than ten feet away from the witness stand, the Senator hidden between the burlier Barnes and Evans as if for protection from the angry glances with which Sarah was to punctuate most of her testimony. He managed most of the time to maintain an expression which was aloof yet curious, as though in wonder that she could remember and relate so plausible a fiction.

Tyler began by asking Sarah where she was born, and she responded with a detailed chronicle of her life. Since coming to San Francisco in 1871, she said, she had lived with her grandmother for about two years, after which her parents' estate

made it possible for her to move into the fashionable Grand
Hotel. She subsequently lived with her brother in various of
the better hotels in San Francisco but, she said, in the fateful
year of 1880 she lived alone at the Baldwin, with a brief summer sojourn across the bay in Oakland.

She testified that she first met Senator Sharon while visiting
friends at Redwood City, where she was introduced to him
and his daughter, Flora, at the train station near Belmont. This
was in approximately 1878. She next saw him in the spring of
1880, in a chance meeting at the entrance to the Bank of California, in San Francisco's financial district. She had been using
her moderate fortune in trading mining stocks, and the Senator
teased her by saying he had heard she was becoming quite a
stock sharp. She modestly deprecated this, and he offered her
an opportunity to buy a stock that he was about to put on the
market, inviting her to visit his office to discuss the matter.

A week later they met on the street by chance again, and
he chided her for not coming to see him. She countered by
inviting him to her apartment to discuss the stock which he
was planning to issue. He took her address and a few evenings
later paid her a short visit. "He did not tell me anything about
stocks, but he repeated some poetry, sang Auld Lang Syne and
made himself quite comical, I thought." Altogether he was
"agreeable and very pleasant . . . for an elderly gentleman."

As her narration progressed Sarah began to weep, particularly while relating their meetings. Her tears made Barnes and
the Senator uneasy and uncertain where they should cast their
eyes or what they should do, but they gave Tyler a rare chance
at gallantry. He offered her the traditional glass of water and
called for a recess. The judge was pleased to grant a brief
respite.

Resuming the stand, Sarah said that she soon visited the
Senator's office to accept his proffered advice. They talked
about "the stocks, and the weather, and all those kinds of
things." On another visit to his office that summer she entrusted
$7500 to his keeping to invest for her.

Tyler then asked if the Senator at any time introduced "a
little love talk" into the conversations, and after an objection

by Barnes was overruled, Sarah said that "Mr. Sharon had been talking to me most every time I went there about liking the girls, and how the girls liked him. I ignored the conversation. I did not care to enter into such a conversation. It was not what I went for and I always laughed it off."

The first "distinct proposition" was to the effect that "he would like to have me love him, and would like to have me let him love me. I said I had no objection to any gentleman loving me. I said there were few people that I loved in the world. Finally he said if I would let him love me he would give me one thousand dollars a month, and give me Flora's horse, that white horse; and I do not know what all he was not going to do."

At this point, a number of the fairer trial spectators arose and, with crimson faces hidden behind their hands, hastily left the courtroom.

Neither his manner of approach nor the terms suited Sarah, she continued. She had replied, "I think, Mr. Sharon, you have made a mistake in the lady. If you wish to make love to women in that style, there are plenty of women that you can get for much less money than that. For thirty millions of money you could not make love to me in that style."

She tried to leave his office, she testified, but the Senator barred the door and "said he was only teasing me; that he really was in love with me and wanted to marry me." Thus mollified, Sarah consented to stay and they talked a long while, the Senator saying that he liked her better than any girl he had met since his wife's death and that he had made inquiries about her and found her to be of good family and background.

He thereafter repeatedly said he wanted to marry her, but said that he wanted secrecy in any such marriage. He explained that he had "a girl" to whom a child had recently been born. He had sent her to Philadelphia to prevent trouble in his impending re-election campaign. He did not think the child was his but wanted the marriage secret to avoid complicating that problem, he had told Sarah.

Sarah had expressed doubt at his explanation, whereupon he drew out a letter, tore off one-half and gave it to her to prove the other woman's existence, she testified. The fragment, which Sarah presented to the judge, commenced "My dear Sweetheart" and read in part, "The baby left me in a sorry condition, continually flowing, and am not able to exert myself without great bodily pain. I was dreadfully lacerated, but can now enjoy your sweet society to its greatest degree. Ain't I naughty?"

During the reading of the letter fragment several more of the fair spectators hurriedly left the courtroom. The male members of the audience felt confident that they could make a sound appraisal of the character of the well rouged ladies who remained.

Sarah said the discussion of marriage had covered a period of several weeks during which they went riding and to dinner several times. She could give no specific dates as she was at first indifferent to his proposals and "he was of no particular consequence in my life until after we were married." He said he would demand an answer upon his return from a trip to Virginia City. At his request she went to his office at the Bank of California on August 25th to give her reply. She was still uneasy about his proposal for secrecy, but the Senator had fortified himself with a number of law books from which he read, to convince her that a private marriage was legal. "So we agreed to be married by an agreement, although I was not quite satisfied about it."

Sarah said she had written the marriage contract while he paced about the room dictating from notes. "I would write a little and then we would talk and then I would write again. I did not suppose that was going to be the contract; I supposed it was a sketching and would afterwards be properly written out. As soon as it was written, Mr. Sharon came over to me, and put his arm around me and said, 'Will that suit you?' "

Sarah said she told him it would not, but it proved to be all she ever got by way of a contract.

The Senator returned to Virginia City immediately after the signing of the agreement, Sarah testified, but soon returned to San Francisco and commenced visiting with her "nearly every evening and every afternoon; he was there constantly." On Sep-

tember 25th, he arranged a discreet meeting through a series
of notes, which were put in evidence, at which he told her that
the frequency of his visits to her hotel was causing talk. He
urged her either to permit him to provide a house for her or
move into one of his hotels, the Palace or the Grand.

With a letter of introduction and instruction to S. F. Thorn,
manager of the Grand, the Senator induced Sarah to move into
that hotel on about the first of October. At the Senator's suggestion she furnished her suite with purchases from the West
Coast Furniture Company, on the shopping trip related by
Mrs. Wilson. She had some trouble with the hotel manager in
getting the decoration and furnishings she wished (she had the
parlor of her suite retinted in lavender) and complained to the
Senator by letter in early October. His reply from Virginia City
was the first of the letters which for brevity throughout the trial
and afterward came to be known as the "Dear Wife" letters.

> My dear Wife:
>
> In reply to your kind letter I have written Mr.
> Thorn and enclose same, which you may read and
> then send it on to him in an envelope, and he will
> not know that you have seen it. Sorry that any-
> thing should occur to annoy you and think my
> letter will command the kind courtesy you de-
> serve. Am having a very lively and hard fight. But
> think I shall be victorious in the end.
>
> With kindest consideration believe me as
> ever.
>
> Wm. Sharon

The "hard fight" to which he made reference was his campaign for re-election to the United States Senate from Nevada,
in which his optimism proved ill-founded, as he was defeated
by James G. Fair.

As court adjourned after the first day of Sarah's testimony,
the spectators felt that it had been time well spent, and the
following day saw the courtroom filled still earlier, with the
exception of the Senator's chair at his counsel's table. He
strolled in jauntily an hour later and was soon brought current

by his Chinese valet, Ki, and one of his bodyguards, who were always in attendance.

Resuming her testimony, Sarah said that from the time she moved to the Grand Hotel the Senator regularly gave her $500 a month for personal expenses, "of his own free will," and his carriage was made available to her whenever she wished to use it. She and the Senator were constantly together until the first of the new year, Sarah said. Virtually all of her nights were spent in his rooms at the Palace, readily accessible from the rooms she maintained at the Grand by the bridge over New Montgomery Street which joined the two hotels. It was to become known as "the bridge of sighs" as a result of the litigation.

The Senator sent her many intimate notes during that period of their idyll. She had preserved a typical note dated December 9, 1880: "My dear Allie: Am going to Col. Fry's to dinner, will be back about 9 o'clock, then hope to have a sight of your beautiful countenance. Till then as ever. Yours, S."

They spent a week end at the Belmont mansion in early November, she said. She had not wanted to go alone with him, as their marriage was not publicly known, so invited another couple. On a subsequent visit at Belmont the Senator also invited his daughter, Flora, who declined to go if Sarah was to be there. The Senator had replied that Sarah had as much right there as anyone, Sarah testified.

The marriage of the Senator's daughter to a titled Englishman, Sir Thomas Hesketh, took place in December. The Senator gave Sarah a number of reception invitations to send to her relatives and friends. She had been free to attend the wedding itself, she said. But as only the close family was attending, she decided not to go in view of Flora's dislike for her. She did attend the reception which followed at Belmont, however, since it was one of San Francisco's great social events of the decade.

The Senator accompanied his daughter and her new husband part of the way on their wedding trip to Europe, but on his return the relationship continued as before. Sarah acted as hostess at a number of week-end Belmont house parties, she said, sometimes inviting her relatives and friends. Among the

Senator's guests were Cornelius Vanderbilt "of New York," and numerous titled foreigners and American politicians in addition to local notables.

In this happy interlude Sarah "used to go everywhere" with him. When they had any little domestic differences she would return to her rooms in the Grand, and he would generally soon send his servant, Ki, to her with a conciliatory note. One such typical note, of April 1, 1881, introduced in evidence, read, "My dear Wife; Inclosed send you by Ki, the ballance [sic] two hundred and fifty, which I hope will make you very happy. Will call this evening for the joke. Yours, S."

She produced another "Dear Wife" note dated May 5, 1881, in which he enclosed money and said she was getting "very extravagant," and still another "Dear Wife" note on October 3, 1881, enclosing $500 for her expenses at a time when he was ill and unable to see her. These and numerous other notes were introduced in evidence. Some merely accompanied money; some were to tell her that he was going out of town; others invited her to his rooms, as one note read, to join him "in a nice bottle of champagne and let us be gay." In all, five were "Dear Wife" notes, while the others saluted her as "My Dear Allie."

The first domestic discord was felt one day in the fall of 1881, said Sarah touching the corner of her eye with a lace handkerchief. The Senator not only failed to take her for a ride in the afternoon as he had promised, but stayed out all night. The next day she went to his apartment and accused him of giving his attentions to a young lady just out from New York. Sarah started to leave but he ordered her to the bedroom and, when she resisted, choked her. She fell to the floor in a faint and became conscious some time later in a closet of his bedroom. He later let her out and apologized, explaining that someone had come to the door while she was unconscious and he had dragged her into the closet to avoid embarrassment. He assured her that her accusation had been groundless, and she stayed the night, she testified.

One evening at dinner a few weeks later the Senator abruptly demanded that she sign a paper declaring that she had no claim on him and that he was paying her $500 a month to be his mistress. She refused, because it would "cause me to be both morally and socially ostracized." She later learned that the Senator's anger was inspired by a suspicion that she had divulged the marriage to an attorney, she wept. But when she protested that she had merely consulted an attorney about the $7,500 which she had invested with him, he brusquely gave her $3,000, a note for $1,500 more and written promise to pay the balance at $250 a month and ordered her out of her rooms at the Grand.

When she refused to leave, he had the carpet removed from the corridor outside her apartment. When she still did not move, he had her door removed from its hinges. At this she went to the Senator and pleaded with him through his unyielding door. "I would do anything in the world rather than have him treat me in that way. I would be disgraced and I did not know what would become of me." He replied, she said, that she could sign the paper renouncing any claim against him or he would have her ejected.

Later the same evening Sarah called at the Senator's rooms again to plead once more for the replacement of the door to her room, at least until she could find shelter elsewhere. Finding his apartment empty but unlocked, she decided to hide in wait for him. Ki stumbled on her hiding place and his frightened screams drove her out. Sarah dejectedly returned to her rooms, where she spent a wakeful night, as the door was still gone.

The next morning men came to rip up the carpet in her rooms, refusing to wait until she had removed her trunks. She left the hotel to the sound of hammers and tearing fabric. After several weeks' wandering, as the year 1882 began, Sarah rented a house on Ellis Street, near the home of Nellie Brackett's family. This young woman had earlier been mentioned by newspapers as "a former friend" of the Senator. But now she was in daily attendance at the divorce trial, sitting at Sarah's side at the counsel table.

In the late spring of 1882, Sarah testified, there had been a reconciliation of sorts. She had dinner and spent the night with the Senator on several occasions, and he visited her a time or two. One evening in May of that year, she said, Nellie accompanied her to the Palace on a visit to the Senator. They were admitted by Ki. As the Senator was not there, it occurred to Sarah to secrete Nellie behind a bureau in the Senator's bedroom on the chance of hearing some connubial language on his return.

The Senator's arrival produced more ardor than Sarah hoped for and she found herself importuned to go to bed with him in the presence of an unwanted and unwilling audience. Finding no way out she did spend the night with him, she said. (As this testimony was elicited, ladies again hastily arose and left the courtroom with downcast eyes.) Sarah closed her recitation of the incident by saying that the Senator's words that night were as conjugal as his actions and she was sure Nellie had heard him.

A time finally arrived, Sarah wept, when all communication between them was severed, and with much reluctance and regret she had determined that she could only vindicate her honor in court.

The direct examination of Sarah eventually came to an end and Tyler surrendered her to the opposition. There was obvious surprise and disappointment in the courtroom when Evans, Barnes' associate, cleared his throat and stood up to commence her cross-examination. Most spectators felt that Barnes would have been more evenly matched against her. Sarah herself, before answering Evans' first question, declared that she would have preferred to be examined by Barnes.

Evans was a good trial lawyer, with the tenacity of a bull-dog and the nose of a blooded bird dog. His cross-examination got a poor press, being described as dull, aimless, tedious or worse, but it was none of these to those who appreciated its purpose. That purpose was to discredit Sarah's case by undertaking to impeach her testimony in every material particular, but Sarah proved to be a wily and elusive target.

She steadfastly refused to commit herself to specific dates of her early meetings with the Senator, despite Evans' tireless — and to the audience necessarily tiresome — efforts. Finally she said, "I do not remember when I met him. I told you I would not like to set any time because I do not remember."

"Q: You do not know what time of year it was?

"A: Some time in the early part of 1880.

"Q: In January?

"A: I do not think it was in January."

In February? March? April? May? June? July? She did not remember but as they were very friendly by July, she guessed it was long before then.

How often did she meet him and where in the month of July? She could not recall.

"Q: Are you positive you met Mr. Sharon at any place during the month of July, 1880?

"A: At his office, I believe."

How many times? Who was there? What occurred? She could not remember, except that she never saw anyone but the Senator, no one else ever being present.

"Q: Can you tell anything in particular that occurred in any other months?

"A: Except the time we were married, I cannot. I know that because the paper reminds me of it.

"Q: You would not recollect it except for that?

"A: I would not remember the date.

"Q: Would you remember the marriage if it were not for the paper?

"A: I think I would."

There was also much sparring over the $7500 Sarah claimed to have invested with the Senator. Evens hardly waited for one answer to be concluded before putting the next question. As one reporter put it, "like a minister galloping through a service," he pressed forward.

"Q: Where did you give it to him?

"A: In his office over the Bank of California.

"Q: In greenbacks or gold notes?

"A: In paper money.

"Q: Were they $5, $10, $20, or $100 notes?

"A: It must have been the $100 and $50 notes.

"Q: When you turned it over who counted it?

"A: Mr. Sharon did.

"Q: How long did it take him to count it?

"A: I could not tell.

"Q: About?

"A: I could not tell.

"Q I want to see if you can come anywhere near it.

"A: I tell you I cannot tell you and you cannot put words into my mouth.

"Q: You do not know how many notes there were?

"A: I do not.

"Q: You do not know what denominations there were?

"A: He said it was correct, and if he chose to accept it for $7500, I was satisfied."

Did she ever receive much investment advice from the Senator? Yes. Could she remember any of it? She said no, but it was bad advice, as she lost money.

The examination was continuing in the same vein as the day finally drew to an end. Judge Sullivan had spent most of the day resting his forehead on his hands as if his brains were bothering him, the *Chronicle* thought. Tyler had remained a silent but interested spectator, apparently feeling that his client could adequately fend for herself.

The loyalty of the undaunted spectators who again filled the courtroom the following morning was rewarded when it became apparent that Evans was shifting his ground and his tactics. He said he was perplexed as to the secrecy provision of the marriage contract. What reason, he asked, did the Senator give for requiring two years secrecy?

"A: He had a young woman in Philadelphia with a child. If we were openly married they would come out and make trouble in Nevada for him. They had nothing to lose and all to gain.

"Q: That is in reference to his re-election to the Senate?

"A: He was afraid they would make trouble and prevent him from being re-elected.

"Q: He was afraid she would come to Nevada and injure his chances?

"A: If he was publicly married and she found it out she would not hesitate to do it.

"Q: If you were married publicly and this woman came on there and raised a row, that would make such a scandal in the State of Nevada that it might defeat him?

"A: He must have been afraid that it would hurt him in some way.

"Q: It was in reference to his re-election as United States Senator?

"A: If you call it 're-election.' I do not know about politics. He wanted to still hold his position."

Evans' carefully guarded purpose in painstakingly establishing Sarah's understanding that the secrecy requirement related to the election campaign was made apparent by his next question.

"Q: Did you understand that it would take two years to determine the question whether he was to be re-elected or not?

"A: No, he was defeated that fall. Mr. Fair took his seat in the following March.

"Q: Was it not determined in November, 1880?

"A: I believe it was. When he came back he found he was defeated.

"Q: Why did you put two years, if it was the object to save scandal and to prevent them injuring his chances of re-election?

"A: He put it in himself. I put it as he dictated it.

"Q: That was objectionable to you, you stated?

"A: Yes.

"Q: You did not like the secret clause?

"A: No.

"Q: You wanted to be publicly married?

"A: Yes.

"Q: You did that with very great reluctance?

"A: Yes.

"Q: He explained to you as a reason why he wanted it done, that he was afraid this woman would come on and injure his chance of re-election?

"A: Yes.

"Q: Did he tell you it would take two years to be re-elected and he wanted it kept secret that long?

"A: Mr. Sharon gave me to understand that just as soon as he would get rid of the woman and settle matters with her, he would make it known. I was not to make it known myself for two years, until he felt ready to make it known.

"Q: What reason did he assign to you for fixing that period of time, if any?

"A: I do not know that he gave me any particular reason for it.

"Q: Then it did not have anything to do with his re-election?

"A: Yes, it did."

Evans abandoned that subject in favor of another to which the defense was to assign much time and, apparently, importance. But, though it greatly entertained the trial's undiscriminating votaries, the relevance of a great part of it was dubious. He began by asking Sarah if she had been in the habit of consulting fortunetellers about the Senator. She primly denied having such a habit, but admitted that she did occasionally have her fortune told.

She would have been a rare person for the time if she did not occasionally turn to the occult. The Senator himself, as well as other prominent San Francisco men and most women, believed to some degree in one or another aspect of palmistry, phrenology, and the "reading" of a variety of things, including, most commonly, cards, tea leaves or chicken entrails. Newspapers regularly carried "scientific" discussions on the topic. There were many "readers" and spiritualists in San Francisco, as in other cities, who advertised widely and some of whom gained no little affluence. The phenomenon was probably largely explainable by the frenetic way of life and the mutability of the quickly made fortunes and status of the leaders of the community.

Evans led Sarah through a series of scornful denials that she had ever put potions or drugs in any of the Senator's food or drink, or stolen or worn any of his clothing for supernatural purposes.

"Did you," asked Evans, laying a package on the counsel table and withdrawing several badly soiled rags, "ever see those?"

Never, said Sarah; she had never seen any of the articles before.

As a matter of fact, asked Evans, weren't they articles of the Senator's clothing which she had stolen from his rooms and, in company with Nellie Brackett, buried beneath the casket in a newly opened grave at the Masonic Cemetery on May 1, 1883?

"I never did anything of the kind in my life, sir," said Sarah indignantly. "You may bring all the world here, and that is a falsehood, and I defy anybody to prove it. If you think you are doing this to dirty me over the world, you are making a great mistake, sir!" She would admit only that she "frequently" took strolls in cemeteries, "all the cemeteries," sometimes with Nellie. Evans passed on to a new topic.

"Are you through with your dirt?" asked Sarah, and when Judge Sullivan amiably asked her to answer the pending question, she observed, "Mr. Sharon seems to smile — a great master stroke." The judge said "I can't help it," and again asked her to pass on to the answer to the next question.

The question concerned whether, in recent years, her family had been as cordial toward her as previously. No, it had not, Sarah admitted.

"Why?" asked Evans. In his zeal he momentarily forgot a cardinal rule of cross-examination: Never ask a "Why" question. When Sarah's eyes lighted and she gathered herself for the answer Evans saw his mistake, but it was too late.

Angry a moment before, Sarah now answered with zest. "My brother did not consider Mr. Sharon my equal by any means, but thinks he is of very low birth. We are somebody by birth, and Mr. Sharon is like a thistle in a field by birth. He said I could receive the attentions of men that were much more elevating than Mr. Sharon. We had many a fight about Mr. Sharon and many a heartache."

Evans sat down dejectedly to marshal his thoughts, and Judge Sullivan took the opportunity to call an adjournment for the day. Tyler had again left Sarah to her own devices, and the consensus among City Hall strategists was that she had carried the day.

The next morning Evans seemed to know both the field and his quarry better. With revived confidence and supplemented ammunition he resumed the chase, guarding against possible pitfalls but ready to take advantage of any lowering of Sarah's guard. In consequence, the day went somewhat better for the Senator's side. Evans briefly pursued a tedious line of questioning about inconsequential matters for the purpose of lulling the wary Sarah.

Then, abruptly, he asked, "In the month of October, 1880, did you in company with two gentlemen and Mrs. Julia Bornemann go to the Fourteen Mile House and take supper there, and return after midnight?"

Evans was referring to a questionable roadhouse some distance from San Francisco. This time Sarah was obviously caught by surprise and off her guard. "I never took supper or a bite of anything at a public house of that kind in my life," she stammered. "I did not know it was the Fourteen Mile House. I did not know at the time what place it was: I never took a bite of anything to eat or drink there."

Evans repeated the question.

"I do not remember what night it was," Sarah replied. "I did go for a moonlight drive with those people. I had never seen nor met the gentleman until that evening. Mrs. Bornemann persuaded me to go with them for a ride. She had even to loan me a shawl, so unprepared was I for such an occasion. We went for a drive . . ."

Evens persevered. "Did not you make up the party yourself, and invite those gentlemen?"

"I do not think I did . . ."

She said she told the Senator about the excursion later. As well as she could remember, it had taken place while he was in Washington in 1881. Evans suggested that perhaps she was thinking of another moonlight ride on another evening. "No!" she hastily replied. "I never went but that once. I was never in the habit of going on moonlight rides with men, women, or children."

Evans indulged his fondness for the technique of suddenly changing the direction of questioning a few minutes later, when he began a series of innocent questions about the Senator's trip east in January 1881 with his daughter and his new son-in-law. Sarah said she had cried when he left.

"Q: Because you could not go with him?

"A: I could have gone with him if I had insisted on it. He was very kind to me.

"Q (Gently): Were you very much in love with him at that time?

"A: I was.

"Q (Sharply): Do you remember a circumstance that occurred on the 10th of May, 1880? A Mrs. Smith was in a gentleman's office downtown and you requested her to permit you to have an opportunity to speak a few words to the gentleman, and she went away and allowed you to do so?"

Evans was being very careful to keep the name of the gentleman out of the trial at this time, even at the cost of clarity.

"A: Not to my knowledge.

"Q: You do not remember that?

"A: No.

"Q: Did not you take poison on that occasion because you were disappointed in love?"

Not at all, Sarah said. She went to a gentleman's office, had a disagreement with him, and fainted, still being weak from a recent illness. When she recovered she thought she would take some laudanum for relief. "As I put the bottle to my lips I fainted again, and I suppose I took too much. When I next came to, I was in Dr. Murphy's office." The doctor insisted that she remain for the night and Mrs. Smith came to nurse her. That was all there was to it.

"Did not you tell her you had taken poison, intending to commit suicide, because the gentleman you were so much in love with, and in whose office you were, would not marry you?" Evans persisted.

"No, nothing of the kind," said Sarah firmly.

Evans changed the subject again, and asked if she ever threatened the Senator's life.

No, she answered, except for saying once to Mr. Barnes that if, having made her appear to be a forger and perjurer, the Senator succeeded in having her wrongfully convicted of any crime, she would take Sharon's life as well as her own.

At this, Barnes, who had been a passive auditor for several days, leaped up and declared that Sarah had never said anything of the sort to him.

David S. Terry's presence at the trial was felt for the first time as, with deliberation, he rose to his full six feet three inches. Looking evenly at Barnes, he said, "General Barnes has attempted to convict the witness of lying, and as it is a question of veracity between the witness and the lawyer, I believe the witness is telling the truth."

George Washington Tyler bounced out of his chair to accuse Barnes of perjury and misconduct, but Barnes, ignoring Tyler and addressing the court, his face taut and drained of color, said that he had never crossed Terry's path, had never sought his good opinion, did not want it, and though he had been insulted, would not send the challenge which Terry apparently wanted.

Terry made several more provocative remarks, at the same time expressing respect for the dignity of the court. But with a little more bluster from Tyler, who had spent most of the day making objections in an effort to give Sarah relief from the unaccustomed severity of the cross-examination, the affray eventually subsided.

The hour of 4:30 was conveniently announced by the courtroom clock and the judge declared the day's adjournment, "leaving everyone weary and fagged except Tyler, whose unfathomable fund of animal spirits has left him fresh as though he had just arisen from a twelve-hour snore instead of having made at least one hundred fifty objections, roared like Bottom, and misquoted a small library of poets," said the *Chronicle*.

The following day Tyler spoke so softly that Judge Sullivan was surprised to find himself asking the attorney to raise his voice. "I speak in this sweet sub-bass," said Tyler, "because of the frequent and unmanly attacks by the press on my voice; and so, in the future I shall simply whisper." To everyone's surprise, he did so, for a full five minutes. Then, unfortunately, Barnes asked a question which Tyler found objectionable, and his voice was again vibrating among the globes of the chandelier until the dust of years came down in a cloud, reported the *Chronicle*.

Sarah was next confronted with ambiguous statements she had made in numerous letters written to friends in the year preceding the trial. Even when it seemed impossible, however, the defense had to concede the plausibility of the ready explanation she always had for her unconjugal sounding words. In one recent letter to the Governor and Mrs. Reigart, for example, she had said she thought the time had come when her friends should know the truth about the relationship existing between her and the Senator. But, asked Evans, hadn't she earlier testified that the Senator long ago told the Reigarts of the marriage?

That was true, said Sarah.

Then, why was it necessary to tell these friends a truth which they already knew, asked Evans triumphantly?

Quite simple, said Sarah. What a person understood from the Senator and what they learned from her were two quite different things, worlds apart, and she now wanted her friends to learn of the marriage from herself. The feminine subtlety of her reasoning, if not enlightening, was at least dismaying to Evans, and he abandoned the point.

He believed he was correct in recalling that she denied having any affair with Freddie Burchard.

His recollection was correct, said Sarah.

Could she please explain then, he asked, what she meant by "that Burchard affair" in a letter to a friend six months ago?

When she wrote that letter, said Sarah, she was about to file the divorce action and had learned that the opposition would falsely claim that she had become engaged to Freddie Burchard. That was what she meant by "that Burchard affair."

Evans finally surrendered Sarah to Tyler, who led her through several denials on redirect examination. With that

Sarah's testimony was closed. It was generally felt that she had tactfully extricated herself from the most dangerous traps that could have been laid for her. As she stepped down from the stand she was obviously pleased with her performance, as were her supporters.

Chapter VI   SARAH'S TESTIMONY CORROBORATED

HE PAPERS noted that it was becoming fashionable to attend the trial. On the day Sarah's cross-examination closed there had been counted among the spectators one marquis, a count, an ex-mayor, the police commissioner, a county supervisor, and the president of the board of education, in addition to the usual number of idle lawyers and City Hall employees who regularly passed the time there.

The City Hall sidewalk and steps were crowded each morning with celebrity seekers, vying for a glimpse of the principals in their arriving carriages. In the main gallery of spectators it was noted that the number of "soiled doves" (a euphemism of the period) in attendance had taken a sharp rise since Sarah had testified that the Senator made a thousand-dollar-a-month proposition to her. The languishing "doves" followed the Senator with their belladonna-brightened eyes as he entered or left the courtroom and whenever he turned his gaze in their direction.

Sarah's principal witness, with the exception of herself, was Nellie Brackett, but if Sarah's attorneys had suspected the turbulence of which Nellie was to be the agent later in the trial, they would probably not have considered her testimony worth the trouble. But even Tyler was not blessed with prescience, and Nellie was in due course called to the witness stand.

Nellie was a modestly dressed comely young woman of "nineteen going on twenty" at the time of the trial. Her dark gray widely spaced eyes, marked by long lashes and brows as black as her hair, looked straight and unwaveringly into the eyes of her examiner, whether friend or foe, it was reported. Her manner and appearance suggested determination to the point of obstinacy.

She said she had met Sarah when they became neighbors soon after Sarah's ejection from the Grand Hotel. When Sarah moved from Ellis Street, Nellie went with her, and had lived with her ever since against her parents' wishes. Her mother had in fact accused Sarah of taking her daughter from her. Nellie's parents were in court while she testified and her eyes were moist, as were theirs, when she spoke of their disapproval of her relationship with Sarah.

The firmness of her new loyalties was apparent as soon as Nellie's examination switched from her antecedents to Sarah. Once started on a story, Nellie could not be stopped. The attorney who happened to be questioning her would first try to stop her, followed by the shorthand reporter, and opposing counsel would finally try to stop her. Only when she finally ran out of things to volunteer would Nellie sit back to gather breath.

She testified that she first saw the marriage agreement along with the "Dear Wife" letters and "everything of that kind" three or four months after first meeting Sarah. Nellie had asked her bluntly if she was the Senator's mistress, because Nellie had heard rumors to that effect before they had ever met and she did not wish to associate with her if it was true. "I did not mention the rumors to her earlier because I did not feel well enough acquainted with her to do such a thing. I waited until I got intimate with her to tell her." To prove to Nellie that she was an honest woman, Sarah had shown her the marriage agreement and the "Dear Wife" letters.

Nellie said she was present at various meetings between Sarah and Senator Sharon, generally in connection with monetary transactions, but the courtroom audience and newspaper readers were interested only in hearing her version of the occasion on which she was hidden behind the bureau in the Senator's bedroom. It had indeed occurred, she said.

The Senator had started off by telling Sarah how much he loved her. "She said, 'Sen, if you love me so, you would not have turned me from the hotel the way you did.' He said, 'That is all right.' Then it was not long after that that he asked her to go to bed with him." Sarah demurred, said Nellie, but on his insistence she capitulated. When he left the room for a moment Sarah whispered to Nellie that she would simply have to stay

hidden until the Senator was asleep after which she could slip
out. Sarah went to bed with the Senator, Nellie said. After the
lights were out she heard the Senator call Sarah his wife several times. At one point he said, "Who is my own little wife and
nobody knows about it?" After some time, when she heard the
Senator breathing heavily, Nellie tiptoed out.

On concluding her recitation of the incident Nellie sat quiet
and composed, as she had been throughout, having shown no
sign of embarrassment. The audience, on the other hand, had
remained breathlessly silent. Barnes looked overwhelmed, and
spontaneously said, "You didn't!"

"I did," said Nellie.

"You did?" asked Barnes despairingly. Nellie nodded her
head.

Resuming, she testified that two months later, in July 1882,
Sarah was having morning sickness and Nellie went to the
Senator's office to report the development to him. "He said,
'Who does she suspect?' I said, 'She does not suspect anybody;
she knows it is you.' He said, 'Well, send Mrs. Sharon down.'"
Nellie testified that she thereafter negotiated with the Senator
for some months for a house, required by Sarah's delicate condition. A house was selected from among his income properties
which the Senator agreed was to be taken in Nellie's name to
avoid embarrassment. When Sarah's symptoms later proved to
have been misconstrued, the transaction was not concluded.

Surrendered to Barnes for cross-examination, Nellie admitted that she was biased against the Senator, but said that it
was caused by his ungentlemanly treatment of Sarah. This had
so incensed Nellie that she wrote him an indignant letter in
which she described him as a coward and a disgrace to his
country and to manhood, and invited God to do his worst to
him for his treatment of Sarah.

Barnes could not otherwise weaken Nellie's recitals despite
lengthy cross-examination, but did gain an admission that she
had been to so many fortunetellers with Sarah that she could
not recall the names of any in particular. As Nellie left the
stand she cast a conciliatory glance at her parents, but firmly
resumed her seat at the counsel table beside Sarah.

Spectators took much interest in Sarah's next witness, Mary E. Pleasant. Newspapers and court records reported her name variously as Pleasant, Pleasants, Plaissance and Pleasance, but noted that she was generally called "Mammy." She identified herself in court as the housekeeper of one Thomas Bell, a San Francisco financier of rather vague connections. Newspapers cautiously referred to her as "a colored pedlar of white laces."

The vagueness was typical of the mystery surrounding everything connected with Mammy Pleasant. She had been reputed at different times to be the owner and operator of a number of expensive boarding houses, some offering more of the comforts of home than a respectable house could properly boast. Out of these operations it was whispered that she had developed subsidiaries, including blackmail, a marriage brokerage, and a market in unwanted babies, amassing a comfortable fortune from her wealthy and influential clientele.

By the time of the Sharon dispute Mammy was nearing seventy and had begun to reduce her activities. From the trial's first day she had been sitting immediately behind Sarah in the first row of spectators. Those who knew her background suspected that if not instrumental in arranging the union between Sarah and the Senator, she at least was in some way intimately connected with the litigation. For those who entertained such suspicions, her testimony proved to be quite bland.

She had first met Sarah about two years before the trial, while Sarah lived at the Grand Hotel, Mammy declared, and saw her a number of times thereafter, one day finding her weeping; Sarah had explained that she had to leave the hotel, and asked Mammy to find and furnish a home for her.

Tyler asked the now routine question — Had she seen the marriage contract? — and Barnes made the routine objection to which the judge made the routine ruling. Mammy said she had seen it, that Sarah showed it to her in pledge of her ability to pay for the services she was requesting. Mammy said she later spoke to the Senator and that he at first agreed, but later refused, to bear the cost of furnishing the home claiming finally that he did not even know a "Miss Hill." Police Captain I. W. Lees called on her later, Mammy said, announcing that he had been sent by the Senator and demanding to know the contents of the marriage contract. Barnes undertook only a cursory, almost diffident cross-examination.

The next witness, a steward at the Palace, testified that he saw Sarah in and about the Senator's rooms many times over a period of about a year and that meals served there to Sarah and the Senator were always on a special silver service. When Sarah complained of a waiter the steward soon received orders from the office to discharge him.

A waiter at the Palace then testified that he had frequently served breakfast for two in the Senator's suite. On such occasions he frequently saw Sarah there, sometimes in a "wrapper." On one occasion she ordered him to take a meal she considered too cold back to the kitchen. The Senator later told him that her orders were to be given the same effect as his.

The greater part of a day was spent in reading into evidence the deposition of Cushman, the Senator's former clerk who had been so oppressively cross-examined that even reporters were scandalized, and who, on being show the marriage contract and the "Dear Wife" letters, had pronounced them all genuine. However interesting the subject matter, the reading into evidence of long depositions is monotonous. Though Tyler and Barnes enlivened the reading with a running exchange of constructive criticisms of each other's examination techniques and other pleasantries, the spectators were relieved when it was concluded. But the time had arrived for another adjournment.

During the adjournment taken over that second week end of the trial, there was for the first time in several months, nothing to report concerning the divorce case or any of its satellites. The *Chronicle* took the opportunity to editorialize on "REPORTING NASTY CASES," posing and answering the moral and philosophical problems confronting newspaper editors in deciding whether unsavory suits such as the Sharon case, covering topics "which are forbidden in society," should be published. The editorial writer conceded that the newspaper with the most sensational reporting enjoyed the widest circulation, but firmly declared that this must not be the test. He concluded that however distasteful to the publisher and editor, "a leading newspaper like the *Chronicle* [has an obligation] to furnish *all* the news of the day. Not part, but all."

When the trial resumed after the week end, Sarah arrived a trifle late, looking "blooming and blushing," but Nellie was absent for the first time. Tyler opened the day by calling Harry Lovidore Wells, age 25, the last witness to be sworn on Sarah's case in chief.

Three years earlier, Wells said, in April or May of 1881, he and an elderly friend, H. M. True, had been strolling on Sutter Street one afternoon when True pointed out Senator Sharon approaching on foot with a lady. True greeted the Senator and the two spoke for a few minutes. As Wells did not know the Senator, he walked four or five paces ahead and waited for his friend. He said he paid no particular attention to the conversation at the time, but recalled distinctly hearing the Senator refer to "Mrs. Sharon" and thought the Senator had mentioned "My wife" or "This is my wife."

He thought nothing further of the incident, Wells said, until he read of the divorce case in the newspapers; and after talking with Mr. True, the two men called on Tyler to offer their testimony. Wells said he believed Sarah to be the same lady because he recognized "the peculiarity of the eye, a rather sharp look."

The substance of Wells' testimony made him a very good witness for Sarah, of course. But a lawyer would call him a "good" witness in another sense as well. He gave his answers promptly, concisely, and confidently and he was undismayed by the stern manner of Barnes' cross-examination which, while exhaustive, produced nothing. Sarah's case was looking increasingly good.

Sarah herself was then called back to the stand to answer a few questions about collateral matters and, as she stepped down, her half-dozen attorneys briefly put their heads together. Tyler extracted himself from the huddle after a moment and announced, "Plaintiff rests."

The announcement was so unexpected that it had to be repeated before Barnes understood it.

Chapter VII   THE DEFENSE IS HEARD

ARNES had been so unprepared for the conclusion of Tyler's case in chief that he had no witnesses available and had to ask for a recess. The Senator was in court and available but principals rarely testify until most or all of their supporting witnesses have been called, and Barnes intended to follow that practice.

The defense evidence was expected to be presented on three general fronts, all calculated to arrive at the same objective; some showing that Sarah always conducted herself as a single woman after, as well as before, the alleged marriage; some directly impeaching the material assertions of Sarah's testimony and that of her witnesses; and some consisting of the testimony of handwriting experts exposing the contract and "Dear Wife" letters as spurious.

Barnes opened the defense case with a series of witnesses called to show that Sarah had never ceased conducting herself as a single woman. The first of these was a "social acquaintance" of Sarah's who lived across the bay in Oakland. She said that Sarah and the Senator had visited her there early in November, 1880. While her husband entertained the Senator in another part of the house, she asked Sarah what their relationship was. She said that Sarah made no mention of a marriage in August, but replied that they were engaged. A few months later, when the witness next saw her, Sarah was out riding with a "Lieutenant Somebody."

In another conversation at about the same time, the witness said, Sarah admitted to a purely monetary interest in the Senator, and asked the witness to intercede for her with Reuben Lloyd, whom she loved "better than any man she ever saw," but

77

with whom she had lately had a misunderstanding. Lloyd was the "gentleman" involved in Sarah's alleged suicide attempt, whose name Barnes had till now managed to keep out of the case. Lloyd was a prominent San Francisco attorney and law partner of the Senator's son-in-law, Frank G. Newlands. Though he was a handsome man and very popular, Lloyd never married; the degree of interest he had in Sarah was never disclosed, but it is clear that there came a time when he wished to terminate whatever relationship had existed. He is remembered principally for his often quoted observation concerning the intimate dining alcoves provided by San Francisco's French restaurants — that no woman ever went upstairs in a French restaurant to say her prayers.

Tyler, before launching his cross-examination of this first defense witness, cast an ominous eye around the courtroom as if to suggest that other defense witnesses pay close attention to what was to follow so that they might be forewarned what was in store for them should they also incur his wrath by false testimony. Then swinging back to the witness, he inhaled deeply and discharged his first fearsome cannonade. The judge promptly asked the court reporter to note that he had previously been compelled to admonish Tyler to modulate his voice and that any further disrespect shown any witness would entail "serious consequences."

Tyler subsided into a study out of which he reportedly came as gentle as a bull with a new ring in his nose, his voice no louder than that of the basso in a travelling opera company. As usual the reform was transitory. Barnes had long since learned how to distract Tyler. Whenever the latter nipped too closely at the heels of a faltering witness Barnes would softly make some inconsequential side remark. Tyler invariably reacted by jumping up to ask the judge plaintively that he be permitted to continue the examination unmolested. Barnes would subside immediately, but Tyler once offended could not be stopped until his outrage had spent itself in an ecstasy of indignation.

Such incidents generally ended with Judge Sullivan admonishing Tyler, who would drop back into his chair with a pained look of bewildered innocence. Occasionally, by pulling on his coat, Sarah or one of his associates would be able to get him back in his chair and on with the cross-examination before the judge's admonitions became too pointed, but more often than not Tyler would end the flurry just short of contempt, while Barnes sat blandly looking out the window.

Nothing was developed on cross-examination of the first defense witness, except Tyler's already well-known volatility.

Mrs. Eliza Stagg was the next witness called by Barnes. She said that she and the colonel, her husband, visiting from the East, had gone to Belmont at the Senator's invitation for a house party the first week end in April, 1881. On the train down they had meet Sarah, along with Cornelius Vanderbilt and a half dozen others who were to make up the party.

Some weeks later, she said, she and her husband had accompanied Sarah and Freddie Burchard on another week-end visit at Belmont. Sarah and Freddie were very attentive to each other, she felt, but were never alone together. One evening after the Staggs had retired Sarah had come in their room, sat on their bed, and told them Freddie had proposed to her. The witness would not say that Sarah ever admitted having accepted Freddie's proposal, despite Barnes' urging, but related that when Colonel Stagg had asked what the Senator would say, Sarah had replied that it would make no difference, for though the Senator was very anxious to marry her there was no use talking about love as she did not love him and she had no more heart than a piece of marble.

Tyler spent more than a day cross-examining Mrs. Stagg, devoting much attention to minutiae. As a result, she became vague and confused about much of her earlier testimony. After a laborious process of elimination, Tyler led her to the admission that Sarah and Freddie could have known each other for two or three days, at most, before the asserted engagement talk. She said she had used her diary to refresh her memory, but close examination by Tyler did not reveal any entries relating to conversations with Sarah.

Tyler asked her when she had started keeping her diary. She did not know. Well, then, about how old had she been when she started keeping it? She did not remember. Eighteen? (Same answer.) Twenty? (Same answer.) Twenty-five? (Same answer.) Thirty? She gave Tyler a look which suggested that it was not polite to assume a lady ever reached the age of thirty years and said she was sure she had begun the diary before she was thirty. The spectators tittered and Tyler, satisfied, said, "That is all."

Barnes, wrathful at Tyler's treatment of Mrs. Stagg, and irritated with her for collapsing under that treatment, vented his frustration on the spectators, demanding that the "gabbling crowd" be excluded from the court.

Spectators and newspaper readers had started the trial curious but detached, but as it progressed most of them became partisan to one side or the other. Judge Sullivan several times felt constrained to admonish spectators to desist from the laughter and applause which was increasingly punctuating the testimony. The audience seemed to be deriving its greatest satisfaction from the discomfiture of Senator Sharon's witnesses, hence Barnes' demand.

To everyone's surprise Judge Sullivan complied, ordering the courtroom immediately cleared and announcing that henceforth the trial would be closed to the public. The disappointed motley of disengaged attorneys, courthouse retainers and women of all ages and callings sadly trailed out of the courtroom; but after some discussion it was agreed that the large corps of reporters might remain, and they were invited back.

Nellie Brackett's continued absence from her accustomed chair beside Sarah was again marked as court convened the following day, but no one seemed able or willing to say what had become of her.

J. R. Reigart, the next witness called by Barnes, was among those at the Belmont party in early April. The essence of his testimony was that Sarah had many times said she was engaged to the Senator but never claimed nor wished to be married to him.

Unable to shake Reigart's testimony, Tyler resorted to attempts to show bias of recent origin. He extracted an admission that Reigart had written to Sarah soon after the suit was filed,

"You will have to encounter a great deal of false swearing if it comes to court. The Senator's dollars will bring forth a great deal of that sort of evidence, but I have a firm conviction that truth and justice will triumph and that you will be fully vindicated."

If he thought they were not married, asked Tyler, what was the truth and justice he referred to?

"Judging from what she told me, I thought if they were not married they ought to be," Reigart answered. He explained that the letter was written at a time when he believed in Sarah. The course of events later convinced him that he had earlier been wrong and that the Senator — though he could — would not buy perjured testimony, he said. Sarah had written several notes pleading with him to "save her honor at the expense of my own" by testifying that the Senator had introduced her as his wife.

Where were the notes? Tyler asked.

He had destroyed them because he was so indignant at the proposals.

Didn't she in fact simply ask him to be a man and stand up and tell the truth? asked Tyler.

Never, Reigart said emphatically, "because she knew the truth would kill her."

Tyler, who had apparently been doing some research, closed by asking Reigart why Barnes always addressed him as "Governor."

"I don't know," he answered promptly. "I never had political aspirations in my life."

Reigart's wife corroborated his testimony, to end the week's parade of witnesses.

Although, pursuant to Judge Sullivan's order, the trial was now playing to an empty house, newspaper readers were still being thoroughly edified. During the week-end's adjournment a "sensational" development was brought to light by a resourceful *Chronicle* reporter much to the satisfaction of his editor and readers. A full column article that Sunday was captioned "A MISSING BRACKETT." Recalling that Nellie "was always a conspicuous person in the courtroom, her ever eager attention to the testimony always attracting observation," the report revealed that late the previous Saturday night Sarah's attorneys had hastily obtained an order from Judge Sullivan permitting them to search a ship which was about to sail from the bay, on report that Nellie was being spirited away by the opposition. The search had been fruitless and Sarah's counsel had apparently learned the following day that Nellie had gone, or been taken, home to her mother.

✓   ✓   ✓

Throughout the week emissaries from Sarah had reportedly urged Nellie to stand firm, but Nellie's mother was attending her closely and Nellie would only say enigmatically that she had done all that she could for Sarah and she thought that she ought now to do something for her parents. Nellie was reported to have told several people that her father was to be paid $25,000 by the Senator for having lured her home.

As court convened the following Monday, April 1, to begin another week of the trial the attorneys' demeanors had become reversed. Tyler looked wrathful while Barnes appeared to be in better spirits than at any previous time during the new three-week-old trial. Barnes opened the session by saying he wanted to disclaim any involvement in Nellie's reported activities but Judge Sullivan ruled that there was nothing before the court concerning the incident warranting any reference to it.

The incident was before the court soon enough, as the next witness called forward by Barnes was Mrs. Mary H. Brackett, Nellie's mother. She met Sarah, she testified grimly, when Sarah, a new neighbor, asked her to furnish meals until she could get a servant. The first time she ever heard the Senator mentioned was on an occasion when Sarah displayed undergarments she said the Senator had imported for her from France while they were engaged; Sarah had said the engagement was later broken off, and that she would not marry the best man living, as she loved her freedom too much.

As Mrs. Brackett's testimony progressed it became apparent that Nellie's volubility had been inherited. Once started, Mrs. Brackett was difficult to stop and, asked by Barnes how frequently she had seen her daughter during Nellie's sojourn with Sarah, her answer provided one of the few poignant interludes of the trial.

"I remember going there one day and they two were going out," she said, "and I walked along a little ways; I thought I could walk along with my daughter and speak to her, and Miss Hill says, 'Nellie, I want you to come along and walk with me.' And I said, 'Nellie, I think it is too bad that I could not see you a few minutes.' And Miss Hill said, 'Come along, I am in a hurry; I have got to go to my lawyer's office, and you must go with me.' Nellie followed along.

"I followed them down to Market and First Street. Miss Hill turned back and said she did not care to have me follow her, as she was going on business. I said she needn't flatter herself, I was following my child. Where my child could go I could go. I followed along until they got to Tucker's Building, where Colonel Flournoy's office was, and they ran upstairs and I followed.

"When they got up to the top stairs Miss Hill turned round and said she was going to the office on business and didn't care to have me follow. I told her I didn't care where it was she was going, I was going to follow my child, and I went into the office to plead with my child.

"I thought it was very unkind in the lawyers for not wanting her to be with her mother. I was pleading with the attorney and Nellie says, 'This is not Colonel Flournoy, it is the clerk.' And I said it didn't matter to me, that I was not saying anything I was afraid of. And then Miss Hill turned and asked the clerk to ring for Mr. Tyler by telephone, and when she said that, I said to Nellie that I would bid her goodbye, for I did not like to meet Judge Tyler, as I thought he had used his influence to have her away from me."

Mrs. Brackett brought her answer to a close with a five-minute monologue on the relative merits of Sarah's various attorneys, at the end of which Barnes sat for a time in silent wonder at what his simple question had wrought. But, whether from trepidation or because he had forgotten the point he was pursuing, he surrendered the witness to Tyler.

On cross-examination Tyler was unable to develop much from Mrs. Brackett except increased hostility and an admission that she did not feel very friendly toward Sarah. As Mrs. Brackett stepped down from the stand with another day's adjournment, there was much speculation on Nellie's probable future role, if any, in the case.

The next morning's *Chronicle* closed its account of the trial day by divulging that all of the reporters who were covering the trial had been invited to dinner that evening at one of the city's most expensive restaurants. Their host was one of the Senator's bodyguards. "Of course, the representative of the *Chronicle* declined such a compromising invitation, but it is said a grand feast was held at Marchand's Restaurant in the evening. It may be added that Sharon is expected to be placed on the witness stand today." The next morning's paper reported that "a *Chronicle* representative" was assaulted in a City Hall corridor by a reporter for another newspaper because of the mention of the dinner. But the enmity its probity had engendered only inspired a more emphatic espousal of virtue. Just as a judge would be censured for attending a dinner given by a litigant in a case under consideration, the article concluded, so also an honest newspaper reporter was obliged to remain objective, impartial and aloof.

Confuting the *Chronicle's* surmise that the Senator was about to testify, the next witness called by Barnes the following day was Mrs. Harriet Kenyon, a "lady's companion," employed in that capacity by Sarah in 1881 in anticipation of a trip East during which Sarah planned to study music. Sarah had told her they might go on from there to Europe, never to return to San Francisco. She was with Sarah almost constantly that autumn, she testified, and the Senator never visited her rooms, although Sarah did spend three nights in his. The first two nights she secreted herself in the Senator's room to find out if he was keeping any other woman there. After the last night, in November, Sarah reappeared saying she and the Senator had spent the night discussing their problems and had a friendly breakfast together. Reporters wondered how this last picture of domestic intimacy helped the Senator's case, but found no answer.

Barnes having apparently abandoned any effort to spare Reuben Lloyd, law partner of the Senator's son-in-law, asked Mrs. Kenyon if she ever knew Sarah to visit Lloyd. She said Sarah went to his law office in the financial district several times. After one such interview, Sarah returned radiant, exclaiming joyously, "Oh, Mrs. Kenyon, he has met me so cordially today. Reuben, how I love him. I love him better than any person I ever knew. I would give up everything I have in the world if he would only come back to me again." The skeptical Mrs. Kenyon said she asked Sarah if she meant she would even give up wealth to marry him, and Sarah said she would. This display of feeling greatly impressed Mrs. Kenyon.

Barnes concluded her direct examination by eliciting testimony that she had accompanied Sarah on visits to a number of fortunetellers, to one of whom Sarah said she was a "Mrs. Something," giving a fictitious name and asking the fortuneteller to do whatever was necessary to get her husband back. Again, reporters felt this contributed less to the Senator's case than to Sarah's.

On cross-examination, Tyler developed that Sarah had sometimes brought articles of the Senator's clothing for her to mend, that all she knew of the Reuben Lloyd matter was what Sarah told her, and finally that Sarah had discharged her for shirking some assigned task.

Barnes next called the "Mrs. Smith" about whom he had questioned Sarah. On about May 10, 1880, she said, Sarah told her she had taken poison in Lloyd's office because he had refused to marry her. Mrs. Smith spent the night with Sarah at her doctor's office, and accompanied her to her rooms the following day. Later in the year, she said, she visited Sarah at the Grand Hotel, and Sarah told her that she was engaged to marry the Senator.

A seamstress, employed at the Grand while Sarah lived there, next testified that Sarah acted as though she was being kept by the Senator, never claiming to be his wife. Late one night Sarah visited her to report that she had been hiding in the Senator's room and saw him come in and go to bed with another woman. Sarah told her that as they undressed the Sena-

tor had jokingly said to the woman, "Look out, there might be
a tiger around." As Sarah told the story, she laughed at the
obvious reference to herself, the witness said.

On cross-examination the witness admitted to Tyler that
her employment at the Grand had been terminated a year or
so ago, but that after talking to the Senator about becoming a
witness she had recently been re-employed.

Barnes next called Mrs. Julia Bornemann, the young woman
with whom Sarah, in the company of two gentlemen, had admitted driving to the roadhouse in 1881. Mrs. Bornemann's
striking beauty affected the whole courtroom as soon as she
stepped forward; it was reported that Tyler even forgot to
take notes of her testimony.

She said, in a voice "soft as a lute," that she had been an
intimate friend of Sarah's, and that in November 1880 Sarah
told her the Senator wanted to marry her but that she wanted
more than the quarter-million dollars he was willing to settle
on her. Sarah had also spoken often of opportunities to marry
various other gentlemen. Mrs. Bornemann recalled trips to
Belmont and the ride to the Fourteen Mile House, much as
Sarah had spoken of them.

On cross-examination, Tyler asked if she ever engaged in
questionable conduct.

Certainly not, she said.

He assumed then, Tyler went on, that nothing in the slightest degree improper had occurred during any activities she
shared with Sarah.

As Tyler expected, she said firmly that nothing at all improper had occurred at any time that she was with Sarah or at
any time she was not with Sarah.

Tyler thanked her gallantly and said that was all he wished
to know.

As she stepped down from the stand, Mrs. Bornemann
favored Tyler with a grateful smile and said to Barnes, "He
isn't so bad at all, is he now?" He had, certainly, attempted to
be on good behavior, but when at one point he had asked her
whether she discussed with Sarah "children she had, or children she might have," the gallant Terry felt constrained to

prompt him to greater gentility, suggesting "children *in esse* or children *in posse*."

The next day saw a number of minor actors called to the stand in quick succession. Among others, a spirit medium testified that Sarah had told her in April, 1881, that the Senator was interested in marrying her, and in October asked her to do something to compel the Senator to marry her.

A San Francisco attorney testified that a year previously a Mrs. Samson had introduced him to a veiled lady who wanted to bring a breach of promise action against the Senator. The veiled lady, who may have been Sarah, said she had been deceived by the Senator, and claimed to have fifty letters from him. The attorney told her that three or four would be enough but, he testified, he never saw her again until the present, if Sarah was the lady — he could not be sure.

The manager of the Grand Hotel confirmed the circumstances of Sarah's arrival and departure. He said he had written a note on the Senator's order, requesting Sarah to leave, around November 19, 1881. When she failed to leave by December 1 the hall carpeting was taken up. On the fifth he ordered that her doors be removed. "Seeing no effort at moving" on the sixth, the manager said, he sent the carpet man to raise the carpet in her suite. When the carpet had been loosened around the edges, Sarah packed her bags, but the manager refused to release her luggage until Sarah paid rent for the month of November and five days in December, whereupon she departed.

✁　　　✁　　　✁

The following day began with Barnes offering to prove that Sarah had buried some of the Senator's clothing in a grave in Masonic Cemetery. Tyler objected vehemently that such evidence would be entirely irrelevant to any issue in the case and could have no other purpose than to prejudice the judge against Sarah, but Judge Sullivan ruled that it might have some bearing on the question of whether Sarah considered herself to be a married woman, and permitted Barnes to proceed, thereby lengthening the trial by at least a week. With a sweep of his hand toward the witness stand, Tyler invited Barnes to "wallow in filth" if he wished.

A cemetery employee then testified that in the spring of the previous year, 1883, Nellie Brackett introduced him to Sarah. They asked if there were any newly opened grave and requested permission to put a package under the casket. They explained that their fortunes had been told and that the procedure was necessary to make predictions of the marriages of each come true. He hesitated but finally consented and Sarah went with him into the grave he selected. Placing the package under the box which was to receive the casket, she whispered something that he could not make out. The witness testified that two weeks ago the casket was dug up and the package, which he identified in court, was removed. The city health officer and other cemetery employees were called to the witness stand to corroborate the identification of the package.

With the beginning of the next day's session, the trial entered its second month. It gave no indication of being soon concluded, though everyone except Sarah and Mammy Pleasant, still in daily attendance, was now reported to be tiring. Public interest did not seem to be flagging despite Judge Sullivan's continuing order excluding spectators from the courtroom; local newspapers were carrying from one to three full columns of the testimony every day, and hundreds of words were pouring over the Associated Press wires.

Barnes that day called a succession of fortunetellers, spirit mediums, astrologists and charm workers, whose testimony was to the effect that Sarah had visited one or another of them at various times from 1880 until shortly before the trial. She had asked their advice, charms and incantations to do various things, they said, including getting the Senator to marry her, inducing Reuben Lloyd to marry her, and to get her Chinese cook to return to her.

Laura Scott, a "New Orleans trained fortuneteller," was typical. Although she "disremembered" a good bit she said that in 1881 Sarah had come to her saying that she wanted a charm to induce the Senator, who was ill and whom she was nursing, to marry her. Sarah had told her she was supplementing his

medicine with a charm given her by another fortuneteller, but
that it was giving him an upset stomach and making him
drowsy and cross; and when she attempted to improve the
charm's effectiveness with a larger dose, it made him twitch.

Mrs. Scott testified that although she was a straight fortuneteller and had nothing to do with charms, she offered to prepare one for Sarah with the secret hope of sparing the unsuspecting Senator more serious consequences from taking the potion Sarah was administering. She asked Sarah to come back
the next day, and in the interval bought a charm book. Finding
a nice harmless-sounding recipe for a love potion, she gave
Sarah a bottle of molasses and sugar in black tea, telling her to
give the Senator three teaspoons daily. Sarah asked if it would
hurt to try hastening the effect by giving him more, and Mrs.
Scott replied that she could give him up to a quart a day if
she chose. Sarah returned in a few days for another bottle, saying the first had not been effective. In another day or two she
was back for another refill, and the next day sent for a fourth.
She later returned, disappointed, to say the charm was no good,
that in fact the Senator was getting more irritable and had
quarreled with her.

Tyler's cross-examination followed the same pattern with
all of the sibyls, and was conducted with obvious zest. He
asked Mrs. Scott if she actually believed that the molasses and
tea had any supernatural effect. She couldn't say, said Mrs.
Scott; she was a God-fearing Christian woman and she had
given Sarah the charm because if she didn't someone else
would. Moreover, she said righteously, she had wanted Sarah to
stop giving the Senator the terrible charm she was originally
using.

How did she determine what advice to give, asked Tyler?

"I goes into the oraculum," she answered. "After you gets
in you oraculums, you examine them, and you ask any part
of the question you please to ask; then you marks down so
many marks; then you get your charm out. You have to understand how to work out these things. If you had your book here
you would see how it done. You asks the oraculum if it will
have the desired effect. You get yes, or no, or so on. The oracu-

lum said this charm would work, so I made it for her, but she said it didn't work."

Both Barnes and Tyler eventually tired of the fortunetellers, and after several days moved on to the testimony and various diversions provided by "Mrs." Mary Shawhan, a handsome, poised woman of about thirty, called by Barnes to relate several conversations in which Sarah had spoken of herself as engaged to the Senator as late as 1882 and 1883. She answered Barnes' questions in a bored, world-weary, well-modulated voice (pronouncing "piano" with a long "I," the press noted), allowing herself an amused laugh when testifying that Sarah had once accused her of having an affair with the Senator. On that occasion, she said, Sarah had told her that her engagement with him was broken and that she intended to bring a breach of promise suit against him. Mrs. Shawhan also testified that Nellie had recently expressed surprise at the filing of the divorce suit, as she had assumed a breach of contract action would be filed.

Tyler took Mrs. Shawhan's manner, indeed her existence, as a personal affront and was barely able to contain himself until being unleashed by Barnes' "You may cross-examine," on the morning of the second day. It was immediately apparent that he had not spent the previous evening in repose. He warmed up with a few questions about her marital status. She was vague as to Mr. Shawhan's whereabouts, or his existence, but, in speaking of her son by Mr. Shawhan, she nodded toward the back of the courtroom.

Tyler, who had been vexed at the order excluding spectators, bounced to his feet to object to any special privileges being accorded friends and relatives of the Senator's witnesses; but as he spoke he looked around and saw sitting alone in the body of the court a boy of about twelve or fourteen. Deprecatingly waving aside his objection, he turned back to the witness.

Wasn't it a fact that she was in the habit of maintaining correspondence with a number of men, using false return addresses?

Mrs. Shawhan, who had been lounging in the witness chair, stiffened and her languid eyes narrowed to focus on Tyler.

Barnes was up immediately to object to that line of questioning as irrelevant but Tyler, flourishing a number of envelopes, responded that he intended to prove "this woman is in the habit of visiting disreputable places in the company of a large number of men."

As Tyler was speaking, the witness's right hand moved surreptitiously to a large pocket buried under a fold in her dress. Tyler and the judge failed to see or interpret the movement, but Barnes, already on his feet, thrust forward a restraining hand, saying, "Stop that. None of that."

Thinking Barnes was addressing him, Tyler opened his mouth to complain to the judge; but then became aware of what was taking place. He said, "Oh, let her go, I can take care of myself," and asked the judge if he might proceed to show that "this woman is a disreputable character."

Mrs. Shawhan again reached into her pocket and Barnes, waving his hands discouragingly to the witness, again objected. Tyler replied that the only ground he could see for the objection was that the witness might shoot, and he did not think he should be required to forebear for that reason.

The Shawhan boy, something more than the child for which Tyler had taken him a few minutes earlier, had quietly come forward in the courtroom and was standing only four or five paces behind Tyler, attempting to draw a gun from his jacket pocket. Tyler's son, seeing this, turned to face the boy, putting his own hand to his hip, while another of Sarah's attorneys, Walter Levy, moved between the Shawhan boy and the senior Tyler who, oblivious, was still arguing the legal point to the judge.

Much switching of seats, running about and demands for searches followed in the ensuing seconds. When a degree of order was finally restored Tyler suggested that the boy be placed on the stand with his mother so that he could face them both. "I fear no pistol," he said.

Mrs. Shawhan concurred in the proposal, saying to the judge, "My life has been threatened; he is my only protection."

Judge Sullivan, until then sitting transfixed in speechless disbelief responded that Mrs. Shawhan needed no protection there. A moment later, coming fully to his senses, he ordered both Mrs. Shawhan and her son to leave.

Loud acrimony ensued among counsel. Evans accused Tyler's son of misconduct in carrying a weapon into court, and Levy retorted that the defense should be cited for permitting a witness to come into court armed.

George Washington Tyler, seeing an opportunity for a dramatic declamation, and unable to resist it despite the absence of spectators, said, "I have carried arms for my country although few know it, for I have never boasted of my war record. I know how to use arms, though I never carry any but those which God has given me. I can take care of myself. Counsel on the other side declare they are not armed. They do not need to be for beyond them sit two armed men, special police officers in the pay of the defendant. They may shoot me down from behind but I shall never swerve one line from my duty."

Tyler was hardly warming to his subject, but the others wanted to be heard also, and as each attorney attempted to surpass the other in his declared dedication to the sanctity of the rule of law over the rule of force, the judge, who had had time to regain sufficient composure to begin to feel outraged, abruptly called a recess and strode from the bench. The attorneys, unwilling to permit the raptures of righteous indignation to be cut off by the judge's absence, continued to argue, becoming louder and nearer violence with each succeeding pacific utterance, until the bailiff demanded that they disperse.

A number of San Francisco policemen were in court as it reconvened at two o'clock. Judge Sullivan announced that he would not proceed with the trial unless assured at each session that no one was armed. He directed the clerk and bailiff to see that his prohibition was enforced. Still hoping to be awakened from an unpleasant dream, he then declared court adjourned for the day.

Police officers were stationed at the courtroom door the following morning, but when they stepped forward to search Tyler as he strode in, he thundered, "Don't you dare lay hands on me," and stomped into court as the abashed officers fell back. Everyone, including newspaper reporters, eventually consented to being searched, and amid much merriment and the exchange of many witticisms and a few practical jokes the search was held. No weapons were found.

When the judge resumed the bench, he permitted further discussion of the admissibility of evidence of Mrs. Shawhan's lack of chastity. Barnes and Tyler managed to utilize the entire day in argument on the point, each rising to new heights of melodramatic eloquence.

At the opening session the following week the judge ruled that Tyler would be permitted to question Mrs. Shawhan further. The courtroom that day, despite the exclusion order, was almost filled. A great many people found that they had official business with the court. It is unlikely that they found what they were seeking.

Mrs. Shawhan was again cool and nonchalant. She admitted having an active correspondence with many men, in which she often used fictitious addresses, but firmly and persistently denied misconduct of any kind, though it was at times difficult to determine what answer she was giving to which question. The flood of objections by Barnes which followed each of Tyler's questions resulted in much disorder.

When Tyler said, "That is all," she asked if she could make a statement regarding his accusations. The judge explained that her denials under oath had been as much as she needed to say, and as much as he could permit. She was later reported to have fainted in the corridor outside the courtroom, and again as she arrived at her home. She was described as suffering from "nervous prostration."

Mrs. Fannie Samson, a friend of Mrs. Shawhan, provided a relatively tranquil interlude with her testimony. She testified to the street corner meeting in which, she said, Sarah had discussed with the attorney the possibility of his representing her in a breach of promise action against the Senator.

She also said that she had been with Sarah and Nellie Brackett one time in 1882 when the Senator had driven by, inspiring Sarah to say, "Why, there is my old darling, beautiful Sen; just come and look at him. He is so fascinating, isn't he, Nell?" Mrs. Samson said she had replied, "I don't see anything

fascinating about him at all; he is a very little man, and outside of his wealth, I wouldn't think he was attractive at all. I
don't see what there is in Senator Sharon for a young pretty girl
like you to be so desperately in love with." Sarah had rejoined,
"I would rather be the wife of a Senator Sharon and live on a
crust in a garret than be the wife of a millionaire and live in a
palace."

During the recital the Senator, sitting at the counsel table,
momentarily appeared to be in a dilemma. Should he evince
gratitude toward Sarah for having so nobly defended him
against the unflattering opinion of the woman who was now his
witness, or should he smilingly encourage the witness not with-
standing her jaundiced evaluation of him, for offering the infer-
ence that at the time of the conversation Sarah was not enjoying
that marital status for which she would renounce a palace?
He resolved the problem in his usual way. His countenance
remained impassive.

Mrs. Samson's direct examination concluded with an assertion that Sarah had recently offered her a hundred thousand
dollars to swear that the Senator had once introduced her to
Sarah as his wife.

On cross-examination she admitted that she, as well as Mrs.
Shawhan, had been actively engaged in finding defense witnesses for some time; but despite Tyler's unbridled outrage
she was not intimidated and her direct testimony stood un-
shaken. She concluded by gratuitously telling Tyler she had
mediumistic powers and the gift to communicate with the
spirit world. Tyler could think of no immediate use to make of
that talent and abandoned the witness.

The week was concluded with a succession of witnesses
whose brief testimony was largely cumulative; among them
was an attorney who testified that Sarah one day asked him
what evidence would be required to support a breach of promise action. He had replied that the kind of evidence referred
to in *Bardell* v. *Pickwick* would not be sufficient.

Tyler cross-examined most of those witnesses indifferently
or not at all, but roused himself to extract from the attorney,
with much effort, the admission that he had recently been

prosecuted for rape in a much publicized trial in Modesto. He had been acquitted, but admitted that the townspeople had been so incensed by the verdict that an unsuccessful attempt had been made to lynch him.

An argument over the admissibility of these peccadillos was in progress as Judge Sullvan declared another week-end adjournment. Tyler and Barnes were as usual enjoying the argument too much to be easily disengaged and the judge had to repeat his adjournment declaration, saying, "This court is adjourned. Fight it out outside."

Chapter VIII PLUMBAGO AND LOOPING W'S

HE NEXT Monday's session was commenced with the now routine search
of all persons who were to enter be-
yond the railing, but although the order excluding spectators
had not been rescinded, so many exceptions were now being
made that the trial was again playing to a full courtroom.

The attorneys had spent the previous week end in Santa
Cruz, some distance down the coast from San Francisco, taking
the deposition of H. M. True, the man who had been introduced to Sarah by the Senator on Sutter Street in 1881, according to Harry Wells. The greater part of the week was taken up
with reading into evidence his deposition and that of Freddie
Burchard. Those who had read of Freddie's deposition were
surprised that the defense would consider it worth using, but
there was no doubt of the value of True's deposition to the
Senator.

H. M. True, sixty-seven, sometimes found delicate health a
convenient refuge, and his deposition was taken in his Santa
Cruz home because he claimed he was unable to endure the
trip to court in San Francisco.

He said he had never seen Sarah and the Senator together,
and did not know the Senator; nor had he ever seen Sarah
before the trial began. Though he knew Wells, he had never
talked to him about the case or about being a witness.

He spoke hurriedly at first, but when his examination was
carried beyond bare denial, True became less eager to volunteer information, pleading a mind weakened by illness, particularly on cross-examination by Tyler. But his memory flagged
even under the friendly guidance of Barnes.

How did he happen to meet Tyler, Barnes asked?

He had introduced Wells to Tyler during the first week of the trial, he said.

Why had he done that?

He didn't know; something about Wells having information about the case.

He admitted that he had gone to San Francisco intending himself to be a witness for Sarah, but said the only reason he went was that Tyler had sent him $15 expense money.

What would he have testified to if called? The truth, he declared, and Barnes urbanely said, "Your witness."

Tyler's voice was distorted by outraged incredulity as he first asked True if it were not a fact that he had come voluntarily to Tyler's office two months before the trial began, asked if there was value in the testimony of witnesses who had heard the Senator introduce Sarah as his wife, and then claimed to have been so introduced.

None of that was true, said True.

Hadn't he thereafter introduced Wells to Tyler as the other man who had heard the Senator called Sarah his wife? Tyler fairly shouted.

"Yes," replied True, but almost immediately corrected himself. "I said that wrong. I introduced him to Judge Tyler, but I did not say he was the other man that heard the conversation. I said nothing. I have not seen him since."

Tyler then showed him a letter, which True admitted having written to Tyler only three weeks past, during the second week of the trial, in which he complained that he was ill and wanted his testimony to be taken at his home in Santa Cruz. The letter concluded, underscored by True for emphasis, "I expect Mrs. Sharon to testify to the introduction of *her* to *me* by Mr. Sharon *before* I *testify*." Asked to explain the letter, True said that his illness had impaired his memory. "I do not know if I can make any explanation. I do not recollect what I was going to say."

Tyler prodded True's memory with another letter written to Tyler shortly before the trial, in which True had written in part, "I want to see you on a/c of evidence *conclusive* which I can give and *substantiate* for Mrs. Sharon, if she remembers the circumstances." Confronted with the letter, True admitted that he had gone to Tyler's office some months before the trial had opened, having read of the case, to see if he "could make anything of it," telling Tyler that he could prove the Senator had introduced Sarah as his wife.

True still maintained, in deposition, that the Senator's introduction of Sarah had never taken place. He now admitted that he had prevailed upon Wells so to testify and had intended to do so himself until thinking better of it. So far as he knew, he said, they had been able to deceive Tyler, who was not a party to the plan, but he assumed that Sarah knew the falsity of the story.

Tyler closed True's cross-examination by asking questions calculated to reveal recently developed animosity. Had he spoken privately with any of the Senator's representatives since the trial had started, Tyler asked as a parting shot?

Not until a few minutes ago during a recess in the deposition, he replied. He had then asked Barnes one question.

What was that, asked Tyler eagerly?

"I asked him if the nonsensical questions that you were asking me amounted to anything. He said 'No'."

All who heard or read of True's testimony were in agreement that he was a reprehensible character. There was, however, much divergence of opinion on its proper interpretation and effect. Clearly, at least part of his testimony was false. Had he and Wells conspired to produce false evidence? If so, was Sarah a party to it? Or had Wells' testimony and True's intended testimony at the trial been true, and had True now been bought off?

Even if the story of the introduction was false, did this mean that the marriage was a fraud? Sensational cases frequently draw unscrupulous or unbalanced people who seek money or notoriety by claiming to have knowledge of material elements of the case. Sarah herself had testified that she did not recall ever having been introduced to True. Thus, even if True and Wells were adventurers — and even if Sarah suspected, or knew, that their testimony was false — would this have any effect on the case other than to discredit Wells' testimony? These and other questions were doubtless going through Judge Sullivan's mind as he heard the testimony, but as to his conclusions he gave no indication.

If the long course which the case had already followed had caused any flagging of public interest, the True testimony revived it. The greater weight of public opinion had, until then, favored Sarah. Her case appeared to have been presented in a straightforward and plausible fashion; moreover, she had the popular advantage of being an underdog, the wronged woman against the ruthless tycoon's millions.

The testimony elicited on behalf of the Senator thus far had done nothing to change popular sentiment. Evidence that after the marriage she still held herself out to be a single woman was entirely consistent with the secrecy provision in the marriage contract. Moreover, Freddie Burchard had been thoroughly discredited in his claim of having courted Sarah. If he could be bought, as he presumably had been, perhaps others of the Senator's witnesses were, as well.

Sarah's asserted suicide attempt had occurred in May, 1880, three months before the claimed marriage; far from inconsistent with the marriage, perhaps the unhappy conclusion of her affair with Lloyd had catapulted her into the unconventional union with the Senator.

True's testimony now unsettled public opinion, inspiring reactions ranging from indignation at True to consternation, from suspicion of Sarah to rejection.

✓   ✓   ✓

All parties having survived the sixth week of the trial, the following Monday, April 21, they bravely faced the seventh, starting off with a pair of witnesses called by Barnes to testify that Nellie Brackett had told them Sarah had offered her $10,000 to remain loyal. Tyler limited his cross-examination to asking one of the witnesses whether he had ever done an honest day's work. After some reflecting, the witness thought he recalled a job he had held for a time, three or four years past.

The next witness was Ah Ki, the Senator's manservant, who had been with him since soon after his arrival from China in

1853. His speech was broken, rapid and high pitched. Additionally, he had much nervous energy which he released by waving his hands about and by jumping out of the witness chair every few minutes to illustrate the incidents related in his testimony, all to the great entertainment of the audience.

Ki said he first saw Sarah about August, 1880, at the Senator's office, where Ki was guarding the door. She visited the Senator's rooms at the Palace three or four times a week during the winter of 1880-81, generally taking dinner there and often staying the night. After the Senator's return from the East in March, 1881, the visits were less frequent, Ki testified, and after June the Senator would not have Sarah in at all. She continued to lurk in the hall, begging Ki to take in notes to the Senator, though he told her the Senator believed she had stolen papers and money and no longer wished to see her.

Several times after the separation Ki made a "mistake" and let Sarah in while the Senator was not there, for which he was later scolded. One evening Sarah, pretending the Senator had invited her, gained entry while the Senator was at home. This time the Senator choked and cursed her and threw her out, telling Ki never to let her in again. Undaunted, Sarah continued to come almost every day, said Ki, until she got tired of being refused. Then she came less often, and occasionally sent Nellie Brackett.

On one final occasion Sarah came to Ki, accompanied by Nellie, saying she wanted his help in making the Senator again love her. The compassionate Ki again succumbed to her plea. "I say, 'What you do?' She showed me a little piece paper and some black powder, then I wanted to watch and see what she was going to do, and she said, 'All right.' Then she put powder on Mr. Sharon's chair right here [indicating], and this dining-room table right on corner [indicating]. Then she went underneath Mr. Sharon's chair, and went down in this way, just like a priest [indicating]. I stayed in other room with Nellie Brackett talking, and I look at her and laugh, and she say, 'You no laugh at me,' and she shut folding door."

He said Sarah also put powders in the Senator's wine and whiskey bottles, sprinkled clove spice under his pillow and busied herself elsewhere in the apartment. When Ki tried to follow to observe what she was doing, Nellie reproved him, saying "She go to water-closet; you no want to follow."

When Sarah had finished, she said " 'Oh, Mr. Sharon marry me sure, and I give you one thousand dollars, and I give you forty dollars every month to help your family.'" She gave Ki a five-dollar gold piece by way of advance, which he said he did not really care for, and left with Nellie, saying, " 'We go home and come two times more — come twice more; three times make it good.'"

When she later returned, Ki had had a change of heart. "I was afraid. I told her to go away; it was played out [a mining term apparently borrowed from the Senator]; and she said, 'You will tell Mr. Sharon?' And I say, 'Yes, I will; what's the reason not? You are going to cut my throat.' Then she went away. I told her not to come back and bother me any more." Although she did come several more times he never again admitted her.

Little but confusion was developed on Tyler's attempted cross-examination of Ki. He soon abandoned the effort and Ki left the stand bowing ingratiatingly to the entire courtroom.

Murmurs arose when Barnes next asked the bailiff to call William M. Neilson, Sarah's early champion. It was apparent that the maneuver had not been anticipated at Sarah's counsel table and Tyler was obviously as interested as anyone in learning what it presaged.

Neilson had been fairly regular in his attendance at the trial, but had been sitting among the spectators and not at the counsel table or with any of Sarah's contingent. So far as was known, he had not defected to the opposition, but had gone his own misanthropic way, devoting most of his energies to stirring up trouble of his own. He had been periodically in the newspapers, both his public disturbance case and the remaining forgery indictment having occupied the attorneys and the press from time to time in connection with various legal maneuvers. Both cases were still pending.

Neilson's manner as he strode forward and took the witness stand indicated satisfaction that his importance in the case was finally being given recognition, but his confidence was clearly not contagious. Barnes, as he cautiously began his examination, looked as uneasy as Tyler, and it was apparent that Neilson was not a witness of whom Barnes was at all sure. His questioning soon was sounding like cross-examination, and Tyler interrupted with numerous objections.

Neilson testified that he first met Sarah and became interested in her case in June, 1883. He admitted he was still a strong partisan of Sarah, but said he had never been employed by her and had no material interest in the case. He had advised Sarah about the divorce action and, he proudly declared, she had followed that advice.

If he was not an attorney, asked Barnes, how had he felt competent to advise Sarah?

He got his advice from a prominent San Francisco attorney, he said, a man he had hoped and expected to have represent Sarah.

Who was that, asked Barnes?

The attorney was General Barnes, said Neilson, blandly.

Barnes stared at Neilson. The Senator stared at Barnes. For a time after Barnes found his voice it was difficult to tell who was testifying, but when calm was eventually restored Neilson said he had met Barnes by chance on the street in the summer of 1883, at a time when the case was not publicly known, and asked Barnes if he could be engaged in a divorce case. Receiving an affirmative response, he testified, he told Barnes the names of the parties and mentioned the marriage contract.

Well, Barnes asked the witness, "Didn't I tell you it was impossible?"

"On the contrary," said Neilson, urbanely, "You said, 'I thought there was something like marriage in that case, for she was too good a girl and of too good a family to give herself away to old Sharon, unless she had something of that kind.'"

Barnes seemed about to have a seizure, but the intransigent Neilson continued, pronouncing each word with deliberation, "I am now talking of the first conversation I had with General Barnes, walking from the corner of Montgomery and California Streets to his office."

Sorrier by the minute, Barnes soon surrendered Neilson to Tyler, knowing that the worst was probably yet to come.

Neilson then recounted his talk with Barnes in great detail, saying that when he told Barnes that the case was against Sharon, Barnes had answered, "If you can give me a dead sure thing there is nothing would please me better than to go after the damned old rascal." Later, Neilson continued blithely, they discussed the case at Barnes' office and Barnes read and explained the law of marriage and divorce to Neilson. Neilson said he had asked whether Sarah should wait until after the Senator's death before asserting her claim, and Barnes had said it would be suicidal, that his heirs would fight the case more vigorously and with less fear of shame than the Senator during his lifetime. It was upon the "very impressive" delivery of the legal opinion by Barnes that the decision was made to file the divorce suit, said Neilson. The looks exchanged by Barnes and the Senator, sitting together at their counsel table, were said to be enigmatic.

At a third meeting, in Barnes' office, Neilson testified, he was astonished when Barnes had greeted him by saying, "Mr. Sharon denies the whole business." Neilson had angrily left the office because of Barnes' unauthorized disclosure to the intended opposition, and never returned. He had helped Sarah retain Tyler soon thereafter.

At several points in the testimony, Barnes had to be restrained from denying Neilson's assertions out of hand. Judge Sullivan told him, as Barnes knew when his mind was less perturbed, that if he chose to do so he would have to take the stand under oath, in due course, like any other witness. But under legal practice in effect at the time, becoming a witness would disqualify him from subsequently arguing the case as counsel. This dilemma did not contribute to Barnes' peace of mind, and when Neilson's cross-examination was finally concluded, Barnes slumped to his chair in impotent despair.

The news editor and the managing editor of the San Francisco *Examiner* were next called by Barnes, to testify to the accuracy of that newspaper's report of the interview Neilson had given the previous September, much of which he now said he did not remember. The judge sustained Tyler's objection to their testimony as hearsay. As the frustrated managing editor stepped down, he complained that "The faithfulness of the *Examiner* has been called in question, and I think I ought to have the privilege of having this matter sifted." The judge was unmoved, but Tyler, in his accustomed good spirits, offered to attempt to establish a good reputation for the paper if there was enough money in it.

ɬ   ɬ   ɬ

Henry C. Hyde was added to the list of counsel for the Senator at about this time, and on the next day Barnes proposed to call him to the stand as a handwriting expert. Tyler vociferously objected that as one of the attorneys for the defense, Hyde would simply be making a defense argument from the witness stand.

Barnes responded that Hyde would be testifying to matters which were self-evident facts, not matters of opinion, so his intended testimony could not be characterized as argument.

If that was true, Tyler rejoined, Hyde should not be permitted to testify for that very reason. If a dog was in court, he said, it would be a reflection on the court to have someone take the witness stand to testify that there was a dog in court. And, if the questioned handwriting was "self-evident," as claimed by Barnes, there was no need of having anyone testify to it.

Judge Sullivan pondered the question over the noon recess and then determined to permit Hyde to be sworn.

Hyde and several helpers then carried into court a series of various sized microscopes, together with magnifying glasses and lenses of one kind and another. Counsel tables were shifted about and more tables brought in, until the courtroom looked like a medical school laboratory. It was the spring of the year, and everyone seemed to enjoy the rearrangement of the furniture, with the exception of the bailiff, who rocked on his feet uneasily.

By way of establishing his qualification as a handwriting expert, Hyde testified that he had been a practicing attorney for over thirty years, had developed "some facility at distin-

guishing handwriting," was a charter member of the San Francisco Microscopical Society, and had been called upon and
accepted as an expert to examine handwriting on a number of
occasions. With his qualifications established, Barnes asked
him if there appeared to be any erasure on the "Dear Wife"
letters. The witness' response provided a portent of the weeks
to follow.

The order requiring the documents to remain in court had
prevented any prior examination. Hyde therefore stepped down
from the stand, selected a letter, and put it under one of his
microscopes. After alternately adjusting and peering for several
minutes, he shifted to another apparatus where the procedure
was repeated. Seeing that everyone was becoming restive, Hyde
muttered that a thorough examination required time and patience. More time was passed in silence, while Hyde squinted
intently through the magnifying lenses. Tyler broke the silence
saying "I hope the glass is not so powerful as to injure the sur-
face of the paper." Sarah reacted to the feeble jest with obvious
alarm, and Judge Sullivan told her he was carefully watching
out for that contingency. Court finally adjourned for the day
with the first question yet unanswered.

On the following day Judge Sullivan ordered Sarah to permit the documents to be examined in court at all times, and
authorized any and all experts named by either side to examine
them. In the interest of time, they were permitted to conduct
their independent examinations while Hyde was on the stand,
but, for the time being, he remained the only expert witness.

In their monotony, the next three days were indistinguish-
able from each other. News reports were captioned "DULL
DAY," "SHARON DOLDRUMS," "EXPERTS AT WORK,
COUNSEL DOZING," and reporters had reverted to describing Sarah's costume. "Sarah Althea tripped lightly into court
yesterday morning, arrayed in a brand new closely fitting costume, a perfect love of a hat, and a coral pin." The following
day she was wearing a wine colored dress of velvet and silk,
and a gold bracelet "an inch and one-half in width".

Tyler spent most of his time hovering about the expert,
helpfully twiddling the microscopes out of focus and jiggling

the table for him. The others, to relieve their boredom, would occasionally troop past to look at something of particular interest under the microscope, but Barnes generally amused himself by idly imitating the signature of the various persons connected with the case, becoming quite adept after several days.

Sarah, it was reported, seemed to get through the first hour each day in the simple enjoyment of being in a new dress, or wearing her hair in a different fashion, but when that palled, she invariably turned to Terry, who, always courtly, joined her in light conversation or politely watched as she smilingly demonstrated her penmanship to him. Court attaches spent their time staring out the windows at the clear late spring sky over Nob Hill. It was now early May and San Francisco was coming to its loveliest season.

For a short time the attorneys appeared grateful to be relieved of the talking which had occupied them for so long, but inevitably minor skirmishes developed. Judge Sullivan, occupying himself at the bench in the study of documents in other pending cases, tried to ignore the wrangles, but occasionally had to settle a dispute. Once young Tyler reached for one of Evans' law books to search a point and Evans objected. The judge, without raising his eyes from the papers on the bench said absently, "Well, I would like to study. Settle your difficulty without disturbing anybody else." All in all, the atmosphere was quite bucolic and on occasion counsel were startled to find themselves whispering civilly to each other.

On the plea of Hyde, who was being made nervous by the atmosphere in which he was having to work, however pastoral, it was agreed that other testimony would be taken while he completed his examination. Finally, ten days after he had been called to the stand, Hyde declared that he had thoroughly examined all of the questioned documents and was prepared to testify.

Barnes and Tyler, on the day Hyde announced his readiness to testify, spent the morning arguing about the way in which he should be examined. A compromise was finally reached. But Barnes then proposed that the documents should also be subjected to chemical analysis. Tyler said he would be happy to agree to it, but as the chemical analysis would destroy the document, Barnes should agree to be bound by the results of that analysis. Barnes declined and Tyler pointed out that as there was also a federal case pending, he could not agree to anything which would provide Sarah with less than a whole document when that case was tried if it ever was. An impasse having been reached, the subject was dropped. The hour of adjournment had been reached and Hyde would have to wait for the morrow.

When the now long awaited testimony of Hyde got under way, it moved slowly notwithstanding his exhaustive preparation. Each time he referred to a writing, or to a particular handwriting characteristic, one side or the other invariably demanded to be shown. Hyde would then step down, locate the document to which he was referring, insert it in and focus the microscope on the particular word, letter, line or scratch in question, and then wait until the judge, Tyler, Barnes, Flournoy, Evans, young Tyler, Sarah and Terry, in addition to anyone else who happened to be inside the rail, had lined up and shuffled past like school children at a drinking fountain, to squint in turn into the microscope. No protocol was followed, and the judge more often than not found himself jostled somewhere in the back of the line. The Senator had not been in attendance for some days and so did not contribute to the congestion.

There were in all six documents which Barnes and the Senator had determined to question. While Sarah had put in evidence over a dozen notes and letters from the Senator, he was presumably going to concede having written most of them. Though many contained familiar, even intimate references, most were as consistent with Sarah being his mistress as with being his wife and so no issue was expected to be made of them.

The questioned documents included the marriage contract itself and five "Dear Wife" notes or letters, four of which were written in pencil and one in ink. The questions which would be asked of Hyde included consideration of whether the notes had actually been written by the Senator; whether they had been in any way altered; and if so how, when, and by whom they had been altered. As to the marriage contract, Sarah had acknowledged that she wrote the body of the contract; so presumably the only question as to that document would be whether the Senator's signature was genuine.

Hyde first turned his attention to one of the pencilled "Dear Wife" notes. Asked by Barnes whether there was evidence of tampering, Hyde began by giving a little lecture on pencil writings. When pencil marks are erased, he said, any substance used for erasure will leave some pencil plumbago embedded in the paper fibers, never being wholly effective. Hence, he said, the way to find erasure in pencilled writing is through discovery of any remnants of plumbago in the interstices of the paper fiber and through seeking the old indentations caused by the pencil point.

Finally getting to the business at hand, Hyde said that in one "Dear Wife" note, there was evidence of rubber or some equivalent substance having touched the paper in the space where the word "Wife" was written. He felt, but could not be sure without more powerful magnification than he had available, that there were particles of plumbago both above and between the letters in that word. He had an impression also that the last two letters of the word "Dear", which preceded "Wife" in the note, had been gone over a second time; and he thought that the pencil at that point appeared to have presented a broken edge rather than the smooth one which preceded those letters.

Questioned by Tyler, he admitted that if a pencilled writing had been folded a number of times, particles of plumbago would be apt to be rubbed from their original place to other parts of the papers. The notes had been folded a number of times, he conceded. He said he also detected multiple abrasions of the paper under the word "Wife," but nowhere else. Although folding would cause abrasion, he conceded to Tyler, it could not explain the kind of magnitude of the abrasions he found under the word "Wife".

Turning to the question of whether a different hand had formed the word "Wife," he said the letters of that word appeared to be formed boldly and firmly, while the remainder of the words in the note showed evidence of a slight tremor. Everyone, including the judge dutifully trooped past the microscope to peer at the tremor. Hyde opined that the tremor was evidence of advanced age of the writer of the note, while the boldness of the "Wife" suggested relative youth of the writer of that word. The tremor could be the result of a transient or temporary condition, brought on by alcohol, biliousness or other temporary indisposition, he conceded to Tyler, but to explain the note the transition in condition would have had to be remarkably rapid.

Many days of testimony were then devoted to analysis of the formation of each letter in "Wife." The "W" did not look like the Senator's, he said. On cross-examination, Tyler occupied the greater part of one day requiring Hyde to locate every "W" in each of the hundred odd documents in evidence, and in the several hundred cancelled checks and other exemplars of both the Senator's and Sarah's handwriting which had been produced. Over a thousand "W's" were finally accumulated. After confessing himself unable to distinguish the various "W's" Hyde conceded that the letter "W" was not a strongly consistent characteristic of the Senator's handwriting, and that this letter might not have any significance in identifying it. That method of identification was "pretty much guess work" anyway, he told Tyler.

Hyde turned to writing characteristics he felt were peculiar to the Senator in the remainder of the word "Wife," with Tyler doggedly challenging each statement. Tyler enlivened the proceedings to his own satisfaction, but to no one else's, by compelling Hyde to join him at the blackboard which had been brought into court. They spent several hours there, engrossed in writing endless "Wife"s, to see, Tyler said, whether any consistent characteristics appeared.

When they had concluded that exercise, Hyde said in response to a question by Barnes on re-direct examination that "The phenomena exhibited under the direction of Mr. Tyler, and which he has illustrated, not to say adorned, by his comments, have not in any manner changed or affected the opinion that I expressed on my examination-in-chief." Hyde became

increasingly cautious and Barnes abruptly interrupted his testimony to call a second expert, George C. Hickox, who had been
examining the documents in the solitude of the court's anteroom. Spectators wondered if the interruption of Hyde's testimony resulted from a fear that he was weakening under Tyler's
onslaught, or was intended merely to give him a rest. Little
time was available for conjecture, as Hickox was prepared to
give his testimony without delay or hesitation.

In his opinion, Hickox said, the word "Wife" was not in the
Senator's handwriting in any of the "Dear Wife" letters. As to
who did write the word, in most of the notes he could not say;
but in one note he was confident the word "Wife" was written
by Sarah. Turning to the marriage contract, he said he had
concluded that the Senator's signature was genuine, but written
before the body of the contract; the Senator had signed a blank
sheet of paper, to which the contract had been later added.

At the conclusion of Hickox' recitation Tyler said, "No cross-
examination." When the judge looked at him in astonishment,
he simply repeated, "No cross-examination," permitting a look
of disdain fleetingly to cross his face.

Hyde had been engaged in additional study during his
twenty-four-hour respite and was then recalled for further examination. He squared his shoulders, inhaled deeply, and with
renewed confidence began. With illustrations and explanations,
his testimony consumed several more days, but its substance
was that his conclusions were the same as those of Hickox. On
cross-examination, Tyler used his earlier approach and again
induced Hyde to admit that the "Wife" could have been written by the Senator, particularly if done when he was ill, nervous, or under the influence of alcohol. This provided Tyler
with the opportunity to ask Hyde, as each exhibit was shown
him, whether the writing was more like the Senator's or more
like Sarah's, and whether it was nervous, ill, or "under the influence" writing. The amusement this aroused wore thin after the
first day or two.

During a lull in the Hyde examination, Barnes quietly
asked permission to recall a number of Sarah's witnesses for

further cross-examination. Tyler did not know Barnes' purpose but felt sure it was not intended to benefit Sarah's case, so he objected. The judge deferred a ruling until the witnesses were actually offered. Tyler looked thoughtful.

Turning finally to the marriage contract itself, Hyde described it as being on a note paper half-sheet, with a number of different foldings, which he delineated in great detail. Getting to the central point at last, Hyde said that the "Wm. Sharon, Nevada, August 25, 1880" was genuine, written by the Senator, but before the body of the contract was inserted. Folds made over dried ink, he said, caused a breaking and parting of the paper fibers, resulting in the exposure of uninked subsurfaces on "cracks" of the paper, whereas writing done over prior existing folds causes the ink to collect and run along the fold. Applying these physical principles to the marriage contract, he said, its folds had had the effect of causing breaks in the ink where the "Wm. Sharon, etc." was written, indicating that that writing had been done and the ink completely dried before the folds were made. In the body of the contract, on the other hand, and in Sarah's signature, the ink was not broken but had run along the line of the folds, thus suggesting that the pen had passed over prior existing creases. With that Barnes surrendered the witness to Tyler.

Tyler began by having Hyde give a variety of demonstrations, folding and writing on numerous sheets of paper, at the conclusion of which, said the *Chronicle,* the most patent achievement was development of considerable animosity between attorney and witness. After the noon recess they devoted the afternoon session to widening the breach.

On the question of whether blurring of the ink on the body of the contract was the result of its having been written after the paper was creased, Tyler asked if it wasn't true that most inks, even after having been dry for a long while, would blot and run if they were again moistened. Hyde admitted that to a certain extent that was true. Well, Tyler asked, wasn't it possible that moisture, for example perspiration collecting in a lady's bosom, could have caused the ink of the contract to become fluid again and to run along the folds of the paper? As the bosom was thrust into the discussion, Hyde affected a blasé studiousness and said that it was possible, but improbable.

Tyler then undertook to put Hyde through a number of moistening tests in which Tyler, Hyde, and the judge, but no one else, took great interest. Hyde had been sworn as a witness on April 29. On May 22, he was still on the stand, counting "W's" and moistening paper. Although there had been brief intervals of testimony by other witnesses, handwriting had been the almost exclusive theme for so long that everyone was wearying of it. Sarah had had an armchair put at the counsel table and spent much of her time napping or daydreaming with her head pillowed on her arms on the back of the large chair.

The proceedings had in fact become so dispiriting that Barnes and Tyler rarely mustered the energy to exchange witticisms or insults, and those which they did hazard were of low calibre. At one point, preparatory to one of the innumerable demonstrations, Tyler was about to moisten the edge of a piece of paper with his tongue when Barnes inquired whether it would be fair first to ask the expert if the validity of the experiment would be affected if Tyler was bilious, had a furred tongue, or had been drinking. Tyler assured Barnes that he felt fine and never drank before noon, and Barnes appealed to Judge Sullivan to admonish Tyler to leave his personal boasts and complaints out of the case.

The result of the cross-examination, when it finally came to an end, was that Tyler arrived at one conclusion, the witness at another, and the judge at, perhaps, still a third. Barnes undertook a short re-direct examination and at its conclusion, Hyde finally stepped down from the witness stand for the last time.

It was now the last week of May and the Senator, chief witness for the defense, had not yet begun his testimony. It was rumored that Judge Sullivan had resigned himself to the trial dragging on until autumn, and had determined to take a vacation adjournment from the first of June until mid-July.

The remaining week before adjournment was to provide as much excitement as anything which had yet occurred and, coming after the dreary weeks with handwriting experts, was a particularly welcome relief to spectators and newspaper followers of the trial.

The office of the San Francisco *Chronicle* at Bush and Kearny Streets, as it appeared in 1884. A crowd is gathered to scan the late news bulletins. Perhaps they were interested in the sensation of the year, the Sharon divorce trial. Or perhaps they were interested in the progress or results of the Blaine-Cleveland contest for the presidency.

— *San Francisco Public Library.*

Senator Sharon's apartment in the Palace Hotel, right, could easily be reached from Sarah's apartment in the Grand Hotel, left, by the connecting bridge across New Montgomery Street. The traffic over this bridge, if not its architecture, led contemporary San Franciscans to refer to it as "the Bridge of Sighs." — *Society of California Pioneers.*

Chapter IX WITNESSES RECANT

ITH HYDE off the stand, Barnes renewed his request for permission to
call back certain of Tyler's witnesses
for further cross-examination. Tyler opposed the motion, complaining that the Senator's large staff of professional and ama-
teur detectives had harassed all of Sarah's witnesses from the
time they stepped down from the stand. He argued that it
would be improper tacitly to condone such conduct by permitting the Senator to reap any benefit from that relentless
badgering.

Barnes answered that the purpose of a lawsuit was to seek
the truth and to do justice, that to this end all admissible evidence should be received without frustration by too strict application of procedural rules, or by too nice a concern for the tran-
quility of false witnesses. The argument was, as always, bitter
and lengthy. Judge Sullivan inclined to Barnes' view, and finally
cut off the argument, saying he would be willing to hear any
and all competent and relevant evidence. It was now to be
learned why Barnes had not aroused the partisan passions of
Sarah's witnesses in their earlier cross-examination.

The first person called pursuant to the ruling was Mrs.
Martha Wilson, Sarah's first witness, who had testified on the
opening day of the trial, some two and a half months previously. She was, Barnes reminded the judge, the illiterate seamstress who testified she had seen the contract in 1880 shortly
after its execution. She now entered weeping and, as she took
the stand, kept her eyes downcast, refusing to look at anyone
in the courtroom.

Mrs. Wilson now testified for Barnes that her previous testimony had been untrue; Mrs. Snow never read the contract to

her, she mumbled almost inaudibly. Sarah had asked her and her husband to testify that they had seen the contract in 1880 and offered them five thousand dollars to do so, the witness said. Both had at first consented, but Mr. Wilson later withdrew. The first time she actually saw the contract was in late 1883, she whispered.

Tyler was barely able to contain his outrage as he began his examination. On the record it was designated "re-direct," as Mrs. Wilson was still technically his witness, but it sounded more like cross-examination and neither Barnes nor the judge attempted to intervene. The witness' voice, still barely audible, constantly trailed off into a faint whimper.

Under questioning by Tyler, she acknowledged that much of her original testimony was true, that she had accompanied Sarah to the furniture store in 1880 and Sarah had at that time told her that she was secretly married to the Senator. But, she reiterated, she had seen no paper then, or at any time, until 1883.

"Look this way. Look at me while you are speaking", Tyler commanded. Under further questioning, she contradicted the testimony she had given only moments before. She now remembered that Sarah did show her a paper in 1880 or 1881, but she "disremembered" what it was. Sarah had read it to her at the time, and it said something about marriage. She also remembered, under Tyler's tutelage, that her earlier testimony about Sarah leaving papers with her in December, 1881, was true. She remembered that when Sarah had returned for the papers later, she had pasted a little patch on the paper at a fold where it was getting worn. (The contract had a small patch on it when brought into court.)

Mrs. Wilson finally decided that all of her original testimony was true, except that Mrs. Snow had not read the contract to her in 1880. She admitted that a statement she had given Tyler in his office before the trial was the same as the testimony she first gave at the trial, and that Sarah had never told her to say anything but the truth.

Tyler climaxed his questioning by asking who had talked to her about the case since she had given her testimony. Still crying and only slightly more audibly, she said Mrs. Shawhan and another lady, two of Barnes' witnesses, had recently talked to her for the greater part of three days. They had told her that Sarah called her a light-fingered darky, not to be trusted. They had also said Nellie Brackett was about to change her testimony. They ended the last conversation, she said by asking how she would like to have a thousand dollars, and whether she would be willing to visit Mr. Barnes who would "treat her nice." She told them she didn't want to talk to anybody and didn't want money. They then said that Captain Lees had been listening to the entire conversation, and that everyone on Sarah's side was going to prison. Mrs. Wilson told them she was sorry she knew anyone connected with the case and would rather never have known anything about it. The ladies had replied that that was all they wished her to do — say that she actually knew nothing about the case; and since she could not read, would this not be closest to the truth? She told them she would consult her husband, who took her to see Barnes last Tuesday. Barnes told her the contract did not exist in 1880 and she decided her testimony about the time she first saw the contract must have been wrong.

When Tyler had concluded with Mrs. Wilson, Barnes did not attempt any further examination, and she stepped down, sobbing loudly.

Mrs. Vesta Snow, who had been Sarah's second witness, the woman who read the contract to Mrs. Wilson, was then called by Barnes. He asked her the same question he had put to Mrs. Wilson and looked at her expectantly. She answered, "The first time I ever saw that paper was in 1880 at Mrs. Wilson's house, just as I stated when I was on the stand before. I read it at that time, and subsequently in 1881. I have seen it several times since."

Barnes stifled a look of surprise and asked her whether she had spoken with anyone connected with Sarah in the last few days. Yes, she had, she said. She spoke to Sarah last night, and to Tyler and Terry a few minutes ago, during the last recess.

Barnes' look was enigmatic as he dismissed Mrs. Snow. Tyler did not examine her. Spectators wondered whether Barnes had merely taken a shot in the dark, hoping that Mrs. Snow would change her testimony to conform to Mrs. Wilson's, or whether she had once changed her story and was now changing it back. Some months would pass before the answer would be known.

Robert Wilson, husband of Martha, then testified that he first heard of the marriage contract at the time the litigation was being "breezed up," when Sarah offered him and his wife three thousand dollars to testify that they had seen it in 1880.

On cross-examination, Wilson admitted to Tyler that his wife did go to the furniture store with Sarah in 1880, and when she got home she had told him Sarah said she was secretly married to the Senator by a contract. She said that if she could read she would have been able to tell him if Sarah was actually married. He said he had at first agreed to support Sarah's cause, but when Sarah showed him the contract he told her it was on too small a piece of paper to be a legal contract, "a very funny written thing," and he decided to have nothing to do with it.

In response to a final question from Tyler, Wilson admitted that he had presented Sarah with a written agreement to pay him three thousand dollars for his testimony, and that Sarah had refused to sign it. He said he wasn't sure he would have had his wife come in to "correct" her testimony if Sarah had signed that agreement.

Newspapers that evening and the next morning carried two and three column articles, setting out the testimony in full with much speculation on which was true. The sensations were not over yet.

Barnes next called Harry Wells for further cross-examination. Looking as unhappy as Martha Wilson, Wells now said that his original testimony had been wholly false. He had first learned of the case from reading about it in the newspapers, and first saw Sarah in Tyler's office after the litigation was under way. He had never seen True introduced to her and had not been in San Francisco at the time he had claimed the meeting took place. He said that True, an acquaintance, had told him it would be worth his while if he recalled their strolling together in downtown San Francisco one day in 1881. True had then arranged to take him to Tyler's office, where he supported everything True told Tyler. He said he had told Tyler he was not sure he could recognize Sarah as the lady in question, and Tyler arranged for him to meet her.

At the introduction in Tyler's office, Sarah smiled graciously, told him he had a pleasant face, and said he looked like the sort of person who would be kind to his sister and mother. He replied that he had no sister. Tyler said that probably he had been kind to someone else's sister, but reminded them that they were meeting for a purpose. Wells replied that he recognized Sarah as the woman he had heard introduced as the Senator's wife. As it turned out, he concluded ruefully, he had testified for Sarah and True had not, but on the contrary gave a deposition for the Senator.

Tyler now apparently concluded that the story of the Sutter Street meeting was false and that Wells was now telling substantially the truth. He therefore limited his redirect examination to questions relating to his own good faith in having used Wells as a witness. At times during his testimony Wells put his head on the railing in front of the witness stand and wept, but there appeared to be little sympathy felt for him. As he stepped down, Tyler asked the judge to place Wells under arrest for perjury, pending the filing of a criminal complaint.

"I have thought myself of taking action, but thought it best to wait until the conclusion of the testimony, in order to see clearly where the perjury has been committed," Judge Sullivan responded. "However, the motion is perfectly proper. Wells, you are in the custody of the Sheriff."

Barnes remarked that Judge Sullivan was in a difficult position, having to decide which of Wells' stories was true in order to frame the perjury charge properly.

The judge said he had already satisfied himself on that question. "The fact is that I never believed that such an introduction took place, and I think that the witness committed perjury when he testified to that effect. True, in my opinion, was not such a man as Sharon would introduce to his wife."

Barnes was elated at this candid revelation by the judge, but elation was short lived.

"As far as Mrs. Wilson's testimony is concerned," the judge continued, "my present impression of her testimony is the reverse. I believe Martha Wilson committed perjury when she was on the stand for the second time. I shall also commit Martha Wilson into custody, as the perjury was committed in the one case as much as in the other. Let bail be fixed at twenty thousand dollars in each case."

The following day the *Chronicle's* editorial was captioned, "THE CRIME OF PERJURY," and observed that while it would probably be unjust to say there was more perjury in San Francisco than elsewhere, the incidence of that crime was increasing alarmingly. "The motives may sometimes be personal hatred," it continued, "but they are oftener the hope of reward, as in the case of Sharon vs. Sharon, on which, according to the public belief, money has been lavishly expended not only in the collection of testimony but in its shameful purchase. We have not the slightest desire to discuss the merits of the case. Whether the arrested witnesses have been led to swear falsely by the prospective sharing of Mr. Sharon's millions before or after his losing them is foreign to the aim of this discussion. It is beyond controversy that the offense has been committed. Our courts have to take action in this matter lest they themselves become infamous."

The perjury case preliminaries excited as much general interest as the divorce trial. Levy and Tyler generally appeared as special prosecutors, with an attorney of the Senator's coterie representing the defendants. As they slowly dragged through the courts both the Wells and Wilson prosecutions were to plague the divorce trial principals for almost a year.

Chapter X THE SENATOR TELLS HIS STORY

HERE were yet three court days left in the month of May when Hyde and the perjurers finally left the stand in the divorce trial. There was much expectancy that the Senator would at long last testify. The surmise was bolstered by his arrival at court after several days of absence, and confirmed when, with no ceremony, Barnes called him to the witness stand. Courtroom strategists speculated on whether the cautious Senator had waited until all of his witnesses had testified so that he might know how far he safely could go in his denials.

The Senator was attired in his usual broadcloth, whose shining blackness rivaled his carefully brushed mustache. Although his manner and posture in striding to the stand, in taking the oath, and in seating himself in the witness chair, exuded complete confidence, his voice was so low as to be sometimes inaudible. Admonitions to speak louder had no effect on him.

The first day was occupied in his direct examination by Barnes, who permitted the Senator to have his head. He delivered most of his testimony in narrative form, with few questions being interposed. About the only interruptions were the frequent pleas that he speak louder. The purport of his narrative was that:

One afternoon around August 1, 1880 he was in his private office at the Bank of California when Ki announced a young lady who wished to see him. He asked Ki for "some little description," as he had been for some time plagued with women and beggars. Satisfied with the description, he asked Ki to show her in. She introduced herself as Sarah Althea Hill. This was the first time he was aware of having seen her or of knowing of her existence. "I think the ostensible idea she presented then

119

was that she wanted to make some little inquiry about stocks. I gave her no advice, because I am not in the habit of giving advice," but for thirty minutes they had "a little chat about indifferent subjects."

She called again in the latter part of August. Another "pleasant little chat of probably half an hour or more" took place. He did not recall inviting her to return on either occasion.

He was away in Virginia City for a few days, but on his return Sarah asked him "to come up and see her. Within a very short period" he acted on the invitation. He visited her three times in all in the month of September. On the second occasion she accepted an invitation to have dinner with him. They went to his rooms at the Palace, where "We had dinner and a pleasant time."

"And after we had talked and spent the hours merrily she said it was time to go home. I believe it must have been twelve or one o'clock at night, and as she walked into the bedroom [to retrieve her cloak] having shown familiarity by calling on me privately in my private room, I said to her, 'Miss Hill, I will give you two hundred and fifty dollars a month to sleep with you.' She said, 'I will not take that.' I said, quite rapidly, 'Miss Hill, I will give you five hundred dollars a month.' She said, 'I want the money, but I don't care about sleeping with you.' I said, 'It is quite late; it is too late to go to the Baldwin Hotel, or to be out this late at night. You might as well take a bed here.'

To that proposal she acceded, he testified, and they retired, she taking one bedroom and he another. "In about three-quarters of an hour she came and crawled into my bed. Coming to my bed was an acceptance of the offer, and she continued to demand the five hundred dollars a month, which I paid her and more."

The Senator's visits to Sarah at the Baldwin, where she was then staying, soon aroused sufficient interest in their relationship that an acquaintance told him that "they had set a watch to catch her and me in bed together at the Baldwin Hotel and wanted, if possible, to get some rumor about me to injure my business and the hotel." He therefore arranged a discreet meeting with Sarah "and I told her she had better take rooms at the

Grand Hotel." The Senator wrote a letter of introduction to the manager, describing her as "a particular friend of mine, and a lady of unblemished character, and of good family" and requesting that she be given "the best." That, said the Senator, "was the circumstance under which she came to the Grand and took rooms."

September 28 he left for Virginia City and Lake Tahoe. While away he wrote the first of the "Dear Wife" letters, the one in ink. The word "wife" in the salutation was, he declared, a forgery, but with that exception, he admitted having written the letter. He was again away in Virginia City from October 18 until about November 2, occupied in his efforts to gain re-election to the United States Senate, but took up the affair on his return.

He arranged a house party at Belmont on the week end of December 6, 1880, which Sarah attended with Mrs. Bornemann as her chaperone, as she had testified. He invited Sarah to his daughter's wedding reception "with a good deal of hesitation," he testified. Between Christmas and New Year's Day, 1881, he went with Sarah to meet her aunt and grandmother.

All told he admitted seeing Sarah "possibly twenty times, a little more or less" up until the time he went East, January 2, 1881. He was "engaged in other pursuits and circumstances," he said. "I did not see a great deal of her at that time. I saw more of her after I returned." He sent telegraphic orders that she be paid $500 a month while he was gone.

He left for New York January 2, 1881, with his daughter and her new husband, Sir Thomas Hesketh, returning to San Francisco about March 14. Sarah visited Belmont a number of times thereafter, at his invitation, once with a party including the Staggs, the Reigarts, Sarah's brother, Vanderbilt, and others. He took her once to Oakland to call on friends and once to the theater.

He admitted writing all of the dozen and a half notes and letters which Sarah had offered in evidence, but the word "wife," whenever it appeared was a forgery.

By July, 1881, Sarah "had become rather impudent in her approach to my room, throwing off the mask of secrecy of the relations that existed." Moreover, "I found on three different occasions specifically that my pockets were picked and there was no other person at night when I took off my clothes that had access to my room." He decided to end the relationship and forbade further visits to his rooms, but without much success. One day in August, 1881, he said, "she climbed over the transom and I heard her fall." He said he told her "I wish you had broken your damn neck" and, to get some peace, he pushed her into the next room where she fell to the floor, refusing to get up. He poured a pitcher of cold water on her and threatened to call assistance to take her out. She then got up and into bed, he said. He had not choked her or dragged her into the closet, he said emphatically.

Altogether, he permitted Sarah to spend the night with him perhaps a half dozen times after his attempt to end the relationship in July, and he suspected that she secreted herself in his apartment a number of times. On one such occasion "I heard an unearthly yell from Ki and he came running, trembling all over, and kind of fell at my feet, and he said, 'She killed me — she killed me,' and I commenced laughing, and I heard her laugh as she went out."

In November he reached a settlement with her, but he said it was not by way of repayment of any money belonging to her. He offered her $5000 to leave him alone; she demanded $10,000. They settled on $7500 to be paid $3000 in cash, with a note for $1500 and the remaining $3000 to be paid at $250 a month through the year 1883. She gave him a receipt in full, but though he placed it in his pocketbook he never saw it again. He assumed Sarah had stolen it on a later visit.

Even after the settlement, he admitted, she had visited his rooms two or three times, but in December he ordered her eviction despite her pleas. In one note which he introduced into evidence, she asked him not to "stoop to injure and wrong a girl." Her pleas became more importuning as the efforts to remove her were pressed, and she wrote again, "I cannot see how you can have anyone treat me so, I who have always been so good and kind to you. The carpet is all taken up in my hall, the door is taken off and away. Ah, Senator, dear Senator, do not treat me so — whilst everyone else is so happy for Christmas, don't try to make mine miserable. Remember this time last year. You know you are all I have in the world. Say I may see you."

He said he had nothing further to do with Sarah after her removal from the Grand, except to make payments on the note when she came for them.

He offered the court a number of letters from Sarah, written in 1882 and 1883. In one she wrote, "Won't you please try and find out what springs those were you were trying to think of and let me know tomorrow when I see you." The letter urged him to go for a picnic or a drive with Sarah and Nellie. "Us girls would take the best of care of you, and mind you in everything. I am crazy to see Nell try and swallow an egg in champagne." It closed, "We'd do our best to make you forget all your business cares and go home feeling happy." He testified he did not respond. But he did not explain the references which suggested that he was still having friendly relations with her in 1882.

In most of the letters Sarah asked for money. Typical was one reading, "Dear 'Sen.': Would you kindly bring or send me some money. I don't think you would care to see me have any trouble — and I know, with all your wealth, you would not care to take from me what you know is my all. Please don't leave this where it will be read. /s/ A."

The Senator's direct examination by Barnes closed with a series of denials inspired by Sarah's testimony. Barnes eventually surrendered him to Tyler for cross-examination. Tyler required the Senator to recapitulate virtually every minute detail of his direct examination, thus consuming much time but accomplishing little.

As to the marriage contract, he admitted a possibility that his signature was genuine, though he had "very serious doubts." The word "Nevada" and the date looked like his handwriting. But he declared categorically that he never put his signature to the document as it appeared in court. He said he first saw the contract in 1883.

Though he spoke softly, the Senator was not a reluctant witness and seemed to make no effort to soften his image as a cold-blooded financier. Indeed, he seemed to go out of his way to emphasize the role.

Reflecting further on the evening they first slept together, he said, "I supposed from her manner and all, after she had laid a little while that she would come in. I think any woman that will go to a gentleman's private room and dine with him until late certainly is not very strong in those higher sentiments."

Asked to explain what he meant in saying that he "saw her regularly," he said, "She spent the night and slept in the same bed with me and I had sexual intercourse with her repeatedly."

Was it his testimony, Tyler asked, that he had hired Sarah at five hundred dollars a month as his mistress?

It was, he replied laconically.

How long was it agreed that he would pay her, Tyler inquired.

"No arrangement was made between us as to how long I should continue to pay her five hundred dollars a month. I understand on such relations either party can quit at any time they please."

Asked by Tyler to explain more fully the incident in which Sarah and Ki said he had choked her and in which he said she fell, he obliged. "Three times I asked her to leave, and then I got up and shoved her into the other room; and she just laid down on the carpet; and I went off and got a pitcher of water, more for amusement than anything else, and poured it over her. She laid there and soaked in the water for some time; it was very cold" and she eventually got up and into bed.

As the second morning of the Senator's cross-examination opened, Tyler asked the court reporter, "Now, where was I when I left off yesterday?" The Senator promptly replied, "You were there where you stand now," smiling as if he had just cornered the stock of a million-dollar gold mine. Tyler, always susceptible to jokes, laughed appreciatively, and, with amicable relations thus established, again took up his cudgel.

Had they not continued consorting long after the claimed separation agreement, asked Tyler?

Sarah slept with him two or three times in the weeks after the settlement, he admitted, but after she left the Grand he had no further relations with her except in making payments.

"In November I had a settlement with her. She had been stopping with me at a salary, and I thought that the woman was disposed to make trouble if I did not settle with her and get a receipt. I had a talk with her and a settlement. There were kind of mutterings and actions that I deemed ominous in a woman of her character, and I thought it best to get a receipt. She was loath to quit. I think she thought she had a pretty good thing of it.

"The woman was sometimes in the habit of coming in under the influence of liquors or opiates, and threatened sometimes to throw herself out of the window, and was particularly annoying to me. She said, 'I am going to write a dirty note about you and take poison, and pin it on my body.'

"I always feel kindly to any human being or animal, or anything that lives and moves, unless they try to destroy me. I certainly never was attached to the woman in any sense of the word. We were friendly. She never aroused my affections in any way. It was merely friendly intercourse."

Tyler invited the Senator to comment on Sarah's testimony that she had seen him in bed with another woman. She never made herself known or made any fuss at the time, he said; but she later "said she was behind the bureau and watched us. I was satisfied from the words she used that she had been there."

Except as to the incidents which he related, the Senator denied, generally and specifically, the testimony of Sarah and her witnesses concerning all other incidents and meetings, despite Tyler's dogged efforts to break him. Spectators were of mixed opinion on the degree of Tyler's success. During one of the recesses Tyler was asked if he thought he had been successful in rattling the Senator. "Rattle him!", Tyler snorted. "Do you suppose I can rattle a man who can bet a fortune on a busted flush and look as if he were going to sleep at the same time?"

Tyler finally announced that he had concluded the Senator's cross-examination, with the exception of one subject, which would require several days to cover. With that introduction, he asked the Senator, "Have you had any mistresses with whom you had arrangements to pay a set sum each month?" A feeble objection from Barnes was overruled, and spectators leaned forward, anticipating many entertaining hours.

Judge Sullivan, hoping to avoid the salacious revelations which seemed imminent, asked Barnes, before permitting Tyler to proceed, if he might want to enter into a stipulation in the interest of time and public morals. Barnes gratefully accepted a chance to consider the suggestion, and a short recess was taken.

After conferring with the Senator and his associates, Barnes said they were prepared to enter into a stipulation. Tyler proposed that it be admitted that "both before and since August 25, 1880, this defendant has had a large number of mistresses to whom he paid monthly an amount of money, an alleged monthly compensation; that as to none of them has he ever invited them to go to his hotel and live; as to none of them has he walked with them in the corridors of the Palace Hotel with them leaning on his arm, or introduced them to respectable families; with none of them has he taken them down to Belmont himself or sent them there with invited guests, respectable people from foreign countries, or from foreign States, or this State, or had anything to do with introducing them to his family or to respectable people with whom his family associated."

Barnes said, "So stipulated," and with that, the Senator's examination came to an end. Followers of the trial had to be content with what their imaginations could provide.

Some of the spectators felt that the admission did Sarah no good, as it merely acknowledged a course of conduct by the Senator with numerous women, Sarah being simply one among them. Others argued that the admission was most damaging to the Senator, not only because it revealed low morals, but because it showed that he had never permitted his mistresses to mingle with his family and friends, and had never been seen publicly with them or taken them to Belmont. As he conceded having so conducted himself with Sarah, they said, this obviously placed her in a different position.

The public was to have the next six weeks in which to ponder that question and others not yet resolved. With the close of the Senator's testimony, Judge Sullivan announced the anticipated summer recess, declaring that the case would resume on July 14.

Chapter XI AWAITING DECISION

HE TRIAL adjournment conveniently coincided with the beginning of the 1884 United States presidential campaign. On June 6 the Republican convention in Chicago nominated James G. Blaine, the plumed knight of Maine. The Democratic convention, held a month later, nominated Grover Cleveland only after a determined band of dissident Californians had attempted to advance the candidacy of Stephen J. Field, Associate Justice of the United States Supreme Court. Field was destined to play a decisive, indeed fatal, role in the Sharon dispute but this was unknown in the summer of 1884. Consequently no special significance was attached to the fact that a number of Field's political supporters and opponents were also arrayed against each other in the Sharon case.

Field, a California Forty-niner who came West to practice law, had served on the California Supreme Court for six years becoming Chief Justice in 1859 when David Terry, now one of Sarah's counsel, had resigned to fight his duel with Senator David Broderick. In 1863 Field had been appointed to the United States Supreme Court by President Lincoln to fill the position created when that court was expanded from nine to ten members. United States Supreme Court justices at the time "rode circuit," Field's circuit being the Pacific Coast states, and his periodic visits permitted him to maintain close contacts in California in the years after going to Washington.

As early as 1877 Field began to have presidential aspirations, and in that year wrote his memoirs for private circulation. In 1880 he was unsuccessful in seeking the nomination and now, in 1884, despite much work ("intrigue," the *Chronicle* said) by his friends, the state Democratic convention not only refused to advance his nomination at the forthcoming national convention, but actively repudiated him. Terry and an associate of Tyler's were among his most vocal opponents.

Field's friends were led by Frank G. Newlands, Sharon's son-in-law, who made a long and impassioned, though unsuccessful, plea for Field's candidacy. Among his most loyal supporters was O. P. Evans, the Senator's second counsel in the divorce trial. Undaunted, together with a group of Field's wealthy friends, they chartered a train to take them to the Chicago convention, where they hoped to obtain Field's nomination despite his repudiation in Stockton. The national convention found him no more palatable than had the California assembly.

Field's later involvement in the Sharon case would introduce antagonisms which went beyond his presidential aspirations. Most of the attorneys on each side were Democrats as was Field, but in California the party was so divided in the 1880's as to make the label meaningless. One faction asserted that the state's prosperity was dependent on the burgeoning railroads and supported the Central Pacific monopoly which by then owned a substantial part of the state and controlled the rest through unrestricted rate manipulation. The other faction felt that agriculture and manufacture could flourish only if the railroads were subject to strict controls.

The Democratic party split resulted in the loss of the state to the Republicans in the election of 1884, although Cleveland, a Democrat, was elected President. Thus the normal political channels were absent and Field, most political of United States Supreme Court justices, sought avidly to gain control of California patronage. He reportedly carried in his hat a list of names of California Democrats who had voted to reject his bid for nomination to the Presidency, tirelessly seeking to prevent the appointment of any of the "communists," as he called them, or even of their associates to any office in the state.

Field's philosophy, which he expressed often, was that "the moment the idea is admitted into society that property is not as sacred as the laws of God, and that there is not a force of law and public justice to protect it, anarchy and tyranny commence."

The Belmont Estate was built by W. C. Ralston and acquired after his death by Senator Sharon. Here he entertained great and near-great visitors. This was the scene of his daughter's wedding reception, one of the most brilliant social events of the decade. — *California Historical Society.*

City Hall was still under construction at the time of San Francisco's sensational divorce trial in 1884. Courtrooms were in the main structure to the right. This was the building, together with its ornate dome which was later added, that collapsed so spectacularly in the 1906 earthquake.
— *Oakland Public Library.*

Senator Sharon's offices were upstairs at the Bank of California, left. Here were his early meetings with Sarah and here, she said, the marriage contract was drawn up. The present head office of the Bank of California is still on this California Street site, at the corner of Sansome. The atmosphere, architecture, and traffic in San Francisco's financial district of the 1880's was in marked contrast to the scene at the same spot today.
— *Bancroft Library.*

In his early years on the bench Field was never known to render a decision against the railroads. When the federal government undertook to regulate them, he argued for states' rights, and when the states attempted to tax or otherwise regulate the railroads he argued that they were engaged in interstate commerce, hence amenable only to the federal government. While the subtlety of his arguments was much admired, his close association with the railroad magnates and their attorneys was greatly criticized. Reporting one of his decisions, the *Chronicle* had said, "Justice Field has peculiar opinions regarding the Constitution which, if they cannot be said to be his own, are certainly those of certain interests in whose cause he is engaged." It was often said of him that while his decisions were not always wrong, his reasons for them generally were.

But Field had long since renounced public acceptance in favor of personal loyalties and his often expressed social and economic dogmas. The Senator's attorneys were almost all prominent railroad lawyers, while Sarah's contingent was made up of men who bitterly opposed the railroads. Some were in fact on Field's blacklist. There would later be speculation on the impact of these facts on Field's role in the Sharon case, but this was yet some time away.

ʎ   ʎ   ʎ

During the summer recess the case, while dormant, was still proliferating. Sarah filed suit against the Senator to recover $750 remaining due on the promissory note which he had now admitted signing — though their explanations of the reason for the note differed widely — charging that the last three payments of $250 each had not been made.

William M. Neilson filed a slander and malicious prosecution suit against the Senator, claiming $120,000 in damages. Quixotically, Neilson wrote an "open letter" published the same day, declaring, "Henceforth, I am out of the Sharon case publicly as I have long been privately." He closed the letter by saying that he still believed in Sarah's case, but that his withdrawal was precipitated by Tyler's production of unspecified false evidence. Sarah, asked by the press to comment on Neilson's letter, expressed surprise at it and declared that his charges were unworthy of reply; she had accepted Tyler as her attorney at Neilson's suggestion.

Tyler was across the Bay, campaigning for a seat in Congress. Barnes was also unavailable but Evans, when located, gave the press his opinion that Neilson was merely a rat leaving a sinking ship. Evans added that there was no possibility of settling the case by compromise. Only Sarah's confession of perjury would satisfy the Senator. He would not pay her one cent.

Though Senator Sharon had gone East for the national conventions, he was not to be denied the privilege of letting his views be known throughout the land. He was dividing his time between New York and Chicago and in an interview with a New York *Journal* reporter said that, though a Republican, he was not sure he could support Blaine's candidacy. Now, if the Democrats had sense enough to nominate Justice Field, he said, a man highly regarded in California, they might beat Blaine. The *Journal* reported that its own poll showed that Field was, on the contrary, "universally disliked" on the Pacific Coast.

Reporters were more interested in the divorce trial than in the Senator's political opinions. They found him in a convivial mood and, to the accompaniment of drinks liberally passed around, he entertained the Eastern reporters with trial highlights. He said that though Sarah was a terror herself, he had to admit she came from a good family. He had had every minute of her life investigated, before taking up with her and since the litigation had begun. A reporter asked him if he had made a practice of investigating people with whom he dealt. Certainly, he said. It was the only sensible thing to do. How else could one gain an advantage or guard against treachery? Well, one reporter asked him, how would he have felt if his daughter Flora's baronet had had him investigated before consenting to marry her? The Senator said he had investigated the peer and assumed Sir Thomas had reciprocated. The results were more flattering to Sir Thomas than the latter's investigation of the Senator would have been, he laughed. As to the trial, he was confident of victory, but declared he would fight it as far as necessary.

Sarah, interviewed again, said that no amount of mere money could buy cessation of the case. Unless the Senator publicly acknowledged the marriage, there could be no settlement.

ᕒ   ᕒ   ᕒ

After one false start, the trial resumed on July 15 with all of the principals in attendance. Tyler had thought of "a few more" questions to put to Hyde, and when he began his first question ("Please point out to his Honor any single place where the W in 'Wife' . . ."), Evans in a wistful aside said, "It does not seem possible that we have been away so long."

Judge Sullivan looked much improved, having benefitted greatly from the long rest. Barnes was sunburned and Tyler as bouyant as ever, notwithstanding his defeat for the Congressional nomination on the preceding day. Young Tyler passed around photographs of wild mountain scenes with reporters and fellow counsel sharing his vacation vicariously. Terry was in his now accustomed place beside Sarah, looking happy.

Hyde, anticipating that he would be recalled to the stand, had spent the recess preparing charts and photographic enlargements. He and Tyler contentedly devoted most of the day to misplacing them. Tiring of that sport, the following day Tyler had Hyde demonstrate various forging techniques. Eventually he concluded his examination of Hyde, and Barnes renewed his request that the documents be submitted to chemical analysis. Sarah, who had been napping, became instantly alert as always when anything affecting the physical well-being of the papers was discussed. She closely followed the hour-long discussion which ensued.

After pondering the matter overnight, Judge Sullivan rejected Barnes' request, saying that analysis of the "Dear Wife" letters would not be conclusive of the main issue, and that he would not take responsibility for having the contract subjected to chemicals unless both sides agreed. Tyler again said he was willing, even if it mean destroying the contract, if the defense would let the cases be decided on the results of the test.

Ignoring Tyler's offer, Barnes said, "We rest our case, Your Honor."

Sarah's attorneys were visibly surprised and Tyler said as much. Barnes rejoined irritably, "State to the court what you want without telling how you feel." Tyler, with a gracious bow, said he was unprepared to proceed, as none of his rebuttal witnesses were in court. An adjournment was therefore taken for the week end.

The following Monday was a typical San Francisco July day, the previous night's fog imperceptibly disappearing as the early morning sun began to make itself felt, the pervasive chill giving way successively to crisp morning, cool midday, and a balmy evening. Sarah wore a sealskin sacque against the morning chill, and once in court, she threw it back from her shoulders to permit everyone to share her pleasure in another new dress.

The session opened with Judge Sullivan asking the attorneys when he might expect the trial to end. They all professed inability to say and unwillingness to hazard a guess, but they were clear that whenever it did end, each side would wish at least one week for final argument. The judge thanked them for their help and asked Tyler to proceed with his rebuttal testimony.

Tyler called a 76-year-old retired clerk and sometime shopkeeper, whom he undertook to qualify as a handwriting expert. With much disconnected talk about his early life, the witness said at age 17 he had once given good money for a counterfeit bill. Ever since then he had been on guard against forgeries. He had run across numerous counterfeits, especially during the Civil War, and was always thanked when he took them to the mint, he said proudly.

Over Barnes' objection that the man was obviously not an expert at anything the judge, who had broad discretion in such matters, permitted the witness to express his opinion of the documents in question, and the witness promptly pronounced the signature on the contract and the "Wife" in the letters genuine.

Barnes did not cross-examine.

It had been generally felt that Barnes' handwriting experts would compel counter-measures by Tyler, but this pitiable effort was only embarrassing. The witness was on the stand for only a few minutes as even Tyler did not bother to examine him at any length. It is unlikely that the judge, any more than the attorneys, gave his testimony much weight, despite having permitted him to testify. Max Gumpel was to be another matter.

Barnes appeared surprised when Tyler next asked the bailiff to call "Mr. M. Gumpel." Though his name rang through the corridors of the City Hall, the witness did not respond. The judge issued a bench warrant to have him brought in and called the morning recess.

At two o'clock, Gumpel was present but requested the protection of the court to spare him the necessity of testifying. He explained his failure to respond to Tyler's subpoena that morning by saying that he had been employed by Barnes the previous November to examine the documents in anticipation of testifying for the defense. Perhaps the judge had noticed that he had been studying the documents in court daily until a short time ago. He said he had finally told Barnes that his conclusions made it impossible for him to testify for the defense. For that reason Barnes had not called him, and Gumpel said he felt that it was not proper to testify for Tyler in view of the fact that he had been paid by, and was available only because of, the defense.

The judge told Tyler to proceed and instructed Gumpel to answer any questions which were put, after satisfying himself that Gumpel's ties with Barnes and the Senator had been honorably severed.

Tyler first asked him to state his training and experience, but Barnes interrupted impatiently to say he would stipulate that Gumpel was eminently qualified as an expert in handwriting. Gumpel then reviewed his various examinations of the questioned documents while in the employ of Barnes. In his opinion, Gumpel said, the Senator's signature and the words "Nevada, Aug. 25, 1880" on the contract were in the Senator's handwriting. He said that no part of any of the "Dear Wife" letters was not genuine, and there was "no evidence of any erasure in any portion" of those notes.

The style of letter formation, the absence of evidence of erasure, and the continuity of the pencil point all proved that the word "Wife" was not inserted later. It would be extremely difficult, probably impossible, to insert a word in the body of a pencilled writing without exposing an interruption in the gradual wearing away of the tip, he explained, adding that he found no such interruption in the notes.

He dismissed as nonsense Hyde's testimony that it was possible, from the writing alone, to say that Sarah had written the word "Wife" in the notes. As far as the formation of the letters of the word were concerned, Sarah could have written the word, but so could the Senator or anyone else, Gumpel concluded.

On cross-examination, Barnes asked Gumpel only whether he thought the Senator's signature on the marriage agreement was in different ink from that used in the body of the contract. He said it probably was, but admitted on re-direct examination by Tyler that it was possible that dipping a pen deeper into the inkwell on one occasion than on another could cause such an apparent difference.

Gumpel occasionally made use of the blackboard, but with the exception of these few interruptions, he gave his testimony with precision and confidence and without digression. Its persuasive impact was evident when he left the stand. Only Judge Sullivan and Barnes managed to veil their reaction.

A feeling that the end of the trial was almost in sight pervaded the courtroom as it convened the following day. In that day and the next, Tyler called more than 25 witnesses to pick up loose ends and to meet assertions made by the defense. A dozen testified that the reputation for truth, honesty, and integrity of various of Barnes' fortunetellers was very bad. Two witnesses testified that Mrs. Samson was indebted to each of them and told them that as soon as the case was concluded she would have a great deal of money with which to repay the debts. Another testified that Mrs. Samson had asked her if she knew anything of the case. Receiving a negative reply, she asked if the witness would be willing to testify if something were "suggested." And Mrs. Vesta Snow was again recalled to testify that Mrs. Wilson, the accused perjurer, since retracting her original testimony, had told her that the retraction was not true but had been made at the insistence of her husband.

The following day the courtroom was as crowded as at the beginning of the trial, in anticipation of Sarah again taking the stand. In honor of the occasion, she wore a silk dress trimmed with flounces of black lace and a brocaded velvet cloak. A black plume erupted from her dark straw hat.

Tyler opened the session by complaining to the judge that he had been denied entry to the Senator's apartment to ascertain whether it was physically possible for Ki to have seen the things he claimed to have witnessed during Sarah's alleged love philter trip. After some argument, the judge decided he would like to view the premises himself and selected David Terry and O. P. Evans, as relative non-belligerents, to accompany him that afternoon.

Sarah then took the stand and Terry, rather than Tyler, conducted her examination. Terry had been most with her of late and probably knew more intimately what she would want to testify to, but it was also rumored that her relations with Tyler had been strained since her published remarks that he had not been her choice of attorney.

She denied in detail the testimony of defense witnesses. She particularly denied that she had been in love with, or had told anyone that she was in love with Reuben Lloyd at any time after she met the Senator. After the signing of the contract she had never told anyone that she was engaged to the Senator nor did she ever thereafter tell anyone anything inconsistent with being his wife. She had not authorized Neilsen to bring the adultery charge against the Senator, she said, nor had she consented to his arrest.

On cross-examination she was confronted with a long resentful letter she had written to Neilson shortly before she was indicted by the Grand Jury, in which she had written, "You asked yourself and begged to begin this fight and promised it should never come to court. Oh, God! If I had kept my trials to myself. These scenes are killing me. You have brought me into this fight, making me believe you would let no harm come to me, and here I am about to be arrested as a criminal. Great God! Nobody comforts me or has one kind word. It is a struggle with the world and I do not deserve it." The letter concluded by urging Neilson to direct his efforts against the Senator and not to engage in petty disputes with people on the periphery of the case, as she complained he was doing. The letter did not change her testimony, she now said.

The afternoon was devoted to the judge's visit to the Senator's apartment. Sharon greeted the delegation at the door as though they were social guests. After introductions, which he apparently felt hospitality required, the judge attempted to duplicate Ki's actions on the day of the love philters. A bellboy climbed through the transom and fell to the floor to illustrate the Senator's version of what had happened to Sarah at the outset of the choking, or water pouring, incident.

Two more days were spent with each side calling a number of witnesses who squarely contradicted each other on a variety of collateral matters. Several witnesses testified that the grave incident occurred, several that it did not, and still others said it did but that Sarah and Nellie were not the women involved. Each faction testified that the other's reputation for honesty was bad.

Sarah again took the stand to say that she now remembered that on the day of the cemetery incident, she had gone to the Thomas Bell home to visit Mammy Pleasant, the housekeeper. Finding her out on a drive and picnic with the Bell children, Sarah had taken lunch at the house and awaited their return in the late afternoon. Her testimony was then corroborated by Thomas Bell, Mammy Pleasant and four other occupants of the Bell home. Barnes and one of the witnesses were locked in a confused and heated exchange about the number and description of the Bell children as the time for adjournment arrived, and Judge Sullivan said pleasantly, if wearily, "We'll give the babies a rest until tomorrow at ten o'clock."

Barnes led off the following morning by calling the former butler at the Bell house, who said he had been in the house all of the day in question, and had not seen Sarah there. On cross-examination, he admitted that he was now employed at the Palace Hotel.

With the end of the trial in view, Judge Sullivan was not disposed to tolerate long wrangles between counsel or digressions by witnesses; but with so much conflict on the cemetery question, however collateral it might be, he ordered Nellie back into court. In response to his questions she said resolutely that the incident had taken place and that she had accompanied Sarah.

Nellie's testimony precipitated a clutch of witnesses including Tyler, Sarah, Mammy Pleasant, several friends of the Brackett family, and even an attorney from Modesto who had happened to be in court as a spectator on the day the cemetery incident was first brought up. (The Modesto attorney testified he had heard Nellie, sitting adjacent to him, spontaneously say, "Oh, what a lie! That is an awful lie.")

Other witnesses testified that since her return home Nellie had told each of them that her father was to be given twenty-five thousand dollars if she changed her testimony and that Barnes had already deposited two thousand dollars to her father's account with the Hibernia Bank.

Finally, the Senator was recalled briefly to say that he had first met Mrs. Samson less than a year previously, having been introduced by Archbishop Alemany, that he had paid her not more than fifty dollars to cover her expenses in seeking witnesses, and had never asked her to procure false witnesses.

Sarah herself proved to be her own last witness in the case. In reading over the transcript of the testimony Tyler had been startled to find that he had neglected to ask her one important question, for which he now called her to the stand. Had the Senator, he asked, signed the marriage contract?

"After I got through and signed it," she replied, "at the same time and at the same meeting he took up the pen and signed it, and wrote the words 'Nevada, Aug. 25, 1880,' in his private office, over the Bank of California."

With that, Sarah stepped down and Tyler said, "Plaintiff rests."

Barnes then announced, almost apologetically, that he had just one more witness, whose testimony would be brief. Granted permission, he called to the stand Joseph A. Casey, the one hundred eleventh witness in the trial, one hundred forty-seven calendar days and sixty-seven court days after the first witness had been sworn. Casey testified that he was the index clerk at the Hibernia Bank and, having searched the records, found no account for and no transaction involving Nellie's father. Tyler did not cross-examine, and Barnes said "Defendant rests."

Without a moment's pause, young Tyler stepped to the lectern to begin the final argument.

Chapter XII   DIVORCE JUDGMENT RENDERED

OUNG Tyler, anticipating that his argument was about to begin, had brought 15 or so law books into court and had them lined up on the counsel table for ready reference. As he rose to address Judge Sullivan he said that he would confine himself exclusively to the law of marriage as it related to the legality and effectiveness of the transaction represented by the Sharon marriage contract. He began by tracing the law from Hebrew customs and ceremonies through the Greek and Roman forms to the practices in England and Spain, finishing with Scotland, whose law he felt most closely paralleled that of California on the subject. Having run through all the reference books at hand, he indicated at the day's adjournment that he had concluded his argument. Overnight, as happens to most attorneys, there occurred to him a number of nice points he had overlooked, and the following morning he was granted permission to share them with the judge. He was still talking at noon.

Tyler Senior then began his own summation, taking up a thorough, if dramatic review of Sarah's life with the Senator as reflected in the evidence which Tyler had produced at the trial. An attentive audience crowded the courtroom throughout the three and a half days occupied by George Washington Tyler's argument and he did not disappoint them. The beauty and force of his argument several times brought tears to Sarah's eyes and even City Hall sophisticates appeared occasionally to have moist eyes.

Barnes managed to avoid falling under Tyler's spell by pacing up and down the empty corridor outside the courtroom, only occasionally stopping at the door to listen as Tyler would rise to one of his frequent oratorical climaxes. Tyler brought his argument to a close at the end of almost four full days of talking with as much force and eloquence as he had begun.

After a week-end respite Evans began his argument for the defense and maintained the interest of everyone including Judge Sullivan for two and a half days. Whether Evans had intended to unleash his emotions in a dramatic close was never to be known, as his final morning was marred by a great deal of confusion in the body of the courtroom, compelling him to stop a number of times while the noise was quelled. Each time it resumed unabated, and the judge finally interrupted Evans and demanded that the source of the disturbance be ejected. It was found to be Neilson, attempting to serve subpoenas on the spectators. He was removed from court under violent protest.

After the previous day's adjournment Neilson had been arrested as a common drunk. This morning the police court proposed to dismiss the case, the normal procedure when one was arrested as a first time drunk, but Neilson as usual demanded "complete vindication" after a "thorough airing of the scandal," and his trial was set for that afternoon.

The cause of the disturbance during Evans' argument that morning was Neilson's effort to subpoena all the divorce trial spectators who had seen him in court the previous day, presumably in the expectation that they would testify that they had seen him sober. Among those subpoenaed were the court reporter and Judge Sullivan, as well as all of the attorneys in the Sharon case, so the divorce case had to defer to Neilson and remain in recess until the drunk trial was concluded. It ordinarily would have taken less than an hour but, because of the number of witnesses, lasted three days. Eventually it was concluded favorably to Neilson, making it possible to resume final arguments in the divorce trial. Flournoy, speaking for Sarah, occupied two days in a meticulous review of various facets of the case, with exhaustive references to the applicable law.

The last week of August had now arrived, and with it the hottest part of the year. San Franciscans found any temperature above eighty degrees insufferable, justifying extreme measures

to escape the cruelties of the heat — so long as the breach of
decorum was not too great — and the courtroom doors were
left open in deference to the attorneys, who might otherwise
have been prostrated. Previously frustrated spectators were
quick to take advantage of the situation, with the result that the
open doorways, which had been intended to provide a breeze-
way, immediately became choked with human bodies extending
well out into the lobby of the City Hall.

A still larger crowd was in attendance as Barnes began the
presentation of his final argument for the defense, and there
was no flagging of interest during the six days consumed by
him. His summation was faithfully reproduced, daily filling
from four to six columns of newspapers whose total size was at
most eight pages. Sarah sat through a day or two of Barnes'
argument but, as his abuse of her became more and more
intense, she found it hard to contain herself and for several
sessions absented herself for the first and only time during the
trial.

Terry had been given the privilege of saying the last word.
Judge Sullivan decided that everyone might benefit by permitting a day to intervene between Barnes' close and the beginning of Terry's concluding address, and declared a one-day
adjournment.

The realization that all of the talking would soon be concluded turned the thoughts of many for the first time to the man
who was going to have to make the decision. With the exception
of his utterances at the time of the perjury arrests of Martha
Wilson and Harry Wells, Judge Sullivan had given no indication of the impressions made by the testimony and the arguments. He had, fact, so eschewed obtruding himself into the
trial, that some found it difficult to accept that this man who
had played such a modest role in the case was to write its
climactic chapter.

Terry spoke for four and a half days, without use of text or
outline, although Sarah occasionally passed him notes suggesting
points she thought should be emphasized. His style of delivery
was simple, direct, and strong. His manner contrasted sharply
with that of all other counsel who had appeared, perhaps be-

cause of the apparently sincere emotion with which he spoke. He brought his argument to a close in a voice charged with emotion, saying, "She goes from this courtroom either vindicated as an honest and virtuous wife, or branded as an adventuress, a blackmailer, a perjurer, and a harlot."

With Terry's final words the case stood submitted to Judge Sullivan for decision on September 16, 1884, six months and one week after the trial had begun with Tyler's opening statement.

Some trial followers were partisans of one side or the other even before it had commenced. As it progressed there appeared to be more general sentiment for Sarah's side than for the Senator and, by the time the last witness had stepped down from the stand and the last exhibit had been marked in evidence, a referendum would have given Sarah an easy victory. The final arguments, while uniformly good, did nothing to change popular opinion.

✓   ✓   ✓

It was expected that the judge would require a month or more to review the evidence and the legal points raised by counsel. No effort was made by the press to keep the case before the public in the meantime. No such effort was necessary; as usual the case proved to be capable of spontaneous generation.

Neilson called another press conference. Now that the case was concluded and no one could be injured, he said, he owed it to his honor to speak out. Several of the "Dear Wife" letters were forgeries, he charged. The next evening reporters found Sarah at her home with Terry as a visitor. Asked for their reactions to Neilson's statements, Terry said that Neilson was insane. "Oh, no," remonstrated Sarah placidly. "I don't think he is insane. There is too much method in his madness." But a few days later she sued one of the San Francisco newspapers, the *Alta California,* for libel in having published Neilson's charges. The action was taken by whim and against Tyler's advice, thus further straining their relations.

Tyler used the free time following the trial to attack again the Senator's long dormant federal suit, the action in U. S.

Circuit Court to have Sarah enjoined from claiming the validity of the marriage contract. Tyler was still hoping the federal case would be dismissed without the necessity of another protracted trial. But the federal court was not eager to give up the opportunity. Judge Lorenzo Sawyer complained that he would have liked to reject Tyler's arguments on technical grounds, but as Barnes did not see fit to raise the right objection, the judge went on, looking down his judicial nose, he would consider and deny Tyler's plea on its merits. This he did forthwith.*

With these exceptions the attorneys turned to other employment. Sarah passed the time agreeably, though the social circles in which she was now accepted were more limited than previously. Judge Sullivan was also conducting his normal daily court calendar, utilizing his free time in consideration of the legal problems presented by the Sharon case. September gave way to October, and another San Francisco winter was heralded in mid-November with the first seasonal rain.

✓ ✓ ✓

It was rumored that the judge was determined to decide the case before the end of the year, and from early December onward interest in the case was renewed, gathering momentum

---

* *Sharon* v. *Hill*, 22 Fed. 28: Tyler had urged that the federal suit should be dismissed since the same dispute was being considered by the state court. "It is true, the same principal issue will arise in both cases," the judge conceded, but "different and inconsistent relief" was sought, and not "by the same party." In other words, since Sarah was plaintiff in one case, and the Senator was plaintiff in the other, and one party sought to have a valid marriage declared, while the other wanted it declared invalid, the lawsuits were not identical and there was no good reason to abate the federal case. Although nothing in his decision suggested that Judge Sawyer felt like a character from Lewis Carroll or, indeed, any uneasiness about his analysis, he declared that in any event the United States Supreme Court had held that "a suit pending in another jurisdiction for the same cause cannot be pleaded in abatement of a suit in the United States courts" and that state courts are "another jurisdiction" for purposes of the rule; so, he concluded, even if he were wrong on the question of whether the two actions here were substantially identical — which he did not for a moment believe — Tyler's point was not well taken.

as the holiday season approached. Finally, at the beginning of Christmas week, it was reliably reported that the decision would be read by Judge Sullivan the day before Christmas. Though no public announcement was made, long before nine o'clock on that morning Judge Sullivan's courtroom had the appearance which for so long had been familiar to so many. It was again crowded to overflowing.

A heavy mist fell throughout the morning of December 24. Sarah arrived at the City Hall wearing a cloak of richly embossed velvet trimmed with otter, with an otter boa thrown about her neck to provide a soft warmth against the cold. Black gloves and a bonnet covered with blue beads completed her outer costume. When she discarded the cloak after entering the courtroom, there was revealed a black silk dress trimmed in velvet of the same blue as her bonnet except on the close fitting sleeves which ended in pink ruffles at the wrist. Altogether it was the most striking of the many costumes with which the auburn-haired Sarah had favored the court during the long trial.

The Senator was reported to be in the building, but did not make an appearance in court. Barnes sat immobile, staring at the floor in silence as he awaited Judge Sullivan's appearance, while Evans played nervously with his watch chain. Tyler looked tense but confident as he kept his eye on the chamber's door through which the judge would momentarily appear, and Flournoy rocked placidly on the back legs of his chair. Spectators wondered if the demeanor of the attorneys reflected a foreknowledge of the decision.

At ten minutes past nine o'clock the trained ears of the bailiff detected the turning of the chamber's doorknob. His call for order precipitated the usual din created when the packed courtroom simultaneously came to its feet, and the judge, looking unusually pale, strode quickly to the bench.

Some thought the judge took the bench as though about to deliver the death sentence in a capital case, while others likened his manner to that of one who was himself mounting the scaffold. But, however great the pleasure of attempting to divine the decision from Judge Sullivan's appearance, it had to be abandoned as he squared the papers before him and cleared his throat. All those in attendance settled back in their chairs attentively.

"As I have informed counsel," said Judge Sullivan, "I am now ready to deliver my decision in the case of Sharon versus Sharon." He had written his opinion in full, and, after the introductory sentence he rarely raised his eyes from the text but read without inflection in a low and deliberate voice.

The judge began with a careful review of each party's contentions, and then marshalled the evidence which had been presented. Early in his analysis of the evidence he said that Sarah had been untruthful in part of her testimony — at which she caught her breath — and that there had been an unprecedented amount of "frightful perjury" by a number of witnesses, a situation which he described as intolerably disgusting. Nellie he dismissed as a "pure and virtuous girl" duped into being an "assistant fabricator," and Neilson as a "malicious trickster."

Barnes roused himself slightly with these characterizations and his spirits improved still more when the judge said that he did not believe that the Senator had ever introduced Sarah to anyone as his wife, nor had he spoken of her as his wife in the presence of other persons.

Barnes' newborn hopes were blighted when the judge declared that the question was not which witnesses were the more truthful, but whether the marriage contract was genuine. For answer to that question he turned to Gumpel's testimony. "It is to be borne in mind," said Judge Sullivan, "that he was a witness summoned by the defendant; he came into court fully accredited; his competence is unquestioned. Under the circumstances his testimony is entitled to great weight." The marriage contract, said the judge, is therefore genuine, written by Sarah at the direction of the Senator and then signed by both of them.

Sarah leaned forward and a single sob escaped her. The judge continued, declaring that the "Dear Wife" letters were also genuine and that, as between themselves, the parties had conducted themselves as married persons. Why had the "malevolent defendant" signed the contract? Because he was a libertine. "The defendant was a man of unbounded wealth, pos-

sessed of strong animal passions that, from excessive indulg-
ence, had become unaccustomed to restraint," said the judge,
to Sarah's increasing joy. "Whatever he had undertaken during
his career he had in great measure accomplished. His passion
may have been stronger than his judgment. He may have regarded as a trifle, light as air, the miserable bit of paper behind
which a weak woman could shelter her virginity and her claim
to a standing in the community."

Although Tyler permitted himself a grimace intended to
approximate a smile, he held himself in check for the time
being, recognizing that the battle was yet only half won. The
judge had not yet touched on the question of whether the contract could establish a legal marriage.

In due course Judge Sullivan, methodically covering all aspects of the case, turned to the legal questions. He had not
found it necessary to accompany young Tyler back to Old
Testament rituals, but devoted substantial time to the history
of the law of marriage. He concluded that a valid marriage
could result from the actions of the parties.

Tyler grew increasingly exultant as he followed the judge
through his legal reasoning. But Sarah, who lacked the ability
or the patience — or both — to follow the legal points, kept her
eyes expectantly on the judge. She finally sighed with a flush
of joy when at last she heard him say, "Under the law of the
state, Sarah Althea Sharon, plaintiff in this case, is entitled to a
decree of the court dissolving the bonds of marriage now existing between her and her husband, William Sharon, the defendant herein."

The judge ordered that a referee should handle division of
the community property, directed Tyler to prepare formal findings and the decree for his later signature, and without cere-
money left the bench. Two and a half hours had been consumed
in reading the opinion.

Evans quickly left the courtroom followed more slowly by
Barnes. Sarah's attorneys stood in a group repeatedly shaking
hands and clapping each other on the back, while the entire
courtroom welled forward to congratulate the radiant Sarah.
She began to cry quietly, touching the corners of her eyes with

a handkerchief. To reporters who clustered about her as she left she said, "The decision is all the congratulation I want. I am prepared now to pass a merry Christmas even though I am a divorced woman."

Tyler told reporters that he was not at all sure the other side would appeal, but said that Sarah would in any case be entitled to support money while any appeal was pending, and he expected that to be at least five thousand dollars a month. In any event, an appeal would be but a shallow hope.

Reporters later tracked down Barnes at the Pacific Club. He appeared cheerful as he said, "What will we do? Well, I haven't had time to collect my thoughts since this morning's shock. It was a little unexpected, I must confess. As a matter of course we will appeal. After I have studied the opinion I shall know on what grounds." What did the Senator think? "I have already told him that the case may outlast his life."

The Senator, when reporters found him still later in his apartment at the Palace, was prepared to speak for himself. Asked what he intended to do, he expressed himself in language similar to that which a British Prime Minister was to use in a somewhat larger cause half a century later. "Fight it to the bitter end," he said. "Fight it in all the courts, and fight it on all sides. I'll never give in to the last."

It occurred to reporters still later that evening to seek a legal opinion on what could happen to the federal case which had been floating idly at anchor for over a year now. Tyler was the only person connected with the case who could be found. He answered succinctly. "Having submitted to the jurisdiction of the state courts, the United States Circuit Court's judgment will be a mere nullity. There is nothing left to decide."

Tyler's opinion was not universally shared. The *Chronicle* felt that the federal case was "more important than many think," and speculated that if that court's decision should hold that the contract was spurious, the one decision would offset the other and the only appeal would be to the Supreme Court of the United States.

Sarah spent the remainder of Christmas Eve on a shopping tour of the city, buying many costly gifts for friends and occasionally finding something for herself. She found special pleasure in asking the deferential clerks to charge the purchases to Mrs. William Sharon, and explained to newsmen who followed her about that she had been too occupied with the trial, and too much out of the spirit, to have done any of her Christmas shopping earlier.

Christmas Day Sarah spent "at home" to visitors. Although she received many, and pressed champagne on all who called, including newsmen, she discovered that the mere rendition of Judge Sullivan's decision had not re-established her standing in the community. Those of greatest social prominence in San Francisco, whose doors had been open to Sarah prior to the scandal, did not call; but if her guests were less than fashionable, she showed no disappointment.

Chapter XIII ALIMONY AND PANDEMONIUM

S THE YEAR 1885 began, there was continuing action on many fronts.

Tyler filed a denial in the federal case styling Sarah "Mrs. S. A. Sharon," urging Judge Sullivan's decision as conclusive on the validity of the marriage.

Tyler was also making preparations, with supporting affidavits, to request of Judge Sullivan an award of temporary alimony and attorney's fees pending final termination of the divorce case.

Sarah's libel case against the *Alta* newspaper was moving along briskly, to Tyler's dismay. The *Alta's* attorney, who appeared to be working closely with Barnes, had demanded that depositions of potential witnesses be taken, starting with Neilson.

Barnes had been occupying the time more usefully. He said he was collecting much evidence, with the help of the Sarah-Neilson disputes, and felt daily more confident that Judge Sullivan would grant a new trial when he saw what Barnes and his investigators had discovered.

The general public had long been curious about the cost of, and methods of procuring, evidence in the divorce case. The Senator did not deny rumors that he was spending more than a thousand dollars a day to prevent Sarah from getting the one cent that he was determined to deny her. A transaction which occupied the weeks immediately following the decision shed some light on the question of the Senator's costs and methods of finding evidence, though its unexpectedness and its sudden complete change of thrust greatly obscured that point.

Barnes began plotting his course as soon as the judge's decision was announced, sending individual agents and teams into the field on a wide variety of missions. Judge Sullivan had relied heavily on Gumpel, the handwriting expert, and Barnes felt that one of the most critical areas of attack would have to be the discrediting of Gumpel's testimony. The insidious Police Captain I. W. Lees, the most implacable of the Senator's minions, was given that assignment.

Within forty-eight hours Lees, working through Christmas day itself, was on a scent which, when reported to the taciturn Barnes, produced an exultant smile. He knew that the information, if true, was of a kind which would require Judge Sullivan to reverse his decision. Barnes and Lees immediately bent all their energies to procuring tangible evidence. At the end of two weeks they were prepared to lay the results before the judge.

Impatient to turn his recent defeat to victory, Barnes sought the earliest opportunity to publish his findings. The opportunity was provided soon after the holidays when Judge Sullivan convened court to consider Sarah's application for alimony and attorneys' fees.

As the judge took the bench, Tyler rose to open the alimony discussion, but Barnes interrupted to say he wished to present indisputable evidence of perjury and collusion not only countenanced by, but actively participated in, by Tyler. Barnes' ominous tone and the unexpectedness of such a serious charge astounded the crowded courtroom. Without visible reaction Tyler blandly objected that such an offer was irrelevant to the alimony hearing.

The judge said that such a serious charge should never be deferred and instructed Barnes to proceed. Barnes opened by saying he would prove the conspiracy by measuring testimony at the trial against a document which would condemn both Gumpel and Tyler as conspiring perjurers. His voice strident with emotion, he first reminded the judge that Gumpel had given the court to understand that he was an unwilling witness, that he had been hired and paid by the Senator, and that although his conclusions after examination of the contract made it impossible for him to testify for Barnes he was reluctant to testify for the other side. Barnes said he was sure the judge would recall that Gumpel had said he had been neither paid nor promised anything by Tyler, and had not even talked with Tyler nor told him what his testimony would be at any time before being called to the stand. Tyler had later under oath attested the truth of Gumpel's statement.

Judge Sullivan's stony silence was underscored by the hushed attention given by the spectators, as Barnes, after a pause, said dramatically that he held in his hand a paper which gave the lie to the entire representation, proving it a deception of the court. Brandishing it momentarily, Barnes then read the document. It provided for a $25,000 fee to be paid Gumpel contingent on favorable testimony and on winning the divorce case. It was subscribed "M. Gumpel" and "Geo. W. Tyler" and was dated two months before Gumpel had testified.

As Barnes concluded his reading attention centered on Tyler. It was obvious that this revelation would mean a reversal of the judge's decision. It was equally clear that Tyler's involvement would likely cost him his career; it would necessitate his disbarment if not a criminal prosecution.

Tyler had buried his face in his handkerchief midway in Barnes' recitation and, as his shoulders shook convulsively, pity vied with contempt in the hearts of the spectators. Tyler with difficulty drew himself to his feet at the conclusion of Barnes' remarks and it then became apparent that he was not hiding his face in shame but was wiping away tears of laughter.

Choked and gasping for words, Tyler converted an explosive laugh to a shout demanding that Barnes be sworn and required to tell how the paper came into his possession. As Barnes, puzzled, was being sworn one of Tyler's associates leaned over, horror still apparent on his face, to demand a whispered explanation of Tyler and, having made some sense of Tyler's garbled words, joined him in his laughter.

Barnes at first refused to divulge his source of the paper, but when Tyler asserted that he could prove it to be a forgery, Barnes with obvious reluctance told how he had been occupying much of his time the past two weeks.

In the week between Christmas and New Year's Day, he said, Police Captain Lees had arranged a secret meeting with John McLaughlin, Tyler's chief clerk, after much furtive negotiation, in a hotel room Lees had hired under a fictitious name. To McLaughlin's surprise, not only Lees but Barnes was present. Barnes told McLaughlin that he and Lees were sure a Tyler-Gumpel contract existed, and that he was willing to pay well for it.

Barnes testified that McLaughlin agreed to make a search, but demanded five thousand dollars if he was successful in finding and abstracting such a document. Barnes instantly replied, "All right, go ahead." McLaughlin did nothing further and two days later told Lees he still did not think such a contract existed and did not wish to go further with the venture.

Several more secret meetings were held in the next few days. Lees reassured McLaughlin that he had nothing to fear, that even if he was found out he would be taken care of for life: "Trust in me," Lees said; "I never did a dishonorable act in my life."

McLaughlin eventually sent word to Lees that he had found and now had in his possession the paper which Barnes wanted. A meeting was arranged with Barnes and Lees in a private room at Marchand's Restaurant. Seeing their eagerness McLaughlin demanded more money, to which Barnes immediately agreed. $25,000 was the price ultimately agreed on, Barnes testified, and he had paid it only last Friday at which time McLaughlin had turned over the damning contract.

When Barnes stepped down from the stand, still perplexed by Tyler's manner, all of the attorneys began to talk simultaneously, hurling accusations of burglary, bribery, and perjury. The noise was quelled before long and Tyler requested permission to be sworn.

On the stand he testified that everything Barnes had said was true, but that he, Tyler, could supply a bit more information for the edification of the court. "I am familiar with all the transactions," he said. Judge Sullivan asked him to confine himself to the facts without indulging in argument. "I intend to do so, your Honor," Tyler replied. "I shall not follow the example of my illustrious predecessor."

Tyler testified that McLaughlin, far from being the disloyal clerk Barnes had tried to make of him, had come to him immediately after being first approached by Lees. Tyler asked McLaughlin to pretend to cooperate with Lees for the purpose of "showing up the schemes used by the opposition throughout the trial." Later, when McLaughlin reported Barnes' great anxiety for the Gumpel agreement which he believed to exist, Tyler determined to manufacture such an agreement. He first tried to get a sample of Gumpel's signature, but finally drew Gumpel into the plan and, with a little coaching, Tyler said, he had written the entire contract a few days past, and had subscribed a facsimile of Gumpel's name.

That was all there was to it, he said, except to say that there had never been any actual contract between himself and Gumpel, before or after the trial.

Barnes, who looked increasingly crestfallen during Tyler's ebullient recitation, demanded dispiritedly that Tyler imitate Gumpel's signature for the judge. After Tyler obliged with several very good likenesses in rapid succession, Barnes said with resignation, "Mr. Tyler's narration of these facts and these interviews bears a sufficient evidence of truth, though filled with a certain kind of exaggeration. It satisfies me that what he says is substantially true. I believe now that the contract is a fraud."

"No, not a fraud, a decoy," Tyler remonstrated.

"I believe it was a decoy," the defeated Barnes echoed, and requested permission to withdraw the "contract" from evidence. He sought some solace, saying that McLaughlin could have talked him out of a hundred thousand dollars, and expressed hope that Tyler would get his share of the twenty-five thousand.

They turned back briefly to the alimony motion but Judge Sullivan decided to put it over to another day for consideration, and court adjourned with laughter from the spectators echoing down the corridors in the City Hall. Small clusters of people talked excitedly as they slowly drifted down the steps, lingering long after adjournment.

Like most developments in the case, the Barnes-McLaughlin transaction died slowly, flaring up several times before expiring. For some time, it was the main topic of conversation at the City Hall and on the street and was for several days given the greater part of a page in the newspapers.

Gumpel and McLaughlin, interviewed immediately by the press, confirmed Tyler's version of the events, and eventually filed affidavits with Judge Sullivan to the same effect. Others came forward to swear that they "heard" that the facts were to the contrary and that the Tyler-Gumpel agreement was genuine. But it was eventually conceded by everyone that it was spurious.

The contest had been of the sort Tyler relished, but though he met Barnes blast for blast in subsequent press interviews, he pursued the matter no further.

Barnes was of a different mold. He was known to hold himself in high regard, being of the opinion that a man could demand of others no more respect than he was willing to award himself. He had now been made the butt of a widely publicized and highly successful joke. Moreover, it was reported that the Senator, irritated by Barnes' clumsy performance, had deducted the $25,000 from Barnes' fee. A man less proud than Barnes would have had difficulty dismissing it lightly or treating it with levity. Barnes could not let it drop without satisfaction. Until now harassment of Tyler had been, for Barnes, incidental to the goal of winning the Sharon dispute. Now the destruction of Tyler became an end in itself, an end which Barnes would pursue remorselessly, aided by the large investigative and financial resources with which he was waging the Sharon fight.

The flamboyant Tyler had won the battle but was ultimately to lose the war, paying the greatest price which can be demanded of an attorney. He would have been wise to take a more serious measure of his opponent.

The questions which kept the incident simmering in the following days were: What crimes or unprofessional conduct had been committed? By whom? What was to be done with the $25,000? Reporters devoted their full time for a period of a week to interviewing the principals, coaxing rejoinders by repeating each man's charges to the others.

Interviewed the day after the court hearing, Barnes said that Tyler was guilty of grand theft in having obtained money by false pretenses and he intended to seek Tyler's disbarment.

Tyler responded that McLaughlin had made no representation of the genuineness of the Gumpel contract and Barnes had received precisely what he bargained for. He would appreciate it, Tyler said, if newsmen would inquire how it happened that Captain Lees, a police officer paid by the public, found so much time to be employed in the Senator's interest. He said he was thinking of asking the Supreme Court to investigate the entire matter. In 35 years of criminal practice he had never heard an attempt to corrupt a man's employee described as legal, "But if the Supreme Court think it correct practice for General Barnes with the assistance of Captain Lees to bribe my confidential clerk to break open my desk, then all right; they're the ones to decide."

The following day Tyler proposed that either the Bar Association or Judge Sullivan take charge of the $25,000 until its proper disposition could be determined. Although Barnes loftily refused to consent, saying it would compound a felony, Tyler nevertheless determined to deposit the money with the judge.

The Bar Association was convened to consider the question of whether discipline should be imposed and, if so, on whom. There was unanimity that some action must be taken, but after lengthy discussion the members differed widely on what course should follow. It was decided to appoint a committee.

An editorial in the *Chronicle* expressed the opinion that "recent events teach us that it is high time" the laws of marriage and divorce were remodeled in California.

✓   ✓   ✓

In the next two months the divorce trial's satellites were so active that the newspaper columns collecting the "Side Lights" generally exceeded the space allotted to the main case. In the month after the judge took the alimony application under submission, for example, the *Chronicle* reported the following:

January 17: The Bar Association committee to investigate alleged misconduct of the attorneys was named.

Item: Neilson filed a second hundred-thousand-dollar libel action against the Senator.

Item: Tyler was convicted and fined one hundred dollars in police court for obscenity in having called Neilson a "puke" during the taking of his deposition in Sarah's suit against the *Alta* newspaper.

Item: At the taking of his deposition, which was still in progress, Neilson spent the day reviewing his life, often breaking down in tears.

January 19: McLaughlin failed to keep an appointment to accompany Tyler to Judge Sullivan's chambers to deposit the $25,000 with him. Tyler expressed hope that he was merely ill "somewhere."

January 20: More affidavits were filed in the alimony proceeding.

Item: McLaughlin and the $25,000 were still missing.

January 21: In a lengthy interview Tyler was unable to give any information on the whereabouts of McLaughlin or the money.

Item: Neilson refused to sign his completed *Alta* deposition, saying that his doctor told him his health was too poor.

January 22: In a further alimony hearing before Judge Sullivan, Barnes again argued criminal conduct by Tyler, but the judge ruled that in considering alimony it did not matter how great a rascal one's attorney was elsewhere.

Item: A San Francisco attorney named Seaton held a press interview and claimed that he knew of the existence of a genuine Tyler-Gumpel contract.

January 23: Tyler said that Seaton was a destitute and disreputable flunkey of the opposition who had several days earlier offered McLaughlin an additional $20,000 if he would disappear and not corroborate Tyler's story.

January 24: Many more affidavits were filed in the alimony proceeding. Tyler objected to any further delays, but William Stewart, a new addition to the Senator's legal staff, said, "This is no longer a San Francisco case; it interests the whole civilized world and involves serious charges of frauds which ought to be fully investigated."

Item: Neilson was charged with embezzling two hundred and fifty dollars from Sarah.

Item: Tyler appealed from the obscenity judgment.

January 26: Further argument was had on the alimony request.

Item: The Grand Jury was in session hearing testimony of Barnes and Lees, leading to much speculation.

Item: Sarah's suit against the Senator for seven hundred fifty dollars on the promissory note was called for trial and deferred until next month, as everyone was busy elsewhere.

January 27: Tyler accused Barnes and Lees of having smuggled McLaughlin onto a Honolulu-bound ship. Barnes accused Tyler of keeping McLaughlin in hiding.

Item: Neilson, seen on the street with a great bundle of documents, said he was about to have Sarah and Tyler charged with perjury for having him accused of embezzlement.

Item: The Grand Jury was still sitting, but unwilling to say what it was sitting for.

February 2: The notary in the *Alta* suit again demanded that Neilson sign his deposition and Neilson refused.

February 3: In the federal suit by the Senator against Sarah to have the marriage contract declared a forgery, S. G. Houghton was designated trial examiner to take testimony in the Appraiser's Building.

February 7: The attorneys argued legal questions before Examiner Houghton and testimony was begun, but as the federal proceedings were closed to the public, its purport was not known.

February 9: It was learned that in the federal case Tyler had raised a technical objection, compelling Barnes to commence taking testimony anew.

February 13: Sarah was ordered to produce the marriage contract for inspection by the *Alta's* handwriting expert, R. W. Piper, who had been brought out from Chicago.

Judge Sullivan made his ruling on the alimony request in mid-February, awarding $2500 a month to Sarah as alimony and $55,000 to her attorneys, divided in proportion to the amount of work they had done, the largest share being awarded to Tyler. Sarah told reporters that it was a nice valentine, though not as much as she had expected, and she hoped people would remember Judge Sullivan as a man who had befriended a poor and defenseless woman, if he should ever seek higher office.

The Senator, asked his reaction to the alimony award as he left court, said Judge Sullivan evidently rated Althea's value a great deal higher than she did herself. "When she and I had to fix her value, she rated it as $500 per month." He was not surprised or unhappy. In fact, the greater the award the better, for "the greater the wrong the sooner it is righted." He said he would pay her no alimony, temporary or otherwise, as he was sure he would eventually win and if he paid anything now it would be impossible ever to recover it from anyone as irresponsible as Sarah.

Asked if he had given any thought to compromising the case, the Senator said, "Compromise, sir? No, sir! This is an infamous conspiracy and I would not lay down one silver dollar this minute to have the conspirators renounce all claims upon me. I will never rest until justice is done me and not a cent of my money — not a single mill — shall these people have."

Three days later Judge Sullivan signed the formal findings and the divorce decree prepared by Tyler, notwithstanding the filing by Barnes of a closely printed 470-page bill of exceptions. Barnes immediately gave notice he intended to appeal. E. J. Baldwin, owner of the Baldwin Hotel, and Lloyd Tevis, a friend of the Senator, signed surety bonds totaling over half a million dollars to stay the proceedings while the appeal was pending.

Meanwhile, like grains of sand in a whirlwind, the various ancillaries were still being stirred:

February 17: In the federal case Judge Sawyer ordered Sarah to produce the marriage contract for examination.

Item: Reporters followed the process server around the city in his unsuccessful effort to serve Neilson with a contempt citation for refusing to sign the *Alta* deposition.

February 18: Sarah did not produce the marriage contract before the federal examiner and was ordered into court. She told Judge Sawyer that David Terry had the contract and had gone to Fresno on another case. Judge Sawyer offered to remand her to jail but Barnes suggested that she be given one week in which to produce it.

Item: The Grand Jury returned indictments against Tyler, Gumpel, and McLaughlin for obtaining money by false pretenses in having defrauded Barnes with the sham Gumpel-Tyler paper. Tyler immediately surrendered himself and, with much merriment, he and Gumpel were released on bail posted by Mammy Pleasant. No one appeared to take the indictment very seriously. Sarah was present and took the opportunity to ask the district attorney's legal advice on how she should go about getting perjury indictments issued against the Senator, Barnes, and Nellie.

Item: McLaughlin was seen in Honolulu, where he was reported to be enjoying a comfortable life.

February 19: Judge Sullivan appointed a referee to determine the amount of community property to be divided pursuant to the divorce decree.

February 20: The Superior Court reversed Tyler's obscenity conviction, holding that the word "puke" applied to Neilson did not constitute vulgar, obscene, or profane language within the meaning of the law.

Item: Young Tyler was charged with obscenity in having called Neilson a liar. Trial was set for the following week.

February 25: Judge Sawyer, in federal court, refused to permit any argument regarding Sarah's failure to produce the marriage contract, and she reluctantly handed it over to R. W. Piper, the *Alta's* erstwhile handwriting expert, and now to no one's surprise the Senator's handwriting expert in the federal case. As Piper began to examine the contract Sarah rushed at him with a nail file. Piper threw out his hands to ward her off and she grasped first one and then the other, cleaning and smoothing the nails, telling him that he must not handle the contract with dirty hands. "You can sometime say that you once had your nails cleaned for you by Mrs. Sharon," she said sweetly as Piper began to relax. She finished by wiping his fingers and his microscope with a handkerchief, and Piper sat down to his work.

February 27: The notary and reporter were still sitting daily, alone, awaiting the completion of Neilson's *Alta* deposition.

February 28: The Tyler obscenity trials were deferred, no one being present.

March 5: Tyler dismissed the libel suit against the *Alta.*

March 7: The United States marshal served on Sarah an order requiring her to produce in federal court the "Dear Wife" letters.

March 9: Judge Sullivan ordered that all documents used in the divorce case be deposited with him, to prevent their removal from the state in the event the federal case should be appealed to the United States Supreme Court in Washington.

Item: All parties appeared later in the day in Judge Sawyer's federal court. He ordered that all documents be deposited with him, saying that Sarah would be held in contempt of court if she put it out of her power to produce them.

Item: Judge Wilson, hearing the Neilson embezzlement case, ordered that Sarah produce in his court all divorce case exhibits.

Item: It was rumored that Levy drew a gun on Tyler during an argument on the division of the attorney's fee in the divorce case. Confirmation could not be obtained.

March 10: The federal court rejected a renewal of Tyler's plea to dismiss the Senator's suit to have the marriage contract declared a forgery.*

Item: Judge Sullivan called five of his associates to sit with him *en banc* to hear argument on whether the Senator should be enjoined from pursuing the federal case.

Item: The impanelment of the jury was begun in the Neilson embezzlement trial. All prospective jurors were asked whether anything they had read about the Sharon disputes would influence their verdict. One man said he had never heard of the Sharon case and was later interviewed by reporters as a social curiosity.

Item: Sarah's suit against the Senator on the promissory note was again called for trial but, as all the parties were occupied elsewhere, it was postponed.

---

* *Sharon* v. *Hill,* 23 Fed. 353.

Item: Tyler protested a six-hundred-ninety-dollar cost bill filed by the *Alta* in the now dismissed libel suit, claimed to be due Neilson, the notary and the reporter as fees in connection with the taking of his deposition.

Item: A restaurant owner filed suit against the Senator for two hundred sixty-seven dollars for meals served Mrs. Samson and her daughters, which the Senator was alleged to have agreed to pay.

Item: The Senator, interviewed about his now overdue first alimony payment to Sarah, said he would go to jail before paying one cent.

March 11: Sarah, dressed stunningly with a diamond brooch at her throat, was the first witness in Neilson's embezzlement trial followed by Tyler. Neilson undertook Tyler's cross-examination personally, with the result that he and Tyler were soon both fined for contempt of court.

March 12: The Superior Court determined that it lacked the power to order Senator Sharon to abandon the federal case.

For a time, Tyler appeared to be withdrawing from the fray, Terry often taking the lead or appearing alone for Sarah. And Sarah's attitude toward Tyler seemed to have changed. Asked about it, she said that though he still represented her as chief counsel she was unhappy with him for a number of reasons. For one thing, she said she had not authorized the dismissal of the libel suit against the *Alta*. For another, she did not think it looked proper for him to have recorded his fee contract, which called for 50 percent of everything gained in the suit, immediately after Judge Sullivan rendered his decision. Tyler was acting as though entitled to the entire 50 percent, she said, when he knew that another person was entitled to half of it. She did not name the other person, but it was assumed she meant Mammy Pleasant. She also felt that he could have prevented the federal trial thus sparing her the burden of having the entire case retried, she said.

Tyler, interviewed, denied her criticisms and said that he was still as actively and as ardently interested in the litigation as ever, but admitted that Sarah's "unfortunate habit of rasping everyone she comes in contact with" had caused him to use

Terry as an intermediary. "She acts very strangely," he said, "and her peculiar conduct has driven nearly all of her friends away from her." He said the *Alta* suit had been dismissed to prevent the marriage contract and the other documents being tied up there; and he had recorded his fee contract because Sarah had not thanked him for his work and he was fearful he could not trust her.

While relations remained strained for some time, they were never completely broken.

Chapter XIV   A PASSING DIVERSION

T WOULD have been unrealistic to expect the course of the appeal from
Judge Sullivan's divorce decree to run
any more smoothly than the trial, and preliminary skirmishes
commenced almost immediately — reckoning by jurisprudential
time — after the filing of the notice of appeal to the California
Supreme Court. The months which followed were spent in
procedural maneuvers somewhat removed from the central
issue of the validity of the marriage; but their fruits could be
substantial, even conclusive, in their effect on the main case.

After some urging Judge Sullivan threatened the Senator
with a contempt citation if he did not commence making the
alimony payments, and Barnes immediately requested the state
Supreme Court to prohibit execution of the threat. Tyler as
promptly countered by asking the Supreme Court to deny that
application, and for good measure requested the Court to dismiss the Senator's pending appeals from the divorce decree and
alimony awards.

Each side's action provided a fertile field for the kind of
semantic exercises peculiarly enjoyed by lawyers and judges,
in which current statutes and past judicial opinions are viewed,
briefed, compared and contrasted in an effort to harmonize and
reconcile them to one's own views.

The Supreme Court considered the applications together and
required little time to give the Senator a clean sweep in dispos-
ing of these initial appellate jousts.* There was no great quarrel

---

* *Sharon* v. *Sharon*, 67 Cal. 185 (7 Pac. 456): The Court held that an
appeal could properly be taken from an order for payment of alimony and
attorneys' fees as well as from a divorce decree, and that alimony need not
be paid pending the decision on appeal. Although the majority of the
Court felt obligated to search the law as far back as the time of Christ
and to probe the Code of Justinian in support of its position, some attorneys felt that the lone dissenter from the decision, Associate Justice Mc-
Kee, argued more persuasively in pointing out that a wife needed support
as much while her divorce was being appealed as before or afterwards.

with the proposition that one should be entitled to appeal from a divorce decree and from an alimony award, but San Francisco attorneys "unanimously," the papers said, were surprised and alarmed by the ruling that the Senator could ignore the alimony award until the appeal was finally disposed of. The result of the Court's decision, attorneys explained, was that a husband who wished to starve his wife to death could provoke her to seek a divorce, appeal the decision, and pay her no support money during the three to five years then usually required for an appeal. One of many attorneys interviewed by the Oakland *Daily Tribune* expressed the general reaction, saying "It is the most infamous decision ever rendered in this state. It is simply made to fit this case and when the Supreme Court descends to such things, I think it is time we had a change in the personnel of the Bench."*

The intensity with which the conflict had been pursued was obviously not to be slackened now that the case had arrived in a more sedate and elevated forum. Tyler promptly petitioned for and was granted a rehearing. Nevertheless, after a very lively argument of the legal questions between Tyler and Barnes, the Court reaffirmed its original order.**

---

* Less than four years previously the same Court, in a prior case, raised the question of whether an appeal would lie from an alimony award and whether support would have to be paid pending an appeal, but left both issues undecided. (*Ex parte Cottrell*, 59 Cal. 417) And only the previous year, a husband who, like the Senator, was threatened with a contempt citation pending his appeal from a divorce decree and an alimony award, requested the Court to let him file a bond to stay the proceedings until the appeal was decided. The Court summarily refused his request. (*Church* v. *Church*, No. 9405) Though Justice McKee, the lone dissenter, felt that the Church decision should be followed, and Tyler's petition for rehearing — "deliberately," the Court said — relied on the Church case, the majority said it was plain that the situation in the Church case was different.

** *Sharon* v. *Sharon*, 67 Cal. 220: Associate Justice Thornton, now speaking for the majority, was again harried by the Church case of the previous year, and he now vanquished it saying it was impossible to say on what ground the husband in that case was denied the relief which was now being given the Senator. "Conceding," he continued, "that some inconsistency appears to exist, we think the ruling in this case is the better one." Justice McKee again dissented.

Tyler immediately filed a new motion to dismiss the appeal, this time urging several technical grounds. Although he had the consolation of putting the Court to the trouble of writing a 16-page opinion, all of his arguments were again rejected as the year 1885 came to a close.*

ⵏ   ⵏ   ⵏ

The vagrant ancillary frolics, meanwhile, pursued their tumultuous courses, and most were resolved in one way or another by the time the summer of that year had arrived. Neilson was acquitted on the embezzlement charge and the obscenity charges against the Tylers were ultimately dismissed.

In the federal case, although Judge Sawyer had refused to abate the suit several times before, Terry made one more unsuccessful attempts while testimony was being taken.**

Sarah obtained a $750 judgment against the Senator on the promissory note. Barnes immediately appealed.

The restaurant owner who had sued the Senator for Mrs. Samson's meals lost his case and appealed.

McLaughlin was interviewed in Honolulu by a reporter for that community's *Commercial Advertiser*. He said he was en-

---

* *Sharon* v. *Sharon*, 68 Cal. 326: Tyler had contended that both Barnes' notice of the appeal and the bond had been defective, and that the record of the trial court proceedings had not been filed as required. All of these were procedural as opposed to substantive arguments. Although laymen frequently characterize such objections as lint-picking and their successful urging as loopholes in the law, they generally reflect the essential ground rules for the orderly administration of justice and, in consequence, provide attorneys with an occasional effective weapon for appeal.

** *Sharon* v. *Hill*, 26 Fed. 722: Among the denials in the formal answer which had finally been filed for Sarah, it had again been alleged that both Sarah and the Senator were domiciled in California, and that the federal court therefore had no jurisdiction of the dispute. Terry wanted to present evidence on that issue, but Judge Sawyer rejected the request, saying that he had already expressed his convictions very clearly two or three times. To Terry's plea that the question had never yet been considered on its merits — that no evidence had been accepted or considered on the question of the Senator's residence — Sawyer answered "The parties are entitled to have an issue once tried and determined. If through negligence or otherwise they do not present their evidence, the fault is their own, and they must abide the consequences."

joying a happy life there and did not care to discuss or think about the Sharon case. Later, it was reported that after spending most of the $25,000 in Honolulu he drifted on to Australia, where he operated a steam laundry with indifferent success and still later died in poverty.

The *Chronicle* had taken to collecting the threads of the case under the caption "Sharon Sideshows." Inevitably new sideshows appeared as old ones were resolved.

Item: The Oriental Lodge of Masons sued the Senator, Barnes, Lees and others for five thousand dollars in damages alleged to have been caused by the desecration of the grave at the Masonic Cemetery during the trial.

Item: Barnes had Gumpel charged with perjury for having testified at the divorce trial that he had spoken to Barnes during an opium prosecution some years earlier. Tyler represented Gumpel. William Stewart, one of the Senator's newly added attorneys, a prominent railroad lawyer, former senator, and long-time friend of Justice Field, acted as special prosecutor. At one preliminary court skirmish Stewart became angry with Tyler for objecting to a remark and reached for a gun. Though Tyler said he chose to dispute only with words, Stewart continued to advance and had to be overpowered by cooler heads. The divorce case was retried at great length in the course of the Gumpel prosecution, as it was in almost every collateral case that arose.

Item: One of the Senator's newer attorneys, Henry I. Kowalsky, was accosted in the lobby of the Baldwin Hotel by two heavily veiled women who attempted to shoot him, but was spared through his agility and their inexperience with firearms.

Item: A watchman at the Palace Hotel was prosecuted for battery in having thrown Cushman, the Senator's former business manager who had testified for Sarah, out of the hotel at the Senator's direction.

The perjury trial of Martha Wilson, the illiterate seamstress, was finally held. It occupied a month with a week required to select an unbiased jury from the hundreds who were called into court. Sarah had employed the special prosecutor and the defendant was represented by four of the Senator's attorneys.

Several score witnesses were called, including all of the principals in the divorce suit, which was of course again gone through in great detail. The Senator, when called to the witness stand, said he wanted to relate all of the facts of the marriage contract forgery, but the judge said he was the wrong court for that.

The Martha Wilson and Gumpel trials were in progress simultaneously, and witnesses were kept busy traveling from one court room to the other, trying to remember where they were in their narration in which court. One witness, held in contempt, gained the distinction of spending a record two weeks in jail. Both Gumpel and Mrs. Wilson were eventually acquitted.

✓   ✓   ✓

Piper, the Senator's new expert from Chicago, precipitated the first lively encounter in the federal trial. At the request of the Senator's attorney William Stewart, Judge Sawyer gave Piper permission to take ink scrapings from and perform chemical experiments with the marriage contract and the "Dear Wife" letters.

Always zealous to protect her documents, Sarah responded by remaining away from the court with them until arrested and brought in after a week's search. She still refused to permit mutilation of the papers and Judge Sawyer ordered her to jail for 24 hours. She obtained a few hours reprieve to arrange her social calendar and then docilely surrendered, receiving many guests during the afternoon and evening of her incarceration, and sharing with them a large basket of food and fruit brought to her by Mammy Pleasant.

A crowd of five hundred people gathered at the Broadway Jail the next day as the hour of Sarah's release approached, spending the last few minutes counting off the remaining seconds in unison. A magnificent carriage was driven up and several large bouquets brought out in time to be graciously accepted by Sarah as she stepped from the jail at the end of the 24th hour. A cheer went up from the crowd and Sarah quieted them with a regal gesture.

"Good people of California," she addressed them, "if ever you have to contend in the courts and believe you have right on your side, I hope you will do as I have done and stand up for your rights no matter what you may suffer." With another cheer the crowd parted, making an aisle down which Sarah walked to the waiting carriage, shaking many outstretched hands as she passed.

After Sarah had left, a reporter, searching her cell for some clue of how she had spent the night after dismissing her guests, found a scrap of paper on the floor. At its top, in Sarah's firm hand was written, "A Voice From the Tombs, a Parody Addressed to Lorenzo Sawyer." Beneath was a neatly written eight-stanza poem, which read, in part:

> "Hark! From the tombs a warning sound,
>   Thine ears attend the cry.
>   Thou unjust Judge, come view the ground
>   Where you may shortly lie.
>
> "Oh, do not let the power of wealth
>   Blind your judicial eye;
>   Nor let Bill Stewart get by stealth,
>   What gold ought not to buy.
>
> "Oh, cursed gold that would corrupt
>   The judges of the land,
>   Give way to honesty and truth,
>   And let them mighty stand.
>
> "Oh, Judge, how could you just for spite
>   Exceed judicial power,
>   And shut me up within a jail
>   For even one short hour."

It was unsigned, but subscribed, "Broadway Jail, San Francisco, April 7, 1885."

✓   ✓   ✓

The attorneys took up the proposed chemical analysis again the next day, but though the question was argued sporadically throughout the trial, Judge Sawyer again ordering Sarah to produce the documents, she again disappeared for a time and the effort was finally abandoned.

Meanwhile, the testimony of witnesses was being taken, but with the exception of Piper, the new Chicago handwriting expert, the people who were filing through the Appraiser's Building day by day were the same witnesses who had testified in the divorce trial and in the various criminal trials which had been enriching the past year.

The federal hearing occupied about the same time as had the trial before Judge Sullivan, following it by almost exactly one year. The taking of evidence, commenced in late February, was concluded the second week of August. Both the time consumed in the federal trial and the fact that it amounted to a repetition of the trial before Judge Sullivan the previous year caused general interest to wane, notwithstanding the titillation occasionally afforded by the sidelights, and reporters appeared grateful that they were not admitted, thus being relieved of any duty to hear or report it.

Attention was also diverted by another protracted trial in San Francisco that spring and early summer, when Adolph Spreckels, sugar magnate, was tried for the attempted murder of M. H. deYoung, publisher of the *Chronicle*. The *Chronicle* had run a series of articles on Spreckels' business activities to which he protested with two pistol balls in deYoung's back. That matter was eventually resolved and public attention was drawn back to the Sharon dispute by a minor incident which occurred toward the end of the federal hearings, and which suggested that despite her generally buoyant manner, Sarah was at least occasionally feeling emotional if not mental strain from the long battle. As the hearing before the examiner reached its final stages, she became so incensed that at one point she interrupted to complain that a witness' statement was false.

"When I see this testimony," said Sarah, ignoring an admonition, "I feel like taking that man Stewart out and cowhiding him. I will shoot him yet; that very man sitting there. To think he would put up a woman to come here and deliberately lie about me like that. I will shoot him."

The Examiner: "Those are not matters which should be brought up now. Don't talk in this way when a witness is under examination."

Sarah: "I say no jury will convict me for shooting a man that will bring a woman here to tell such things on me . . ."

The Examiner: "Mr. Tyler, can you put a stop to this interruption?"

Sarah persisted and Examiner Houghton again pleaded with young Tyler (Tyler Senior not being present) to put a stop to it, saying that he would adjourn the hearing unless Sarah stopped. Young Tyler remonstrated mildly, but Sarah said that she got so worked up when she heard false testimony that she could not contain herself.

Houghton suggested that she try, until the day's proceedings were over and she agreed, with one last glance at Stewart, saying, "I can hit a four-bit piece nine times out of ten."

Houghton again admonished her, saying that if she interrupted the proceeding any further he would adjourn it indefinitely.

Sarah: "That is enough; you needn't say anything more."

The Examiner: "But I propose to say something more."

Sarah: "All right; then I'll talk."

The examination was at length resumed, and the attorneys had commenced with the next witness when Sarah drew a gun from her reticule, held it for a moment on the table, aimed nonchalantly at Evans, then dropped it to her lap.

Evans, noticing it, said, "What do you want? Do you want to shoot me?"

Sarah: "I am not going to shoot you just now unless you would like to be shot and think you deserve it."

Evans: "No, I would rather not be."

The Examiner: "Unless you will give that pistol into my custody, I shall adjourn the examination and report this matter to the court."

Sarah said she wasn't going to shoot anybody, and gave him the gun, but Evans declined to proceed further, and the matter was referred to the court. Two days later, Associate Justice Stephen J. Field of the United States Supreme Court, in California on his summer circuit, sitting with Judge Sawyer in Circuit Court, ordered that thereafter while the case was pending before Examiner Houghton, Sarah should be disarmed each day before the session commenced.*

Young Tyler, the sole attorney with Sarah at the time, made a bold attempt to follow in his father's footsteps. He said at the conclusion of the judges remarks that, in view of other incidents (apparently having in mind Mrs. Shawhan and her son before Judge Sullivan and Stewart's assault on Tyler) the order should apply not only to Sarah but to everyone entering the hearing room. Both Field and Sawyer loftily said they had no evidence of misconduct by anyone but Sarah, and that "witnesses will be likely hereafter to conduct themselves with propriety."

After suffering a few judicial platitudes, Tyler persisted. "Where witnesses do come armed . . ."

Justice Field: "Then report the fact to the court. That is the proper way."

Mr. Tyler: "That will not stop a bullet."

Judge Sawyer: "Then arrest the parties in advance. The laws are very severe."

Mr. Tyler: "The laws are very severe but it is harder on the man that gets the bullet."

With the impetuosity of youth young Tyler persisted in asserting a man's right to appear armed anywhere if he had reasonable fear of violence. If his arrogance was encouraged by Justice Field's benevolent manner, it immediately collapsed as Field ominously declared that any attorney who threatened wilful defiance of an order of the court was very close to commitment for contempt. Abashed and red faced, young Tyler mumbled a hasty and profuse apology, and the matter ended.

While the colloquy between Field and young Tyler distracted some from the purpose of the hearing, at least some of

---

* *Sharon* v. *Hill*, 24 Fed. 726.

those in attendance recalled the order which had been made, and the day was brought to a close with deputy United States Marshals racing to the office of their chief to volunteer for the delicate assignment of conducting the daily search of Sarah's person.

A few days earlier, Sarah had been reported to have invaded the state Supreme Court chambers to accost the judges, expressing herself rather freely on the subject of justice. Interviewed later while strolling with Terry, she said it was greatly exaggerated; she had simply visited to ask when the Court was going to decide whether to let her have alimony pending the appeal.

These incidents, in addition to her recent differences with Tyler and others who had been close to her, led some to wonder if the strain of the litigation, combined with Sarah's well-known volatile nature, was not perhaps bringing on emotional stresses too great for her to cope with. It would all soon be over, however, and even her closest acquaintances did not worry greatly about her — though they might have some concern for themselves when she was "riled."

✓   ✓   ✓

The usual number of subsidiary cases were spawned throughout the remainder of the year. Sarah had the Senator's new handwriting expert charged with criminal libel, but the charges were ultimately dropped. Both sides filed scores of affidavits throughout the summer in connection with Barnes' effort to reopen the divorce trial, Barnes filing 46 affidavits in one two-day period, according to press tallies.

One of the Senator's detectives accused a notary public and one of Sarah's trial witnesses with procuring a false instrument in having obtained an affidavit from an insane inmate of the Almshouse. Both were convicted after a trial lasting several weeks in which most of the usual witnesses testified and the divorce was substantially retried for perhaps the tenth time. The convictions were eventually reversed by the Supreme Court, after the defendants had served two years in prison.*

---

* *People* v. *Brown,* 74 Cal. 306 (16 Pac. 1).

It began to seem that there was no limit to the litigation fever which afflicted everyone connected with the case. That fall the governor appointed Walter Levy, one of Sarah's attorneys, to fill a vacancy created on the superior court when a member of that court was committed to a sanitarium as insane. Within a month after Levy's appointment, his predecessor recovered and sought to regain his office. The county treasurer, being in doubt, refused to pay Levy his salary and as the year ended Levy was suing for his salary and being sued by his predecessor for the recovery of the office. After more than a full year of litigation the Supreme Court confirmed Levy's position.*

Sarah was responsible for one light interlude during the otherwise sober autumn of that year. Curiously, it had its inception the same morning she had offered to shoot Evans in the federal examiner's hearing room. She had arrived at the Appraiser's Building that morning wearing a brocaded velvet dress and a Langtry cloak and in the gay spirit which a new costume usually generated in her. One of the reporters who followed her to the door of the hearing room — beyond which the public was barred — asked her about a rumor that she was contemplating a concert tour.

"Quite true," said Sarah, "that is, if my lectures are not a success as I hope they will be."

What lectures, she was asked?

"Let me see," said Sarah attempting to look serious, as she rummaged for a note in her reticule — the same reticule from which she was to draw a gun a few minutes later. Pretending to refresh her memory from a scrap of paper, she said, "I think I will call the first lecture, 'Perversion of Facts in the Sharon Case' — 'Facts' or 'Law'? — I don't know which will sound best; but it will be something like that anyway." Then she favored the reporters with a gracious smile and a bow, and disappeared into the hearing room.

Two months later, in the largest and boldest caption the affair had been awarded in some time the *Chronicle* pro-

---

* *People* v. *Levy,* 71 Cal. 618 (12 Pac. 791).

claimed: "ALTHEA AS PORTIA — MRS. SHARON AS A STAR IN SHAKESPEARE." The intrepid reporter had heard another rumor and pursued it by interviewing "Signor" Mc-Greachy, manager of the San Francisco Grand Opera House, to ask if it was true that he had contracted with Sarah for dramatic ventures.

At first reluctant to talk, McGreachy eventually admitted that, having read of Sarah's lecture plans, he had solicited the privilege of acting as her agent. She had laughed and told him it was absurd; she had not been serious in her reported interview. Undiscouraged, he had visited her several times in an attempt to persuade her to go on the stage in a dramatic production he would provide for her.

"On the stage?" Sarah had said incredulously. "But I can't act."

Eventually, after a discussion of possible financial benefits, she had signed a two-year contract to appear in plays locally and on tour, McGreachy said proudly.

What would Sarah open in, he was asked?

She would first play Portia in *The Merchant of Venice,* he said. It was scheduled to open at the Opera House three weeks hence and Sarah was now in Fresno in the seclusion of Judge Terry's ranch, which he had generously offered, where she was learning the part under the tutelage of a retired Shakespearean actress. It would not be too difficult for her to learn, he said, as a talented writer was revising the play to have Portia come on only in the third act, to heighten audience interest.

What did the supporting company think of playing with the inexperienced Sarah, he was asked?

Sarah's name had not been mentioned to the cast, he said quickly; he had felt it adequate to merely tell them that their lead would be more interesting than Lillie Langtry.

On Sarah's return from Fresno several days later the *Chronicle* reporter, calling at her home, heard a firm feminine voice declaiming, "The quality of mercy is not strained," as he was ushered in by a maid. He caught a glimpse of a slight figure in male costume gliding through the sitting room doorway but, after a short wait, was received by Sarah in her normal dress.

"Yes, it is true," she said in answering the reporter's first question. "My decision is not from any desire of succeeding as an actress, or because I have discovered that I have talent in that direction. The case is simply this: I have maintained a long fight against great odds, and have had to rely upon myself alone. Lawyers must be paid and the expenses of trials must be borne."

The Supreme Court decision depriving her of alimony pending the appeal was compelling the course she was following, she said. "To obtain the necessary money to push my case, I have determined to go on the stage. I ask the people to assist me in that way."

Had she any dramatic experience?

"No, but I will do my best. I am told I have the voice, and my troubles and battles in the courts have given me confidence in myself. I do not expect to make what they call a great hit but will endeavor to make the performance at least worthwhile listening to. And, when people consider what motives I have for going on the stage, they will make allowances for my inexperience."

Drawing herself up with a stern expression, she said that as Portia she would "endeavor to represent all the dignity of a federal judge disbarring an attorney for refusing proper deference, and all the legal knowledge of a justice reversing an unsatisfactory decision."

Two weeks later playbills were out, but McGreachy had run out of funds from which to pay the salaries of the company. He postponed the opening from time to time, eventually abandoning the venture altogether. Sarah would have to continue to confine her dramatic talents to the courtroom.

*   *   *

The testimony in the divorce trial before Judge Sullivan had filled 1142 printed pages. Testimony in the federal case before Examiner Houghton, now finally concluded a year and a week later, consumed 1731 pages of legal cap. The completed transcript was in mid-August presented to Judge Sawyer and District Judge Matthew P. Deady of Oregon, sitting together as the United States Circuit Court for review and decision.

While Sarah's legal staff had been reduced to Tyler and Terry, the Senator had for some time been adding recruits, and now at his counsel table, in addition to Barnes, Evans, and Newlands, the Senator's son-in-law, there appeared William Stewart, Henry Kowalsky, and three other attorneys. In the ensuing weeks each platoon was daily to come to court on the third floor of the brick Appraiser's Building with great numbers of transcript volumes, casebooks, statutes, and copies of exhibits. These were distributed on the counsel tables like a barricade, over which the troops belligerently peered at each other from time to time.

A month was devoted to selective reading of testimony, giving the public its first opportunity to learn what had been taking place before Examiner Houghton. The testimony was about the same as in the trial before Judge Sullivan, most of the same witnesses having testified. The principal difference lay in the testimony of the handwriting expert Piper, who had been imported by Barnes since the trial before Judge Sullivan.

In the presentation of Piper's testimony, spectators and newspaper readers were treated to what they first took for a joke. Making innumerable photographic enlargements and myriad microscopic analyses, Piper had determined that the Senator's signature on the marriage contract was forged. This was surprising enough to those who remembered that the Senator's experts at the divorce trial had unanimously pronounced the signature genuine though written before the contract. But Piper went further and testified that after close comparison with exemplars of the forger's handwriting, he was prepared to and could say positively that the Senator's signature had been forged by Max Gumpel. The "Dear Wife" letter in ink was a tracing, Piper said, and at least the word "Wife" in two of the other letters was traced, but he could not say whether that was Gumpel's handiwork.

Hyde, in his testimony in the federal case, it now was disclosed, had decided that he was in error in testifying, as Barnes' chief expert before Judge Sullivan, that the Senator's signature was a genuine autograph written before the body of the marriage contract. He now agreed with Piper that the signature was a forgery, though he apparently did not feel competent to say that it was perpetrated by Gumpel. He still maintained, however, and Piper agreed, that the forged signature was written before the body of the contract and in a different ink. Neither expert was willing to hazard an explanation of such perverseness in the forger, however.

The presentation of the case to the court, including the argument on the law, consumed approximately six weeks, paralleling the closing arguments in the case before Judge Sullivan a year earlier. The coincidence was carried still further when the Circuit Court held the case under submission for three months, as had Judge Sullivan, and then announced its decision in Christmas week, on December 26, 1885, one year and two days after Judge Sullivan had rendered his decision. There the similarity was to end.

ʎ　　　ʎ　　　ʎ

Meanwhile there took place an event whose consequences would be subject to speculation for some time, but which ultimately had little effect on the outcome of any of the litigation. The Senator, whose health was never good, had become ill in the fall and was confined to bed in his apartment in the Palace in early November. His condition rapidly worsened and after a brief illness he died.

The Senator's obituaries were lengthy, as was fitting for the man who had at one time been the wealthiest of the mining speculators, the owner of the Palace Hotel, one of San Francisco's most lavish hosts, and a former Senator. The obituaries were, on the whole, also friendly. So far as his personal life was concerned, the worst that was said was that even his closest friends rarely knew what he was thinking and that after making his fortune he took very little interest in civic affairs but spent most of his time reading or playing poker.

His funeral at Grace Church on November 16 was one of the most splendid in San Francisco history, despite rain which fell steadily throughout the day.

On the day of the Senator's death, former Governor Stanford had executed the documents by which a great part of his estate was transferred to create a large educational institution. Perhaps that coincidental contrast was not needed, but when the Senator's disposition of his estate was published, there was some criticism of the evident modesty of his benevolences. The following week, the criticism had become so sharp that the *Chronicle* felt constrained to print "SHARON'S GOOD DEEDS," in which it was pointed out that he had left fifty thousand dollars to Golden Gate Park, and an equal sum in several small gifts to various charities, principally orphanages and lying-in homes.

There was much general speculation on the legal effect of the Senator's death, and the attorneys were of course interviewed. Tyler said he thought the death would end all proceedings where they were, thus leaving Judge Sullivan's divorce decree in effect; and, he said, as the judge had awarded Sarah half of the community property she would be entitled to have that order enforced against the Senator's estate.

Barnes said he was sure the Senator's death would have no such effect, but if it did abate the various proceedings then the divorce decree itself would have to fall since it was not yet final.

In fact, the Senator's death was to be little felt, though it inevitably caused some delay in the litigation. So far as Sarah was concerned, depending on the outcome of the cases, she was either a divorced woman if Judge Sullivan's decision was upheld, the Senator's wife if it should be determined that the marriage contract was valid but Judge Sullivan's decision erroneous on technical grounds, or an adventuress if the cases should ultimately be decided against her. The second possibility was simply now replaced with another — that she was a widow.

In his last illness the Senator spoke often of the dagger in his heart. To ease his mind Barnes had prepared, and the Senator signed immediately before his death, an assignment of his entire estate in trust for the benefit of his children, expressly excluding Sarah, declaring that he had no relationship with her by blood or marriage. That document would have no effect on the outcome of the litigation since California law provided that a husband could only dispose of his half of the community property. Thus, if the marriage was sustained, Sarah would be able to ignore the trust and claim her estimated 15 million dollar share of the estate. If she ultimately lost, her exclusion would be unnecessary.

Chapter XV THE FEDERAL COURT DECIDES

HE FEDERAL case was unaffected by the death of the Senator, and when it was announced a month later that the decision* would be read on December 26, interest in the dispute quickly revived. The federal courtroom in the Appraiser's Building was as crowded on that morning as Judge Sullivan's had ever been.

It appeared that Judges Deady and Sawyer each wished to unburden himself at length, and each was therefore to read his separate opinion, although they agreed on the goal of their jurisprudential forays.

Judge Deady led off on the question of domicile, so long urged by Tyler. It was true, he conceded, that the federal court could not consider the case unless Sarah and the Senator were domiciled in different states. But domicile, he said, is where the heart is. If the Senator wanted to be a Nevada citizen — and he said he did — then it mattered not at all that he had actually lived in San Francisco for the last ten years, or for his lifetime, said Judge Deady.

The judge then turned to an equally cogent and lengthy rejection of Tyler's plea that the state court had settled the Senator's marital status. He acknowledged the rule that one court's judgment bars another suit on the same subject, but said that Judge Sullivan's decision was not yet final. Hence it was no bar to the federal suit.

Turning finally to the evidence, Deady said the ultimate question was whether the marriage contract was a forgery, and he promised to dispose of that question briefly. In hardly more

---

* *Sharon* v. *Hill*, 26 Fed. 337.

180

than an hour's time he did so. Clues to the answer, he said, could be drawn from a number of sources, among which was the demeanor of the parties during the trial. Sarah had made it virtually impossible for Piper to examine the documents. Her adamant refusal to permit scrapings or chemical analysis, her "contumacious, frivolous, and contradictory" conduct, could only be interpreted as admission that such inspection would tend to prove the falsity of the documents. Both the Senator, a man with "a vein of sentiment and love of pleasure that has led him into illicit relations with the other sex" and Sarah, "an attractive woman of about 32 years of age, but she is not certain as to the year of her birth," were parties to the case, he said, and it might be thought that the assertions of the one merely offset those of the other creating a stalemate as far as their testimony was concerned. But there were other considerations to be weighed "in estimating the relative value of the oath of these parties."

"It must not be forgotten," said Judge Deady, "that the sin of incontinence in a man is compatible with the virtue of veracity [and] does not usually imply the moral degradation and insensibility that it does in a woman." Therefore the Senator's admitted unchastity was irrelevant, but unchastity in Sarah would raise grave doubt as to her credibility.

However much one might agree with the proposition Judge Deady was stating, it was hard to understand how it aided him in deciding the case. For Sarah was unchaste or incontinent only if she was found to have been the Senator's mistress and not his wife. But as that was the very question at issue, it required a man of Judge Deady's talent to use that "fact" to support itself. He could have made his apparent point even more succinctly; he seemed to be saying that a woman accused of being unchaste could not be believed when she denied the charge.

But that was not the only reason for giving greater credence to the Senator's testimony. "It must also be remembered that the plaintiff is a person of long standing and commanding position in this community, of large fortune and manifold business and social relations, and is therefore by all that these imply specially bound to speak the truth."

And what of Sarah?

"On the other hand, the defendant is a comparatively obscure and unimportant person, without property or position in the world. Although apparently of respectable birth and lineage, she has deliberately separated herself from her people and, so far as appears, is only amenable to legal punishment for any false statement that she may make in this case, which all experience proves is not sufficiently certain to prevent perjury in legal proceedings."

Lest his auditors miss the point he repeated his moral. "Other things being equal, property and position are in themselves some certain guaranty of truth in their possessor."

Even beyond what he considered these fundamental truths and laws of human nature, Judge Deady found Sarah's testimony in many respects to be patently "reckless, improbable and false." He illustrated this conclusion with the conflicting stories of the $7500 obligation the Senator acknowledged at about the time of the separation. He accepted the Senator's version of the transaction on the authority of the judgment entered in the state court and affirmed by the state Supreme Court only the previous month on Sarah's suit for the outstanding $750.* Why he was willing to rely on the state court's judgment in that matter and not in the divorce trial he did not say.

Deady then turned to the handwriting experts. As for Gumpel, "his relation to the case and his conduct as a witness therein are both suspicious and unsatisfactory, and lead me to regard him and his testimony with distrust. His opinions on the subject of the writings are mere bald assertions, unsupported by any intelligent or convincing reasons. [He] simply compared the one writing with another and came to a conclusion from their resemblance or dissimilarity." Deady did not say how the methods of the Senator's experts differed.

As to the Senator's experts, Piper was the most important, said Judge Deady. "He appears from his own account to be an expert of celebrity." It was true, the judge said, that Piper came to California with the understanding that at the conclusion of the case the Senator would pay him any fee that he named and

---

* *Sharon* v. *Sharon*, 68 Cal. 29 (8 Pac. 614).

"upon this arrangement his compensation may be contingent upon success." But there was no reason to believe that such a consideration had influenced his testimony.

Turning to Piper's testimony, the judge noted with approval that Piper relied largely on the writing of the letter "t," having said that the line used to cross the "t" is generally made carelessly and unconsciously, "from which he deduces the conclusion, and a very plausible one to say the least of it," that a forger will be most apt to give himself away in his "t." Sarah's "t" he found to be crossed with a blunt heavy line and the Senator's with a light tapered line.

The "Dear Wife" letters he found to have blunt "t" crossings. One might expect him to have concluded that they were entirely written by Sarah. Inexplicably – but apparently understandably to Judge Deady – Piper concluded merely that the word "Wife" in the letters had been written by her, and the Senator's signature on the contract by Gumpel. The paucity of "t"s in "Wife" and in the Senator's signature caused some to wonder at his conclusion but Judge Deady, far from wondering, said that Piper "has accumulated a great mass of material facts from which any person of ordinary intelligence and power of observation and deduction may draw a comparatively safe conclusion."

Piper's presentation was in fact impressive, exhaustive almost to the point of being overwhelming. At the Senator's expense he had written a book of over a hundred pages, liberally illustrated with costly reproductions and enlargements of the disputed writings. It had been the Senator's practice, throughout the litigation, to have his attorney's more impassioned speeches printed in booklets (Barnes' speech before Judge Sullivan was 381 pages long) which were then distributed, "courtesy of" their author, to the Senator's friends and other prominent people throughout the country. Piper's book had been so distributed, and those who had struggled through its intricacies agreed with Judge Deady that Piper's work was thorough.

Three of the other experts called by the Senator were his employees, very familiar with his writing through long years of loyal service, said the judge, but apparently not thereby rendered partisan. The Senator's last expert, Hyde, described by Judge Deady as "an experienced expert," now agreed with Piper that the Senator's signature was a forgery; his contrary testimony in the divorce trial a year earlier was dismissed by the judge as done "without having made any special examination of it." Apparently he had become an experienced expert in the intervening year.

"On the whole," said Judge Deady, "the expert testimony preponderates largely" in the Senator's favor. Neither the experts nor Deady favored spectators with an explanation of why Sarah would have had Gumpel forge the Senator's signature before she wrote the body of the contract, or why she would have him do it in a different ink, though the judge suggested that perhaps she purloined an "innocent forgery."

Hazarding some independent deductions from a scrutiny of the marriage contract, the judge found it suspicious that the agreement appeared on note paper instead of legal paper, though allegedly written in the Senator's office, where stationery for business purposes was readily at hand. Moreover, it was written on the second page, and finished with a crowding of the final words on the unruled top of what should have been the first page, with the Senator's signature then appearing on the top line of the first page, "where it might have been written as an autograph or imitation, or even without any purpose." He also found the addition of "Nevada, Aug. 25, 1880" useless, hence suspect.

The judge acknowledged that there was "force" in Tyler's suggestion that those and other peculiarities supported the document's genuineness, as a person contemplating a fraud of such magnitude would certainly have practiced with other sheets of paper and could easily have created an instrument without defects. But, he said, "this is not the first time in which persons engaged in an illegal or criminal transaction have strangely or foolishly" been inept in their effort.

As to the "Dear Wife" letters, the judge concluded that they had been altered, but did not explain how Sarah's blunt "t" crossings got into the body of the letters which the Senator had acknowledged as genuine. To the judge the explanation was *"clear* and convincing." (Emphasis that of Judge Deady.)

Turning to other witnesses, the judge placed much reliance on the testimony of Nellie Brackett who in federal court had testified in detail to participation in the forging and artificial aging of the "Dear Wife" letters.

Sarah's corroboration, the judge declared, depended entirely on Mammy Pleasant and on Vesta Snow, who had again testified that they had seen the marriage contract. He found Mrs. Snow to be of "doubtful repute" and "unworthy of credit," but except for the fact that she "appears to be keeping a cheap lodging house" he assigned no evidence to support that evaluation.

Mammy Pleasant the judge described as a "conspicuous and important figure" in the case, "a shrewd old negress of considerable means" who admitted having advanced more than five thousand dollars to support Sarah's "fight," as she described it. It was her practice, the judge remarked, to "care for women and girls who need a mammie or a manager, as the case may be." He dismissed Mammy, saying, "In my judgment this case, and the forgeries and perjuries committed in its support, have their origin largely in the brain of this scheming, trafficking, crafty old woman." He again declined to favor his listeners with any reference to the evidence on which he based the conclusion.

Sarah's account of the courtship and marriage was such that "the pages of fiction furnish no parallel," said the judge, turning to her own testimony. It was ridiculous, he said, to think that a man in the Senator's position and of his experience and willingness to enter illicit relations, would be so quickly catapulted into a marriage, notwithstanding Sarah's admitted "prepossessing appearance." If he had been so swept off his feet, would he immediately have left for Nevada without spending even his wedding night with her, without, as she admitted, even kissing her before the parting? Far more likely, their relationship was the commercial venture the Senator described.

In none of Sarah's post-separation letters did she demand any of the rights of a wife. On the contrary, the judge pointed out, she described herself repeatedly as an injured "girl," spoke

of the Senator as having been "kind" to her, expressed her gratitude, and appealed to their "friendship," pleading with him to
do nothing to create "gossip." How were any of these words or
sentiments consistent with the existence of the bonds of marriage? The judge answered his own question at length that
they were not.

Having determined that the marriage contract and the letters were forgeries manufactured by Sarah and her conspirators, Judge Deady pointed out that this was all that he was
required to decide and all that was at issue. Nevertheless, he
could not resist some gratuitous sermonizing about Sarah and
the State of California before bringing his opinion to a close.
"A woman who voluntarily submits to live with a millionaire
for hire ought not, after she finds herself supplanted or discharged, to be allowed to punish her paramour for the immorality of which she was the cause by compelling him to recognize
her as his wife. If society thinks it expedient to punish men and
women for the sin of fornication, let it do so directly. But until
so authorized, the courts have no right to assume such function." The force of his indignation was somewhat blunted by its
irrelevance, since Sarah was not seeking the court's endorsement of concubinage. Apparently recognizing this, Judge
Deady shifted his maledictions to Judge Sullivan and the State
of California. "A community which allows the integrity of the
family, the cornerstone of society, to rest on no better foundation than a union of the sexes, evidenced only by a secret writing, and unaccompanied by any public recognition or assumption of marital duties except furtive intercourse befitting a
brothel, ought to remove the cross from its banner and symbols, and replace it with a crescent."

The judge had apparently forgotten his statement that the
only question for decision was whether the contract was forged
or genuine. The matter of what constituted a valid marriage in
California was not before the court and had no relevance to
his decision; but had that question been in issue, Judge Deady
would have been required to accept California's interpretation
of its laws and not impose his own, whether under the crescent
or not. Having unburdened himself on his views, he closed

succinctly. "The plaintiff is entitled to the relief prayed for; and it is so ordered."

Judge Sawyer, seated passively beside Deady, then leaned forward and commenced reading his decision. Though slightly shorter than his colleague's, it took over two hours to read.

Sawyer spent the better part of the first hour reviewing the convolutions of the case and explaining why it was not now possible to question the jurisdiction of the court. Shifting "very generally to some of the salient points developed in the testimony," he travelled much the same road Deady had followed, reaching the same destination.

It was unlikely, he thought, that the Senator would seriously enter into such a secret marriage as Sarah claimed. And it was unthinkable that a man of "respectable position in society" would through the "basest of motives" deceive a young woman and thereby accomplish her ruin. The existence of such a union could not be sustained on the unsupported testimony of Sarah, "an unusually intelligent and experienced party, capable of entering into a secret arrangement so extraordinary."

Sawyer, like Deady, seemed to some of his auditors to be saying that a woman who would enter into such a marriage contract should not be believed when she said she did. But this created a nice revolving paradox: If she was not to be believed, then she did not enter into the extraordinary contract; if she did not enter into it, then she should not be discredited as a person who would do so; if she was not discredited, then her testimony should be believed; if her testimony was accepted then she did enter into the contract.

While the judge found abhorrent the attribution of base motives to the Senator, he had no such distaste for the alternative: the conclusion that Sarah had sold herself to the Senator for five hundred dollars a month. That conclusion he did reach in due course. At the end of two hours he had proven himself to be a skilled tautologist, but modestly said that Deady had so thoroughly and searchingly covered all salient points that "I can add nothing." He concurred in Deady's conclusion, he said, and ordered judgment entered, decreeing that Sarah and anyone who might ever claim under her were "hereby perpetu-

ally enjoined from alleging the genuineness or the validity of"
the marriage contract, "and from making any use of the same
to support any right claimed under it."

The demeanor of the attorneys suggested that they had
anticipated the decision and, although some spectators and
readers were surprised, the most common reaction was uncer-
tainty. The *Chronicle's* report was typical: "What the ultimate
legal effect of the decision may be," it concluded, "is impossible to predict."

For perhaps the first time in her life, Sarah gave no interviews, and newspaper readers were consequently denied the
benefit of her reaction. There was little doubt that her holiday
season this year of 1885 was not as gay as had been that of the
previous year.

Chapter XVI   SARAH AND TERRY — AND TYLER

HE YEAR which followed was to pass with little further happening of public note in either of the main cases.

Barnes' motion for new trial before Judge Sullivan was finally submitted for decision after the hundred odd affidavits were all filed and after extensive argument. The affidavits provided few revelations of any importance but, like the Barnes-McLaughlin abstraction, some reflected the great intensity with which the dispute was being fought by both sides.

One James Nolan, in an affidavit filed on Sarah's behalf, exposed some typical measures Barnes and the Senator were willing to take to obtain evidence. Nolan, a friend of Mrs. Snow, swore that Captain Lees — also a friend — had been employed by the Senator throughout the trial to locate and intimidate witnesses, generally using police officers as messengers, and that Lees had ceaselessly importuned him to induce Mrs. Snow to change her testimony and say that she had lied about seeing the marriage contract in 1880. She had remained adamant, as her testimony had proved when Barnes recalled her to the stand, despite a last minute offer of the gift of a lucrative saloon and any sum of money she might name, declaring that as poor as she was, Sharon had not money enough to bribe her to tell a lie.

Judge Sullivan denied the motion for a new trial in October, 1886 and Barnes immediately appealed.

With the appeal from Judge Sullivan's divorce decree already pending, some felt that an appeal from his denial of the new trial application was redundant, as the state legislature was to agree several years later. But at the time of the Sharon litiga-

189

tion such appeals were still tolerated, providing yet another
opportunity for its prolongation, and providing also a vehicle
for the most painful jurisprudential contortions the litigation
would experience. But much time and many events would intervene.

Meanwhile the attorneys were researching the law and preparing their briefs for submission to the state Supreme Court
on the appeal already taken from the divorce decree and the
alimony and fee awards. Tyler was also preparing an appeal
from the federal court injunction. Little public attention was
given to these preliminary procedural matters, but the dispute
was not permitted to be forgotten, as collateral matters were
inevitably developing from time to time throughout the year.

Barnes succeeded in inducing the Grand Jury to indict Tyler
for conspiring to procure the false affidavit for which two of
Sarah's witnesses had already been sent to prison the year before. If he was not previously conscious of it, the enmity aroused
the previous year was made clear to Tyler by Barnes' unremit-
ting efforts to harass him. Additionally, the two people already
convicted of perjury later charged that the district attorney had
offered to gain their release if they would place the blame on
Tyler. Both had declined.

Tyler was subjected to a lengthy trial, at the end of which
the jury was discharged hung ten to two for Tyler's acquittal.
A retrial achieved the same result and the prosecution of Tyler
was ultimately abandoned with the reversal by the Supreme
Court of the conviction of his alleged co-conspirators.

✔　　　✔　　　✔

A happier event also took place in the first week of the year.
A dispatch from Stockton reported that Sarah and David Terry
were married at the parsonage of the Catholic Church there, the
State Treasurer acting as best man. The license recited Sarah's
age as thirty-two and Terry's as sixty-two.

Terry's wife had died the previous year, and for some time
there had been conjecture that his courtly attentiveness to
Sarah, steadily increasing as the various proceedings progressed,
was inspired by more than an attorney's solicitude for a client's

well-being. With the death of the Senator, Sarah became eligible to marry, regardless of the outcome of the various cases.

The marriage was generally felt to be a good one for Sarah for a number of reasons. While not of great wealth, Terry was of more than adequate means. With a comfortable family home in Stockton, a ranch near Fresno and a lucrative law practice, he was also still of some political as well as financial prominence notwithstanding the cloud under which he had lived since his fatal duel with Broderick in 1859. And to some, his early life, including other fights and altercations with the vigilance committee, Civil War service as a Confederate officer, and his term as Chief Justice of the State Supreme Court while still in his thirties, made him a romantic and enviable figure. Standing six feet three inches tall, with penetrating eyes and striking features, he was a man of unquestionable courage — some said insensibility to violence — reputed never to have permitted an affront to go unsatisfied, thus giving him still more luster.

Whether Terry had made an equally good match was not so readily conceded and was to become increasingly doubtful with the passage of time. In any event Sarah's increasing agitation, sometimes released in extreme emotional outbursts, was quickly abated — for which the marriage was probably properly to be credited — and they lived together happy and contented. But, although Sarah for a time exhibited more restraint, her ardor for the litigation did not slacken, and newspapers from time to time published her letters to the editor on a variety of subjects related to the dispute.

In the summer of that year Terry, probably at Sarah's urging, petitioned the state legislature to impeach Chief Justice Morrison and Associate Justice Sharpstein of the state Supreme Court, charging that they had become totally incompetent by reason of physical and mental infirmity. San Francisco attorneys were of mixed reactions, some declaring that Terry was performing a public service. The legislature entertained the request but Terry's charges were ultimately held groundless.

✓   ✓   ✓

While Sarah and Terry were happily adjusting to their conjugal life, Tyler's affairs were not following such a tranquil course. Although he had thus far frustrated every effort to destroy him in his profession, the attacks were not yet at an end.

Now he was charged with unprofessional conduct, in having six years previously wrongfully withheld money from a client. Many assumed that Barnes was the agitator for the prosecution, as that seemed the most likely explanation of an effort in 1886 to discipline Tyler for conduct taking place in 1880. But the charge arose from a matter which was wholly unrelated to the Sharon case and there was no direct evidence that it was inspired by Tyler's role in the divorce dispute; Barnes did not openly participate, either as accuser, witness or prosecutor.

In 1880 a widow, one Charlotte Hedge, had employed an attorney, J. M. Hogan, to collect a claim on a promissory note of approximately ten thousand dollars. Through insidiously applied pressure Hogan induced one of the widow's profligate sons to assign a half interest in the debt to him, and the unhappy widow thereupon retained Tyler to recover what he could for her. Tyler proved to be more wily than Hogan, inducing the latter to let him act as stakeholder of the ten thousand dollars.

As soon as Tyler had the money in hand, he caused a suit to be filed against Hogan and, through various legal devices, managed to keep the case dragging out for over a year. After this time he permitted it to be dismissed, having found no legal defense to Hogan's claim to half the money.

Hogan sued Tyler, who compelled him to carry the case to the state Supreme Court,* and then tried to collect. But Tyler claimed to have spent all of the money and to be insolvent. His appeal sureties — people who had promised to pay the judgment if Tyler did not — also proved to be insolvent. Hogan was therefore unable to collect his judgment.

Now in 1886, whether unilaterally or at the urging of others, Hogan filed charges of professional misconduct against Tyler with the state Supreme Court, requesting that he be disbarred. The decision was rendered December 3 of that year.** From the evidence presented to it, but which it did not recite, the

---

* *Hogan* v. *Tyler,* 2 Cal. Unrep. 489 (7 Pac. 454).
** *In re Tyler,* 71 Cal. 353 (12 Pac. 289).

Supreme Court concluded that Tyler intended to keep Hogan from collecting by using sureties known to be irresponsible. The Court further found that Tyler had acted as Hogan's attorney in collecting the debt, and had violated the duties imposed by such a confidential relationship. This was much more serious, but how the Court arrived at it was less apparent. One member of the Court disagreed, pointing out that Tyler had given Hogan a receipt stating, "I have received foregoing papers at the request of Charlotte Hedge [the widow], that said J. M. Hogan should deliver same to me as her attorney." It was obvious, he felt, that Tyler received the papers as the widow's attorney and not as Hogan's. Whatever agreement with Hogan Tyler may have breached would not justify punishing Tyler as Hogan's attorney, the dissenting justice concluded.

The Court had yet to determine what discipline should be imposed for Tyler's misdeeds. The sins were generally felt to be venial, if not trivial, and the popular sentiment in his favor was enhanced by a feeling that Hogan, in making a very great profit at the expense of the widow and her profligate son, was much more to be censured than was Tyler. But courts are not often swayed by popular sentiment and the Court duly entered its order, five members having agreed on the punishment to be imposed, "that respondent George W. Tyler be deprived of the right to practice as attorney or counselor in any and all the courts of this state." The order was to be effective for a minimum of two years, and thereafter until he had satisfied the five-thousand-dollar judgment held against him by Hogan. The distraught Tyler immediately appealed to the Court to reconsider its order, but two months later the Court in a brief memorandum denied the petition.

Tyler's active leadership of Sarah's forces, as well as his entire career — at least for a long period — was now at an end. Henceforth David Terry would have to take the lead.

Barnes, whether he had instigated the proceeding or not, now had the revenge he had been seeking against Tyler as a personal foe for two long years. He also had the favorable federal decision now behind him. It only remained to obtain reversal of Judge Sullivan's divorce decree to make sweet victory complete.

Barnes himself was now confronted with the prospect of having some of his activities scrutinized. This proceeding proved to be of interest only in its contrast with Tyler's disbarment. Barnes was charged with two acts of professional misconduct arising from dealings with Gumpel. It was claimed that he had offered Gumpel a large sum to testify that the marriage contract was forged, even after Gumpel had told him that his examination showed it to be genuine. The other charge was that Barnes had wrongly procured McLaughlin to steal the decoy Gumpel-Tyler contract.

One might think that charges of attempting to suborn perjury and of conspiring to commit theft would be at least as serious as the charge against Tyler that he had failed to pay money owed. But the same court which had disbarred Tyler, after reviewing the evidence "entirely from the standpoint" of Barnes, by the court's own candid boast, did not think so.[*]

Barnes admitted that after Gumpel told him the documents were genuine he had still urged him to testify they were false, offering him a substantial increase in his previously agreed compensation. But Barnes "thought he was merely attempting to get more money," said the judge. "I do not believe that Barnes thought that the money would cause the witness to change his opinion. He regarded, as he well might, the arguments of the witness as mere intimations that he wanted some money. Under such circumstances, no doubt, it would have been more in accordance with exalted ideas of propriety for Barnes to have denounced the witness and dismissed him, but I doubt whether many practitioners would have acted very differently." As to that charge, the judge concluded, "While I think his conduct according to his own testimony may justly be criticized, I do not think it sufficient ground for a disbarment." As to the other charge, if there had been evidence that Barnes encouraged McLaughlin to burglarize Tyler's office and misappropriate any document, the judge said sternly, "Barnes' position would be indefensible." But fortunately for Barnes the judge found no such evidence. "It is bad enough, no doubt, as it is," he con-

---

[*] *In re Barnes*, 2 Cal. Unrep. 847 (16 Pac. 896).

tinued, "but detective work must be judged by an ethic of its own. It is deemed proper to deceive and practice stratagems upon a public enemy, and the criminal is the common enemy of all."

The judge said he regretted that a man so high in the profession as Barnes should engage in conduct which required explanation. But since he had satisfactorily explained it, the judge concluded the disbarment application should be dismissed. Three of his associates concurred with the author of the court opinion that Barnes should be judged by the ethic of the detective rather than any exalted ideas of propriety, declaring that "the evidence utterly fails" to show any ground for disciplining Barnes.

Two justices did not participate, but Thornton, dissenting, felt that Barnes' attempt to influence Gumpel's testimony with money was unethical.

*   *   *

A relatively quiet year ensued, during which both the state and the federal cases dropped from public notice. Sarah and Terry, apparently both serene in a marriage of love, enjoyed for a time an alternately urban and pastoral existence, dividing their time among Terry's family home in Stockton, an apartment in San Francisco and his ranch in the lower San Joaquin Valley, near Fresno. Sarah's interest in the divorce litigation did not flag, but at least its intensity was muted. Sarah had still not received even the one cent which the Senator had vowed to deny her, but, with her comfortable life with Terry, the money was now probably of less interest to her than the abstract challenge of almost realized, but yet elusive, victory.

Sporadic efforts by Tyler to persuade the Supreme Court to reconsider his disbarment were to no avail. He adamantly maintained that he had not defrauded Hogan and refused to reimburse his "client," though he easily could have done so.

The Senator's large estate was contested by heirs and creditors at some length, but ultimately all conflicting interests were resolved save that of Sarah, and the estate was settled, subject only to the effect of the final determination of the litigation with her.

Chapter XVII   PREFACE TO CALAMITY

HE APPEAL from the divorce decree to the state Supreme Court was quiescent for a long while, but was finally decided in early 1888.* Decisions of that Court were not read from the bench and the opinions in the Sharon case were merely filed with the court clerk with copies being delivered to the attorneys.

The long delay and absence for a full year of any newsworthy happenings in the Sharon affair had greatly reduced public interest. Word of the decision spread, nevertheless, throughout the downtown area as soon as it was filed in the early afternoon of January 31. Despite a light but steady rain large crowds quickly gathered in front of newspaper offices to read hastily printed excerpts pasted to the windows.

A decision either way required a clear majority of the seven-man Supreme Court. It had been surmised that the long delay in reaching a decision might reflect a difficulty in finding such agreement. The surmise now proved to be correct. Associate Justice McKinstry wrote what was to be credited with being the main or majority opinion for the Court, some forty-five pages in length, concurred in by two of his associates and by the Chief Justice.

Pointing out that the trial testimony was not at issue before the Court, the judge said it must be assumed for purpose of the appeal that Sarah and the Senator had executed a genuine document and that thereafter they secretly lived together for a time. The question was whether Judge Sullivan was correct in determining that such conduct could under California law create a marriage.

---

* *Sharon* v. *Sharon*, 75 Cal. 1 (16 Pac. 345).

To answer that question, said the Court, it was necessary to consider the marriage statute, which then read, "Marriage is a personal relation arising out of a civil contract. Consent alone will not constitute a marriage; it must be followed by a solemnization, or by a mutual assumption of marital rights, duties or obligations."

That statute, like most of California's laws, had been adapted from a code of laws which many years earlier had been prepared for, but never adopted by, the state of New York. The Court therefore turned its attention to the East, comparing at some length the California statute with its progenitor.* Having done this, it determined that the Sharon marriage satisfied the requirement of the law unless the two-year secrecy clause somehow voided it. The Court gathered and dissected a great number of earlier authorities and at length concluded that "the law does not make it indispensable to the validity of the marriage that the relation between the parties shall be made public." It was thus decided that since the marriage contract and their subsequent cohabitation supported Judge Sullivan's conclusion that Sarah and the Senator had been legally married, Sarah was entitled to the divorce decree, which the Supreme Court thereupon affirmed.

The Court had decided to consider and determine at the same time the appeals from the alimony and attorneys' fee awards. As to these Sarah did not fare so well. The entire award of fees was set aside on technical grounds. "Moreover," said the Court, "it would seem to be an undeserved reflection upon the administration of justice in the superior courts to hold that at

---

* The reference to California's debt to the rejected New York statutes touched another of the Sharon dispute's many coincidences. In the 1840's Stephen Field's brother, David Dudley Field, had been one of the prime movers of a New York Code Commission which, with great effort and talent, had proposed a coherent and comprehensive codification of that state's statutes. The codification was rejected in New York, but Stephen Field, having migrated to California, was a member of that state's early legislature, which was faced with the problem of carving a complete set of laws from a wilderness. He resurrected and proposed his brother's rejected New York codes, which were gratefully received and quickly adopted. They still remain the framework of statutory law in California, hence the Court's reference to them in its 1888 Sharon decision.

least six lawyers were 'necessary' to present the merits of plaintiff's cause." The Court acknowledged that perhaps it was unaware of the full extent of the difficulties at the trial, but it could conceive of no situation requiring so many attorneys. No reference was made to the fact that appearing for the Senator on the appeal in addition to Barnes, Evans, Stewart, Newlands, and Kowalsky were William F. Herrin, S. M. Wilson, J. P. Hoge, and John Currey.

Turning to the alimony award, the Supreme Court felt that Judge Sullivan had abused his discretion in awarding her more support money than she had been getting during the more tranquil period of the marriage. As she had been given five hundred dollars per month then, the Court felt that was sufficient to maintain her now. At a time when a working man's monthly wages averaged less than one hundred dollars, that was no doubt true, but as the income from the Senator's estate was reputed to be around one hundred thousand dollars a month, some felt that the Court was concerning itself with trifles.

Arrayed against the four justices who affirmed the divorce judgment were the three remaining members of the Court. Judge Thornton, who had written Tyler's disbarment decision, joined by Judge Sharpstein, whom Terry had attempted to have impeached two years earlier, felt that regardless of what Justinian or common law had been, California statutes required that a marriage be open to general public view. As Sarah and the Senator had not publicly acknowledged their union, the dissenters said, no valid marriage came into being.

Associate Justice McFarland agreed with his fellow dissenters at florid length ("Jurisprudence here is not called upon to stand with drawn sword among the broken arches and prostrate columns of old common law.") declaring that assigning ordinary dictionary meanings to the words of the California statute, a secret marriage was clearly prohibited. It was nonsense to say that secret sexual intercourse amounts to "assumption" of marital duties. "To call a horse 'an animal with four legs' is to give no definition of a horse; and so to describe marriage, or the assumption of its rights, duties, and obligations, merely as secret copulation is to give no definition of marriage."

The majority of the Court had said that if the legislature intended to require openness in a marriage, it could have made this clear by providing for "*open* assumption" of marital obligations. "It is possible" dissenter McFarland answered, "that to some mental visions the adjective referred to might have made the meaning more satisfactory; just as some minds, perhaps, could not entirely grasp the idea conveyed by the word 'ball' or 'globe,' unless it were accompanied by the word 'round'."

The *Chronicle* captioned its report of the decision, "THE FINAL CHAPTER IN THE SHARON DIVORCE CASE IS ENDED." With this judgment many attorneys agreed. The federal court's decree had merely required Sarah to refrain from asserting the validity of the marriage contract. Now that the divorce decree had apparently been made final, she no longer needed to rely on the marriage contract but had the power of the decree to sustain her in pursuing her marital rights.

Even Barnes shared the general view that the case had now come to an end with victory for Sarah. He attempted to avoid reporters, but when finally reached that evening, said, "There is nothing left to say. The child is dead and that's the end of it. I have worried and worried, and there is no use of worrying any more. I feel very much like David did when his child was sick. He put on sackcloth and ashes and did penance, and when the child died, his people were afraid to tell him. But when he finally was told, he said, 'All right, no more sackcloth and ashes,' and went to breakfast."

What did he expect to do? "Well, we can sit down and think it over, and we will probably have a little talk."

On the other side, young Tyler and Flournoy were the only available members of Sarah's legal team and both were elated. Young Tyler predicted that the appeal from Barnes' motion for a new trial would now quickly be dismissed.

A month later the attorneys were, for the first time in a long while, back in the familiar atmosphere of Judge Sullivan's courtroom where Sarah's attorneys hoped to begin realizing some of the fruits of the now affirmed judgment. George Washington Tyler was permitted to participate by reason of his personal interest in the fee award, and he and Terry urged the

judge to award attorneys' fees in the "reasonable" sum authorized by the Supreme Court order and requested that alimony
be enforced. They also wanted the judge to require an immediate community property accounting by the Senator's heirs
and trustees. But at the request of William Herrin, appearing
for Barnes, the judge determined to defer action until the still
pending appeal from his denial of the motion for a new trial
was disposed of. He did order payment of accumulated alimony
of $6600 and of court costs of almost a thousand dollars. Barnes
immediately appealed this order.

✓   ✓   ✓

Pending the appeal from the divorce decree, Barnes had
done nothing to make use of the federal judgment enjoining
Sarah from using the marriage contract. If the divorce decree
had been reversed, there would be little need to enforce the
injunction. Now that the decree had been affirmed, Barnes
immediately set about reviving the somnolent federal judgment.
The first step toward its enforcement was to compel Sarah to
accede to that decree by having her threatened with imprisonment for contempt of court.

On the morning of September 3rd of that year, 1888, the Circuit Court room in the Appraiser's Building was again crowded
as it had not been in some time to hear the Court's decision.
Stephen J. Field, United States Supreme Court Justice, again in
California on circuit, read the decision of the Court.* Sitting
with him were Judge Sawyer and a district judge.

Though Terry had opposed it for a variety of reasons, it was
generally felt that the revivor was largely perfunctory as the
Court was merely reasserting, in the names of the now dead
Senator's representatives, the decision it had long since reached.
This proved to be the case.

Terry's objections should have been raised on a direct appeal, said Field, but could not be raised now, though he acknowledged that Terry had been faced with a dilemma. "There
was an attempt to appeal, but as this was before the case was
revived, it was without any efficacy. Where a suit has abated by

---

* *Sharon* v. *Terry*, 36 Fed. 337.

the death of the plaintiff after judgment, no appeal can be taken by the defendant until the case is revived."

Thus two questions which had been bothering followers of the case were answered simultaneously. Barnes had delayed in substituting the Senator's representatives in the federal case to keep Sarah from appealing the decision. And Sarah had not taken an appeal from the federal injunction because the absence of a living adversary prevented it.

The Senator's heirs were entitled to the fruits of the earlier judgment, Field concluded after a lengthy review of both the state and federal actions. He thereupon ordered Sarah to turn over the marriage contract for cancellation and enjoined her from ever asserting its validity.

The hearing would have been of little public moment, notwithstanding the large audience in attendance, had it not been for Sarah, who was present at the counsel table with Terry. As Field got to the point in his decision of directing her to deliver up the contract, she rose from her chair, and apparently calmly and in full possession of herself, pointed a finger at Field.

"Are you going to take it upon yourself to order me to give up that contract?"

Field, momentarily disconcerted, finally said, "Sit down, madam."

"I will . . ." she began, apparently intending to get in one last word, but Field interrupted.

"Marshal, put that woman out!" he directed U. S. Marshal J. C. Franks.

"Judge Field, how much have you been paid for that decision? I know it was bought," Sarah cried as the marshal strode toward her.

"Marshal, put that woman out," Field repeated evenly.

No one but Sarah seemed perturbed. Some spectators in the back of the courtroom stood up to gain a better view. Terry, still seated, told the marshal to stand back. "Don't put a finger on my wife," he warned, adding that he would take her out himself, some witnesses later said. The marshal hesitated, then attempted to push past. Terry jumped to his feet and struck him in the face. The marshal fell to the floor, a tooth broken, blood streaming from his mouth. Deputy marshals, assisted by several attorneys and spectators, leaped on Terry, threw him to the floor, and pinned his arms down when he appeared for for a time to be trying to get his hand inside his coat. Sarah attempted to rescue Terry, asking a bystander to hold her reticule. After being buffeted to the floor she was drawn to her feet and led away.

"Let me go," said Terry, ceasing his struggle as Sarah left. "I only want to accompany my wife and I'll go quietly." Released, he turned and walked out of the courtroom straightening his clothing. The deputy marshals fell back. Half of those in attendance pushed out after Terry.

During the entire brief affair neither Field nor his associates had visibly reacted. After a sip of water, Field finished reading his decision without change of tone or demeanor.

Sarah was taken to the marshal's anteroom off the corridor adjacent to the courtroom. Terry walked directly there and, finding the door barred by a deputy he drew a bowie knife from under his coat. A second deputy cocked his gun and held it at Terry's head. Terry ignored him and took a firmer grip on his knife. "Stand back," he said to the men barring the door. "I'm going to my wife and no man shall stop me." The marshal gave way and Terry started into the room. At the doorway several deputies leaped on him and another fight ensued. Terry cried out several times during the battle, "Why do you stop me? I want to go to my wife."

Despite his age and several hard blows to his face, Terry's size and strength engaged the full attention of three or four men. A bystander named David Neagle wrenched the knife from him while he was held, but the fight was still in progress several minutes later when an order came from the courtroom to place both Sarah and Terry under arrest. Marshals easily executed this order by permitting him to join her, after which the door was placed under guard.

They were held in the anteroom for several hours. Terry, solicitous of Sarah's well-being, at one point was heard to ask, "My Dear, why did you bring on all this trouble?" She replied that it was because her case and the corruption of the court must at all cost be kept before the public. She had succeeded admirably. Transcontinental newswires were soon humming as they had not been since the days of the divorce trial itself four years earlier.

Field ordered court reconvened that afternoon to consider what should be done about the morning's altercation. Sarah and Terry were not brought into court, only learning of the proceeding at its conclusion when reporters were admitted to the anteroom to interview them. They told Terry that Sarah had been sentenced to 30 days in the Alameda County jail, across the bay in Oakland. "I'll go with you," said Terry, gently stroking her cheek.

"You have been sentenced to six months," said the reporter.

"What! Damn them!" Terry shouted. He was obviously surprised by the severity of the sentence. "What am I to be in prison for?" He said his embroilment was simply the result of efforts to protect Sarah and to get to her.

"Yes," Sarah laughed, "it was as hard to get in here as it now is hard to get out." Terry chuckled appreciatively.

Sarah repeated her charge that Field's decision was the product of bribery. Both suggested that reporters inquire why Field was always a non-paying guest at Senator Sharon's Palace Hotel while in San Francisco and frequently took dinner and visited socially with the Senator's son-in-law.

Later that afternoon Sarah and Terry were ferried across the bay to jail in Oakland. The jailer, flattered at having such distinguished guests, was a deferential host. He escorted them to the unoccupied death cell, telling them it was the best in the house. Permitted to share the cell, Sarah and Terry received many friends and gifts of flowers and fruit. Both seemed to be in good spirits throughout the month of Sarah's stay. At the completion of her term she hired a room nearby. She continued to spend long hours with Terry, for whom time now began to drag.

Friends suggested that Terry ask Field to reduce the sentence. Field himself as an attorney had been threatened with imprisonment for contempt under similar circumstances in 1850, but avoided punishment by successfully urging that a judge should not use a contempt order to vindicate his own character.* Terry's friends hoped that Field would be equally compassionate. Terry loathed the role of supplicant and doubted its success, in view of their long-standing mutual antipathy. Nevertheless, he did prepare an affidavit disclaiming any intentional disrespect in the courtroom and emphasizing his pacific purpose of merely wanting to escort Sarah out. Terry did not relish the prospect of giving Field the opportunity to use the clemency plea simply as a vehicle of denunciation. He therefore entrusted the affidavit to one of their former associates on the state Supreme Court, pledging him not to use it until he had talked informally with Field, and then only if there appeared some likelihood of success.

The intermediary called on Field in his rooms at the Palace Hotel. After it was read to him, Field asked to look at the affidavit, then pocketed it and the friend left assuming that Field wished to think about it. Instead, Field immediately set about secretly obtaining countervailing affidavits from Marshal Franks and others. When he had them in the form in which he wished them — there is evidence that Field dictated the language of some of the affidavits — he filed them in court along with Terry's affidavit. No formal application had been made, of course, and Field, choosing his words carefully, said in his written order which he filed at the same time, "We have *received* a petition," but he did not mention that he was acting without notice or hearing, and with no one appearing for Terry.

As Terry had feared, Field saw no analogy with his own 1850 experience and used Terry's penance to scourge him fur-

---

* Field had gained the distinction of being the first person ever to be held in contempt of court in California (*People ex rel. Field* v. *Turner,* 1 Cal. 152, 187), as well as the first attorney to be disbarred there. (*People ex rel. Field* v. *Turner,* 1 Cal. 190). The state Supreme Court set aside his sentence, declaring that contempt punishment "should be used with great prudence and caution. A judge should bear in mind that he is engaged not so much in vindicating his own character as in promoting the respect due to the administration of the laws; and this consideration should induce him to receive as satisfactory any reasonable apology for an offender's conduct."

ther. Terry's conduct had been an "indignity and insult to the emblem of the nation's majesty" and his claim that he meant no harm was an appeal to "childish credulity." It was too offensive to be purged by any mere apology, Field decreed, and Terry must serve the entire six months.* Friends immediately appealed to the U. S. Supreme Court on Terry's behalf but with no greater success.** Field was by then back in Washington but took no part in the decision.

Terry occupied himself in reading, legal research and writing on various pending aspects of the cases, meanwhile brooding on the injustices of which he felt Field guilty. He continued to joke with visitors, but also uttered threats toward the judge. Many of these found their way to Washington. Field remarked that Terry was "under great excitement and unless he cools down before his term of imprisonment is finished, he may attempt to wreak bodily vengeance upon the judges and officers of the court." He said he would not be deterred by Terry from doing his duty as a judge.

Both federal and state criminal law provided for time off for good behavior amounting to cancellation of five days of each month of one's sentence. Learning that the sheriff considered Terry to be an exemplary prisoner and intended to give him the time credits, federal Judge Lorenzo Sawyer, maintaining a vigil in Field's absence, hailed the sheriff into court. Greatly admired for his prolixity, Sawyer's skill at marshalling reasons for his decisions was sometimes favorably compared with Field's, whose protege (toady, some put it) he was said to be. He managed to find four separate technical reasons for denying Terry credit

---

* *In re Terry*, 36 Fed. 419. Field said he was equally displeased by Terry's failure to apologize for "violent and vituperative language" outside of court. After imposing the jail sentences the previous September Field had explained to puzzled reporters that it was legal to order a person to jail in his absence and without a hearing "when the offense was committed in the presence of the court." His allusion now to remarks made out of court was understandable if not legally sound. Marshal Franks had reported that while held in the court anteroom after the scuffle Terry said, "Tell that bald-headed old son-of-a-bitch, Field, that I want to go to lunch."

** *In re Terry*, 128 U. S. 289.

and directed the sheriff to hold him to the final hour of the last day.*

The full six months, Field predicted, would give Terry time to "cool down." If he actually believed it would achieve that purpose, he did not know Terry. Shortly before his release Terry tried to vent his frustration by suing Marshal Franks for false imprisonment, demanding that Field's deposition be taken. The effort was quickly neutralized by the simple expedient of having the case transferred to federal court where it was promptly quashed. Field concluded, however, that further chastening was called for, as Terry obviously had not learned humility while in jail; so at the urging of the United States District Attorney the federal Grand Jury was induced to indict Terry for assault and Sarah for impeding an officer, basing the charges on the courtroom affray. The jury issued the indictment without reading it. The district attorney refused its request to hear from several witnesses favorable to Terry, telling it to hurry and sign the indictment as Justice Field did not wish any delay.

Terry was ordered to appear at the marshal's office to surrender on the new charges immediately upon his release from jail in Oakland. Heavily armed and nervous deputies were strategically placed throughout the office and corridors as he and Sarah arrived at the Appraiser's Building. But, though he glared menacingly and Sarah was disdainful, there was no incident, much to the disappointment of the large crowd which had gathered. Both posted bail and were released. Terry promptly complained to the court that the Grand Jury had been coerced. Federal Judge Hoffman refused to dismiss the case, however, saying that while the district attorney may have been overzealous in guiding the jury, such bad judgment could not defeat the indictment.**

---

* *In re Terry*, 37 Fed. 469. Two of Saywer's reasons were particularly nice legal inventions. The statutes granting credit applied to persons guilty of public "offenses," Sawyer pointed out; "offense" meant "crime" and since contempt of court was not technically a crime, Terry's case did not come within the purview of the law. Additionally, the federal and state laws applied to prisoners in their respective penal facilities; but since Terry was a federal prisoner serving his time in a state jail he was not entitled to the benefit of either law, Sawyer said regretfully.

** *United States* v. *Terry*, 39 Fed. 355.

Chapter XVIII   ADVERSITIES ACCUMULATE

HILE IN jail Terry prepared an appeal to the United States Supreme Court from Field's decision reviving the federal decree requiring Sarah to give up the marriage contract. This appeal was dismissed by the Court in May* on the ground that it was idle, even frivolous. Terry's arguments should have been directed against the original decree, said the Court.

Field discreetly abstained from taking part in the decision. It might have dispelled the confusion in some minds if Field had participated and explained his views. In his revivor decree he had said that the Senator's death had made appeal impossible until the substitution was made. The Supreme Court was now saying that the appeal should have been taken from the original decree notwithstanding the Senator's death and, as it had not been taken, the attempted appeal now (when Field said it should be taken) was frivolous.

Ignoring the federal judgment, Sarah now petitioned Judge Sullivan to make a division of the Senator's estate and to compel payment of her accumulated alimony, as she had still received none of the fruits of her affirmed divorce decree or the modified alimony award.

The attorneys for the Senator's estate countered by threatening to have Sarah and any attorney who appeared for her jailed for contempt of the federal court order. The six months Terry had just spent in jail were sufficient to discourage him from risking punishment, but Sarah herself was not daunted. She therefore appeared alone before Judge Sullivan to plead for an order enforcing his decree. He was inclined to make such an

---

* *Terry* v. *Sharon*, 131 U. S. 40.

order, but at Barnes' suggestion he again deferred his ruling until the Senator's last appeal was concluded.

ɤ　　　　ɤ　　　　ɤ

Terry had requested the state Supreme Court to dismiss the appeal from the denial of the motion for new trial in the divorce case, for failure to vigorously prosecute that appeal. His request was denied but it stimulated great activity, and that appeal was in short order briefed, argued and submitted to the Court for decision. Finally, on July 17, the Court filed its decision.

The decision* on the appeal from Judge Sullivan's denial of the new trial motion was, like its predecessor, filed by the state Supreme Court without oral rendition, and those interested, of whom there were still a great many, again had to read it while standing in front of a newspaper office or wait until papers were on the streets.

The Court first honored the now well established custom of reviewing the state and federal proceedings, and then pointed out that the evidence produced before Judge Sullivan was now before the Supreme Court for consideration for the first time. Preliminarily, however, the Court had to dispose of the usual clutch of technical points raised by each side.

On the Senator's side it was urged that the federal decision prohibiting Sarah from asserting any rights under the contract required the Court to honor that decision. The problem was stated by the Court more succinctly than at any previous time:

"Here are two courts of concurrent jurisdiction, both of which have assumed and are exercising jurisdiction over the same subject matter and parties, and the federal court renders a judgment in direct conflict with that of the state court. [But this does not] prove that the judgment of the state court is either void or erroneous. Both may be valid, and as they may have been rendered upon different evidence, it may be that neither of them is erroneous." As a matter of public policy, the Court said, one or the other of these conflicting judgments must prevail over the other. This Court, however, would not now attempt to resolve the conflict, since it had never received offi-

---

* *Sharon* v. *Sharon*, 79 Cal. 633 (22 Pac. 26).

David S. Terry cut a melodramatic figure in the early years of California's statehood. At the time of the Sharon litigation a man in his sixties, he would have appeared somewhat older than in this photograph.

— *Wells Fargo Bank.*

Justice Stephen J. Field, California's first contribution to the United States Supreme Court, served there from 1863 to 1897, longer than any other man before or since. — *Bancroft Library.*

cial notice of the existence of the federal case and would therefore treat it as though it did not exist.

Sarah and her supporters took heart at these words, and
were elated when the Court then declared that Judge Sullivan's
finding that Sarah and the Senator both signed the marriage
contract was supported by clear and positive evidence and was
therefore binding on appeal. But those were the last encourag-
ing words Sarah was to hear from the Court.

Though the marriage contract was genuine, "the fact of
secrecy must become a most important element in determining
whether their cohabitation was such as is usual with married
people, and whether they did mutually assume marital rights,
duties and obligations," the Court now held. This, of course,
was directly contrary to the same Court's decision the previous
year that "the law does not make it indispensable to the validity
of the marriage that the relation be made public; direct proof
of consent is at least as effective as evidence of reputation."
Many marvelled at the ease with which the Court now dismissed its earlier ruling by saying, "Doubtless much was said
on that appeal that was unnecessary to the decision." But while
the Senator's attorneys had been unsuccessful in inducing the
Court to recognize the federal judgment, Terry was equally
unsuccessful in urging the Court to remain steadfast to its own
earlier decision.

The explanation of the difference was to be found in the
changed complexion of the Court itself rather than on the face
of the decision. It was only legally the same Court. Of the
four members of the Court who had decided in Sarah's favor
the previous year, three were no longer on the Court. On the
other hand, all three of the previous year's dissenters — the men
who had voted against Sarah on the earlier appeal — were still
very much on the Court. Thus the previous year's decision was
now being scrutinized by three men who had disagreed with it,
in addition to three who had not been on the Court at that
time, and only one man who had both been on that Court and
agreed with that decision. That the judges took as much time as
they did in neutralizing that decision was commended by some
as a tribute to their integrity.

After laying the previous year's decision at rest the Court turned to the assignment it had carved for itself. The controlling question, the Court said, was whether Sarah and the Senator assumed marital rights and duties, acting like married people. To answer this, it was necessary to review at length all of the now well-known evidence Sarah had been able to produce to see if it supported Judge Sullivan's conclusion.

"It seems to us," said the Court after its grand tour of the evidence, "that this evidence shows conclusively that these parties did not live and cohabit together 'in the way usual with married people.' They did not live or cohabit together at all. They had their separate habitations in different hotels. Her visits to his room and his visits to hers were occasional, and apparently as visitors. They had no common home or dwelling place."

The relationship was more like that of a man and his mistress, said the Court. It was true that the Senator introduced Sarah to his friends; with some men this might suggest that she was a wife rather than a mistress. "But this man has sinned so long and so openly in this respect that he did not care to conceal his wrongdoing even from his own family." The Court was forgetting Barnes' stipulation at the trial that the Senator had kept many mistresses but had never been seen publicly or openly with any of them, had never introduced them to friends or family, and had never had them to Belmont.

Though the marriage contract was genuine, the Senator supported Sarah, they had frequent sexual relations, he addressed her occasionally as "My Dear Wife," and though they thought they were married, something more was required, the Court concluded. The law demanded an "assumption" of the marital relationship. And that was impossible when the parties pursuant to the secrecy provision denied the marriage to the world, the Court said.

"We think just such results were intended to be prevented by the statute we are considering, and that it was clearly intended that they should so conduct themselves toward each other as to give evidence to those with whom they might come in contact that they were husband and wife."

The preceding year the majority of the Court had also probed legislative intent and reached an opposite conclusion. "Shall a man be permitted to say, 'We are not married, because we did not discharge a marital duty, to wit, make public the relation between us'?" And the Court had then answered its own question, "Surely, if the legislators had intended consequences such as would flow from upholding a party in a position like that, they would have expressed their purpose in unmistakable terms."

The Court coasted on to its final conclusion, having now made a complete break with the interpretation given the law the previous year, pausing only to castigate Sarah's attorneys for having cited no authorities on the secrecy issue and indeed "dismissing the question, so important to their client, in a general statement." (Perhaps Sarah's attorneys had thought the Court would find its own previous decision to be authority enough.) The Court drew its discussion to a close, quoting "with approval the dissenting opinion on the former appeal," thus conceding that it was deserting the previous majority decision and wholly embracing the dissent. Judge Sullivan's decision must be reversed for retrial, the Court decreed, at which time Sarah would be permitted to produce any evidence she might have to show an open assumption of marital responsibilities.

The main decision was signed by one of Terry's earlier impeachment targets and by the Court's new members, one of whom had written it.

Associate Justice McFarland, author of the most caustic dissent the previous year, concurred in the Court's adoption of his former position, saying that it was barely possible that the decision of the Court could be construed as indicating that the earlier decision had been correct and still had some force. It was futile to try to square the present decision with the previous majority opinion, he said, and the Court should confess the previous error and expressly disapprove it. Another dissenter of the previous year also wrote a concurring opinion, embellishing the main opinion's tautologies at tedious length.

Associate Justice Paterson, the only remaining member of the previous year's Court who had decided favorably to Sarah, stood by the earlier decision, saying that "The combined wisdom of all who have attacked the reasoning upon which the judgment was affirmed" had not shaken it. "I agree," said Paterson — with whom he did not say — "that if there be a consent to marry, and any mutual marital duty performed in good faith in pursuance of the contract to marry, the marriage is complete." Perhaps he meant he agreed with Terry, as that had been the position taken by Sarah's attorneys; certainly there was no one on the Court with whom he could now agree.

General opinion was that Sarah had now finally and irrevocably lost the entire case. From having won, to having the victory placed in doubt, to having success again almost within her grasp, she was now finally and firmly defeated. She remained in seclusion and would not speak with reporters.

Undaunted, Terry almost immediately filed a petition for rehearing, arguing that the Court should not render a decision so flatly inconsistent with the same Court's ruling in the same case barely a year before. But Sarah and Terry were apparently running out of money, and had the petition printed by a Fresno newspaper on the cheapest kind of newsprint.

The Supreme Court would consider and determine whether to grant a rehearing within thirty days. Terry would never hear the result.

Chapter XIX TRAGEDY

IELD returned to California that summer to sit on federal cases in the Ninth Circuit. He was given a bodyguard by order of U. S. Attorney General William H. Miller as a result of Terry's various threats. U. S. Marshal Franks in San Francisco gave David Neagle the assignment.

Neagle had tried his hand at a number of occupations with indifferent success. He had been a migratory mine worker, a saloon operator and police chief in Tombstone, Arizona Territory, where he ran unsuccessfully for sheriff. He then drifted on to Montana Territory for awhile before returning to San Francisco in 1883. Here he became active in politics and was soon appointed deputy sheriff. While on city business, September 3, 1888, he happened to enter the Appraiser's Building just in time to disarm Terry in the melee at that time. He grabbed the knife by the blade, twisting it out of Terry's grasp. Neagle was unscathed, and his invulnerable valor in that encounter earned him the role of Field's bodyguard.

Field held court in Los Angeles in early August, and on the evening of the 13th entrained, with Neagle at his side, to return to San Francisco. Always apprised of Terry's whereabouts, Neagle knew that he and Sarah had been at their ranch near Fresno. Consequently he stayed up to see the train through its midnight Fresno stop. As he stood with the train conductor in the shadow of Field's sleeping car, he noticed Sarah and Terry boarding a day coach a few cars away. They were required to appear in federal court in San Francisco the next morning on pending criminal charges arising out of the court incident the previous September. Apparently ignorant of the presence of Field, they had been driven by wagon to Fresno from the ranch, arriving barely in time to board the train. Neagle reported the new passengers to the judge. Field instructed him not to be rash, but said that if any incident took place he wanted to be protected at all hazards. As the train started the conductor told Neagle that the Terrys appeared to be making themselves comfortable for a nap in their coach. With no encounter imminent that night, Neagle relaxed his vigil.

Early in the morning the train stopped for breakfast at Lathrop, near Stockton as Field was completing his morning toilet. Neagle suggested that he eat at the buffet on board the train but Field insisted that he had had good breakfasts in the station dining room and preferred to eat there. Neagle shrugged and followed him into the dining room, where the two men took a table near the middle of the room and seated themselves facing the door.

In a few minutes they saw David Terry enter with Sarah. She wheeled in the doorway and returned to the train. The dining room operator, who knew Terry, escorted him to a table near one corner of the room. He asked Terry if he thought his wife planned anything desperate.

"Why?" asked Terry. "Who is here?" Seeing Field he said, "Well, you had better go and watch her." He sat for a moment, then rose and with deliberation walked to Field's table. The restaurateur, at the door to intercept Sarah on her return, watched helplessly as Terry stopped and paused behind Field's chair while Neagle eyed him warily. Standing to the side and slightly in back of Field, Terry leaned over him and struck him twice — lightly, the restaurateur said later — on the cheek with the back of his hand.

Neagle immediately jumped up, wheeled, putting himself two to three feet from Terry, and drew a revolver. Thrusting its barrel against Terry's chest at the heart he fired. Terry stood motionless for a moment, then his legs began to give way. As he fell, Neagle fired again at his head.

Most of the restaurant's guests were unaware of the identity of the participants in the violence. After a moment's shocked silence, the room erupted in great confusion. Some attempted to leave while others began to crowd around Terry's body. A bystander mechanically straightened a leg which was bent underneath. Terry was obviously dead.

Some of the dining room guests tentatively moved toward Neagle to restrain him. He backed against a wall and, fanning his gun at the hundred-odd people still in the room, declared that he was an officer of the United States and no one should touch him.

Sarah arrived at that moment. Wild-eyed with foreboding she tore her way through the cluster of people standing around Terry and dropped to the floor at his side. Ignoring the great mass of blood she cradled his head in her lap. Alternately she caressed and kissed his face, moaning, "Oh, my darling! Oh, my sweetheart! Can you realize that he is dead? Can you realize it? Oh, my darling, my darling, how can I live without you? Oh, to think I had just been asleep in his arms on the train, and then to awaken to this! Oh, those dear hands! My God! My God!"

Then she noticed those who stood silently about. "Why don't they hang the man? The cowardly murderer! He was too cowardly to be given a trial, but hired an assassin. They shot him down like a dog in the road. He was the soul of honor."

Again caressing Terry's face, she swayed despairingly back and forth. "Oh, if I could be in your place! If it was only I, instead of you who have so many to love you! Oh, how can I give him up! My love, my love!"

Sarah was drawn from Terry's body long enough to permit several men to carry it to a barber shop next door. Her clothing was covered with blood. Running from train to dining room to barber shop, she imploringly accosted first one person, then another. At one moment concerned with Terry, at the next she demanded revenge on his murderers.

Field and Neagle had withdrawn to their railway carriage and locked the door. Sarah approached it a time or two and Neagle warned that if she was not kept out he would kill her, too. The town constable boarded the train, and pledging impartiality, he was permitted to talk with Field and Neagle in their carriage. Lengthy negotiations ensued, the trainmaster acting as arbitrator. They finally agreed that Neagle would submit to detention pending the coroner's inquest. In Lathrop sentiment was already hardening against Neagle. As a precaution against possible mob violence the train would first proceed to Tracy, the next stop on the way to San Francisco. There Neagle would be removed for delivery to the San Joaquin County sheriff in Stockton, the county seat.

Many who had witnessed the incident felt that Terry had intended the slaps as the first step toward a challenge to a duel. He had several times hinted at such an intention when he was in jail that spring. He had said he would slap Field or twist his nose the next time he saw him. Many assumed that he would have been satisfied merely to humiliate Field. To a man who lived by Terry's code it made no difference whether the challenge resulted in a duel. Exposing a man as a coward was quite as good as killing him.

Others among Terry's acquaintances remembered his background and violent temper. Such a man, goaded by the events of the past year, and importuned by Sarah, could easily become desperate enough to kill a man in cold blood.

Most people felt that Neagle had acted more precipitately than necessary. This impression was reinforced when a search of Terry's clothing revealed that he had been totally unarmed. Some even charged that Field had deliberately created the incident. It was learned that Field had not been scheduled to travel to California on circuit that year, but had intended to spend the summer in Europe. A delegation of well-intentioned friends forgot that it had been his practice to visit California only in alternate years and visited him in Washington where they told him of Terry's grumblings and cautioned him against coming to California. He promptly cancelled his European trip and arranged that summer's circuit.

The Lathrop constable took Neagle from the train at Tracy and delivered him to the sheriff in Stockton. Field proceeded to San Francisco where a *Chronicle* reporter later found him in his room at the Palace Hotel "as calm as though the killing of a man at breakfast were an everyday occurrence."

The Stockton district attorney was incensed upon learning that Field had not been arrested. He said that every person, no matter how exalted his position and not excluding the President of the United States, must be amenable to the criminal laws. He vowed to go personally to San Francisco to arrest Field, if necessary.

Meanwhile, Sarah was near collapse but withdrawn and mute after her frenetic activity at the station. Silently she followed the carriage taking Terry's body to the Stockton morgue where she stayed through the coroner's examination and inquest. Refusing to leave, she remained with the body that night and all the following day and night as well. She had neither eaten nor slept for two days by the time the funeral was held August 16.

It was conducted with much confusion. Terry's family and Sarah declined to consult with each other, each attempting to make the arrangements. An estimated thousand people were in the chapel. Another thousand milled about outside. Few in the mob appeared in dress or manner to be mourners. No clergyman officiated, but a vestryman read from the Episcopal funeral service while Sarah rocked to and fro, moaning.

*   *   *

Every daily newspaper in the country carried accounts of the killing. It provided grist for editorials descrying a wide variety of moral truths. The New York *Herald* interviewed a number of "Washington lawyers" and reported their general feeling to be that Neagle's conduct had been unjustified. They thought it beyond the necessary and reasonable bounds of his authority. "Here in the East," one was quoted as saying, "we look on matters of this sort in a different light from that in which they are seen by people west of the Rocky Mountains. Out there they kill a man and explain or apologize afterward."

Most papers, particularly in the Midwest, emphasized Terry's life of violence and arrogance toward law. However questionable the particular circumstances under which he met his death, such a man could expect to die as he had lived. The New York *Star* felt that his death provided a "useful lesson."

Even in the West a man may not go through life lawlessly with impunity. The New York *Sun* declared that David Broderick was, after thirty years, avenged. The paper did not intimate, if it knew, how appropriate was the irony of Field's role as avenger.

Terry, as was generally known, had resigned as Chief Justice of the state Supreme Court in 1859 to fight his duel with and kill United States Senator David Broderick. Field, one of Terry's associates who had worked under him for two years, having indeed been sworn into office by Terry, had gained a chance benefit from that duel inasmuch as he was elevated to the position of Chief Justice on Terry's resignation. In all probability his status as Chief Justice of the California Supreme Court at the time the United States Supreme Court was expanded to ten members in 1863 — ostensibly to recognize the fast growing West — was the greatest single factor responsible for his elevation to that Court and subsequent role in the Sharon case.

Less known was the fact that Field in his younger days had not himself been above violence, and more than once had turned to dueling to settle his differences with members of the judiciary and of the legislature. For a few months in early 1850 at the time of the transition of California's government, he had been *alcalde,* or chief magistrate in Marysville, a booming foothill mining town above Sacramento, which he had helped found. By his own account he amassed over a hundred thousand dollars in less than six months as judge.

The governor under the newly formed state government then appointed another man named Turner to be the local judge. It might be expected that Field would be resentful, but according to his later account he took it with good grace. The new man proved to be insufferable, however, and after a number of difficulties including being held in contempt and disbarred by the new Judge Turner, Field asked the state legislature to impeach him. An ensuing debate with a friend of Judge Turner became so heated that Field determined to challenge the man to a duel. A complication developed when he solicited someone to act as his second, however, as the newly adopted state constitution barred any man who participated in a duel from thereafter holding public office. Everyone Field approached begged off on that ground; but David Broderick, then a state legislator and a slight acquaintance, finally agreed to second Field, and set about making the arrangements. Field's antagonist hastily gave satisfaction by apologizing on the floor of the legislature, and the duel was never fought. A few days later, Field and Broderick were solidifying their newfound friendship in a saloon when Broderick suddenly thrust Field out a side door, afterward explaining that he had seen the brother of Field's tormentor, Judge Turner, gun in hand, looking for Field.

Field felt that Broderick had saved his honor and his life and later reminisced, "For years afterwards, I felt there was nothing I could do that would be a sufficient return for his kindness." Shortly after Broderick's death at Terry's hand, Field had written, "I could never forget his generous conduct to me; and for his sad death there was no more sincere mourner in the state."

Broderick could have asked no better avenger.

Chapter XX CONFUSION REIGNS

HE NEW YORK *Herald* predicted that a number of interesting legal points would doubtless be raised by the killing, saying that the tragedy had no parallel in criminal annals. "Meanwhile," the editorial concluded, "has the last act in the eventful drama been reached?" Apparently implying a negative answer, it concluded, "Sarah Althea Hill, the leading actress still lives."

It was in fact already apparent that David Terry's death was going to have the same effect as had virtually every other event connected with the Sharon case. It was spawning a wealth of litigation as bizarre as any that had preceded it.

Sarah signed murder complaints in Stockton the day after the killing. She charged Neagle with murder and Field as his accomplice. Neagle was already in custody, and great precautions were taken at the jail, not to keep him in, but to keep Terry's many Stockton friends out. The San Joaquin County sheriff immediately took the train from Stockton to San Francisco to serve the warrant of arrest on Field.

Field received the awed sheriff in his rooms in the Palace by appointment, urged him to be at his ease, and agreed to accompany him back to Stockton the following afternoon. The sheriff was to pick him up in his chambers at the Appraiser's Building.

A great crowd had collected in the courtroom and outside chambers as the hour for Field's surrender arrived the following day. For the benefit of the press Field made a nice little show of it. He said to the sheriff, "I am glad to see you, sir, and wish you to perform your duty." The diffident sheriff hesitated, intimidated as much by the large audience as by Field. "Because I may be a judge," Field encouraged him," I am not excused from the proper processes of law. Judges should be all the more amenable to the laws which they are selected to maintain."

The sheriff mumbled that it was an unpleasant duty he had to perform.

"I am in your custody," prompted Field.

"You are," said the sheriff. Some thought it more a question than a statement of fact. Satisfied that form had been honored, Field immediately called Circuit Judge Lorenzo Sawyer's waiting clerk, handed him a petition for a writ of *habeas corpus* which had been prepared for the occasion. Judge Sawyer, waiting a few steps away, promptly signed a previously prepared order requiring the sheriff to produce Field before Sawyer forthwith and prohibiting him from taking Field to Stockton. The entire party then trooped into Judge Sawyer's court where he had preceded and was awaiting them. The United States District Attorney was fortuitously present. He generously offered to prepare a written "return" or rejoinder for the sheriff so that the matter could proceed quickly yet legally. The court waited a moment while he did so. The hastily prepared return consisted simply of an admission that Field had been placed under arrest. The trustful sheriff signed it, assuming that someone present must know what was taking place.

To prove that Field was not the only person there with a sense of humor, Sawyer winked slyly at the appreciative reporters. "What shall be done with the prisoner?" After a few minutes' witty repartee, five thousand dollars' bond was agreed on and immediately posted pending hearing the following Thursday. This meant that the sheriff could not in the meantime hold Field nor take him to Stockton. The preliminary hearing on the murder charge was scheduled to take place in Stockton on Wednesday.

The *Chronicle*, not known for irony or cynicism, concluded its account of the afternoon's frolic by reporting that Field then "retired with his friends, having given the best proof possible of the equality of all American citizens before the law."

The sheriff returned to Stockton that evening. He was obviously flattered by the attention he had been receiving. Reporters who met his train were favored with a full account of his adventures in the City, ending with the declaration that he had been "treated very well" in San Francisco. The sheriff was surprised and offended when the district attorney rudely reminded him that he had made the trip to bring back Field. His hope for status as a local celebrity was further thwarted by another disclosure. Not only had he failed to arrest Field, but he had brought along an attorney already carrying a writ of *habeas corpus* to remove Neagle to the jurisdiction of the federal court in San Francisco.

A subscription was well under way in Stockton to provide funds for Neagle's prosecution. Great feeling was aroused by the prospect of having to surrender him without a trial. The subscription committee, attorneys, and citizen groups separately conferred to discuss the legality and necessity of relinquishing the prisoner. Many simply wanted Neagle prosecuted and punished in their presence. They were incensed at losing the spectacle. Others saw it as a much larger question of the division of powers between state and federal authorities. What right had the federal government to take a man from the custody of state officers while a charge of violating state law was pending against him?

The arguments continued throughout the night, but the disputants might have saved their energy. The sheriff failed to mention one thing at his press conference that evening. A special train had been chartered by Neagle's protectors to take him to San Francisco without delay. The sheriff had been honored with the privilege of accompanying the prisoner and his attorneys. In the dead of night, at 3:30 a.m., the train quietly pulled out of the deserted Stockton station.

The escape was not generally known until the next day. Sarah somehow learned of the planned flight soon after the funeral and tried throughout the early evening to reach the sheriff in an effort to dissuade him. He refused to speak with her, apparently piqued at the contrast between his treatment at home and the respect accorded him in San Francisco.

A reporter happened to be at the station while the special train was being made up. He was invited aboard, perhaps to keep him from spreading an untimely alarm, and he accompanied the small party to San Francisco. Later he reported that Neagle was in fine spirits and not at all reticent about the killing, relating it as though it had been a bear hunt.

Friends, associates, and federal officials flocked to visit and encourage Neagle in jail in San Francisco, but a group of young women appeared one day outside the jail and hurled threats of violence and death at the window of his cell. The general feeling in California was of shock and impotent rage. As far away as New York, the *Sunday Mercury* in a lengthy editorial demanded that the United States Attorney General, W. H. H. Miller, be immediately arrested and indicted as an accessory to murder.

A large crowd was on hand in the Appraiser's Building as Judge Sawyer convened court to hear the *habeas corpus* petitions. Neagle was brought in by a Secret Service agent but his fellow defendant, Field, strolled out of chambers where he had been visiting with the Court. The hearing provided spectators with an opportunity to see Field and Neagle, but little else. The Stockton attorneys objected to the proceeding and Field's petition was argued at some length. The matters were then put over to the following week for further argument and decision.

The trial in Stockton, with no defendants present, was put off from day to day awaiting their return. The Governor of California had meanwhile been subjected to much pressure on Field's behalf. He in turn requested the state attorney general to do what he could to have the prosecution against Field dropped. The Stockton district attorney remained adamant for several days. Finally he yielded to the charge that his county and state were being made to appear ridiculous throughout the country, and consented to dismiss Field's prosecution.

When the *habeas corpus* hearing next convened it was announced that state proceedings against Field had been dropped. Federal Judge Sawyer said it was a disgrace that the state of California should for a moment have entertained the thought of prosecuting Feld on such reckless charges. One of Neagle's six attorneys arose and said that they were prepared to waive all irregularities and proceed directly to a trial of the facts before the federal court.

The Stockton district attorney protested that it was the people of Stockton and not Neagle who were complaining of irregularities. He said the State objected to the jurisdiction of the federal court, which he charged had no power to act while the state prosecution was pending.

Judge Sawyer said he wanted to hear the evidence and would consider whether he had jurisdiction later. The state attorneys thereupon withdrew from the case, declaring that they had never heard of a court acting on a case without first determining whether it had power to do so.

Newspapers around the country were now regularly editorializing on the affair. A majority still sided with Field and Neagle, but the federal government's intervention caused a great many to join the New York *Mercury* in expression of alarm and disapproval. So far as Terry's death was concerned, the general view was still that "he married his tragic fate." But this cavalier rejection of the state's right to pursue its regular procedure seemed to set a baleful precedent.

When Neagle's *habeas corpus* hearing finally began several days later, no state attorneys were present to protest the granting of the writ. The hearing lasted two full weeks, even in the absence of any opposition, but proceeded amicably. Justice Field, the case against him dismissed, sat in the unused jury box, making of it a sort of reserved spectator's gallery. He sauntered into and out of chambers with Judge Sawyer at each recess. He was to be a major witness, of course, but perhaps he wished to assist Sawyer by interpreting and explaining the evidence as it was presented.

A parade of witnesses testified to Sarah's and Terry's antagonism and threats against Field. The spectators had heard all this many times before. Several witnesses also related unflattering remarks they had made about Judge Sawyer. With no opposing attorneys to question the competence or relevance of testimony, there were no adversary clashes to enliven the proceedings. Spectators could only assume the pertinence of evi-

With no candid camera present to record the scene, it was necessary for a contemporary journalistic artist to reconstruct the Terry-Field-Neagle confrontation in the Southern Pacific restaurant at Lathrop.

— *Bancroft Library.*

Various participants in the legal altercations between Sarah and the Senator found themselves housed from time to time in the Broadway Jail, whether for contempt of court, perjury, "obscenity," or disorderly conduct. Here Sarah composed her poem to Judge Sawyer.

— *Bancroft Library*

The old fortress-like Appraiser's Building at Sansome and Washington
Streets, San Francisco, was the scene of the loud and sometimes violent
disputes which punctuated the federal litigation in the Sharon cases. It
was in the office of the U. S. Marshal here that David Terry was disarmed
by David Neagle. — *U. S. General Services Administration.*

dence from Sawyer's apparent interest. But public interest flagged.

When it was time for Field's testimony, the courtroom was again crowded in anticipation. He walked briskly from the jury box when called and after a few introductory questions was permitted to give his testimony in narrative form. He first reviewed his judicial career, recalling that Terry as Chief Justice had sworn him in as associate on the state Supreme Court. He said that by reason of their early association, "No one knew better than Judge Terry that I would resent any personal indignity."

Apparently aware of the undercurrent of feeling that he had deliberately brought on the confrontation, Field detailed the important cases which had brought him to California that summer. The suspicion was not allayed when he told that he had gone to the dining room at Lathrop in the face of Neagle's efforts to keep him from leaving the train, adding, "I did not think what he was driving at."

He said he saw Terry rise from his table in the dining room but did not bother to watch him further, being busy eating. The next thing he was aware of was two violent blows to his head. Remaining seated, he looked around to see Terry looming over him with his fist crashing down for a third blow. He said Neagle cried, "Stop! Stop! I am an officer! Stop!"

"Instantly," Field testified, "Two shots followed," and Terry fell. "I am firmly convinced that had the marshal delayed two seconds, both he and myself would have been the victims of Terry. It was only a question of seconds whether my life or Judge Terry's life should be taken."

Next day Neagle testified to a packed courtroom. Reviewing his childhood and early career, he recalled that the boys all talked a great deal about Terry's exploits in the late 1850's. He then related the events at Lathrop much as Field had, but curiously their testimony diverged at the most crucial point. Field had said that Terry was in the act of launching another blow at him, his fist crashing down and averted only by Neagle's shots. Neagle now said that he had jumped between the men as Terry was *reaching for his knife* to attack *him*. Unfortunately with no opposing attorneys present to raise embarrassing questions, the spectators were given no explanation of the conflict in the testimony. Both Judge Sawyer and defense counsel were too circumspect to allude to it.

Field and several other witnesses had explained the necessity for Neagle's second shot by saying that Terry appeared to be unaffected by the first. Neagle's attorney, leading him toward the same explanation, asked what had happened after the first shot. Terry started to sink, said Neagle. His attorney hastily dropped the subject. The delicacy about the second shot was futile, as Neagle volunteered a few minutes later that he had been shooting to kill.

Several Lathrop diners were then called to give their recollections of the killing. Immediately after the incident, a number of people had reported it to the press, describing the blow or blows as "slaps." Strangely only one of these people was called as a witness.

When the testimony had been concluded at the end of the week, the Stockton district attorney again appeared to argue the lack of jurisdiction of the court. A week later Judge Sawyer was prepared to read his lengthy decision* to an again crowded courtroom. Field sat in the jury box, nodding sagely from time to time during the reading. Sawyer began inevitably with a review of the Sharon litigation. He then recited Field's version of the killing, following with a lengthy discussion of the law he deemed applicable to the case.

The question, he said, was whether the killing was "an act done in pursuance of a law of the United States, or an order of a court thereof." If not, Sawyer conceded, the killing could only properly be dealt with by state authorities; but if Neagle was pursuing his duties as a servant of the federal government at the time of the killing, and did not overstep the proper scope of his employment, "then we must hear him, willing or unwilling," Sawyer said. Few feared that he might be unwilling to hear the case.

---

* *In re Neagle*, 39 Fed. 833.

Sawyer acknowledged the Stockton district attorney's assertion that the question was one which the state court would have inquired into in the course of Neagle's murder trial, if permitted to do so. "This would be but to put the state to *great, useless expense*," said Sawyer with emphasis, as the scope of Neagle's authority was a question exclusively for the federal courts to determine.

His power to make the determination being settled to his satisfaction, Sawyer then turned to the question of whether Neagle had acted in pursuance of a federal law in killing Terry. After a few tentative assaults on the problem Sawyer drifted to a lengthy speculation on what might have happened had Neagle not been with Field. Had the federal government relied on the state to protect "one of their most venerable and distinguished officers," it would have "leaned upon a broken reed and there would now, in all probability, be a vacancy on the bench of one of the most august judicial tribunals in the world." That the state could not be relied on was evidenced by the fact that it now wanted to prosecute Neagle instead of arresting Sarah, "the conspirator in the contemplated murder" of Field, Sawyer said indignantly.

Sawyer reluctantly returned eventually to the question at issue, acknowledging that he could find no statute expressly justifying the killing. "So we must look to the powers and duties of sheriffs at common law." One major duty was the maintenance of order in court and the protection of his judge from outrage; but a judge could perform certain official acts in chambers, at his residence, or at any other place, Sawyer said. Could it not be said that the bailiff had a duty to protect the judge at all times and places? No one was surprised to hear him supply an affirmative answer. Therefore, he concluded, since Field could have performed judicial functions in the dining room at Lathrop, Neagle had the duty to protect him there as much as in court. The fact that Field was merely eating breakfast did not alter the matter. It was beyond question, he said, that the killing was done for Field's protection.

The only remaining question, Sawyer then said, was whether the measures taken by Neagle were excessive. "When the *de-*

ceased left his seat, walked *stealthily* down the passage in the rear of Justice Field, and dealt the unsuspecting jurist two preliminary blows, doubtless by way of reminding him that the *time for vengeance* had at last come," Neagle "with abundant reason" felt the killing was the only recourse, said Sawyer, with emphasis.

Perhaps uneasy over the absence of testimony that Terry had been stealthy and recalling Neagle's testimony that Terry had paused for several seconds behind Field while Neagle merely stared at him, and probably recalling the local talk that Field had wanted the confrontation, Sawyer felt that italicizing alone might not convince, so he further supported his conclusion in a way unique in the annals of jurisprudence. "The almost universal *consensus* of public opinion of the United States," he declared, "seems to justify the act." Thus the rule of the Roman arena was called upon — newspaper editorials supplanting thumbs — in aid of his decision.

He conceded that public opinion was not undivided, mentioning an Eastern law journal "ordinarily entitled to great consideration and respect." But he admonished, "It is not for scholarly gentlemen of humane and peaceful instincts — gentlemen who in all probability never in their lives saw a desperate man of stalwart frame and great strength in murderous action — it is not for them, sitting securely in their libraries three thousand miles away, looking backward over the scene, to determine the exact point of time when a man in Neagle's situation should fire at his assailant in order to be justified by the law. It is not for them to say that the proper time had not yet come. To such, the proper time would never come."

Sawyer brought his decision to a close after revelling in some more pious indignation at the state, saying that Neagle's killing of Terry was not merely justifiable, it was "commendable. Let him be discharged."

Field immediately sprang from the jury box to shake hands with Neagle, standing at the counsel table with his half dozen attorneys. Field had foreseen the outcome and presented Neagle with a package which contained a gold watch bearing an engraved inscription saying in part, "With appreciation, in great peril."

Neagle smiled deprecatingly.

Field left for Oregon that evening, in the company of two bodyguards.

✓   ✓   ✓

The state attorney general appealed the portion of Sawyer's decision which held that the state had no power of control over the acts of federal employees in Neagle's situation. The United States Supreme Court rejected the appeal six months later.* Field again circumspectly declined to take part in the decision. The majority of the Court determined that Sawyer was right in ordering Neagle's release, but for a reason that had not occurred to Sawyer. Commencing with the now traditional "history of the incidents which led to the tragic event," the Court reviewed everything from the filing of the Senator's injunction suit in 1883 on down to the killing itself, which it characterized as so extraordinary as to be without exact precedent.

It followed with a summary of many remarkable cases which did not quite fit the situation nor provide the answer the Court was seeking. Finding no judicial precedent, it turned to federal statutes for the answer, and found one which provided that United States marshals had the same power in executing laws of the United States as local enforcement officials had in executing local laws. How did this general provision help? California law provided that county sheriffs were obliged to "preserve the peace." A man assaulting a Justice of the United States was obviously disturbing the peace of the United States. Moreover, the United States Attorney General had expressly commanded that Neagle protect Field from assault. Hence, Neagle was acting in purusuance of his duties in killing Terry and his exoneration by Sawyer was proper.

The Chief Justice and one associate dissented in an opinion which was concise but almost as lengthy as that of the majority. They declared that the propriety of Neagle's conduct and his innocence or guilt of crime was immaterial to the issues presented. It was elementary that a prisoner in custody of a state court could not compel his release through a writ of *habeas*

---

* *In re Neagle,* 135 U.S. 1.

corpus simply upon the claim that he had committed no crime
or that the state court might make a mistake in the course of
his prosecution. The rule applied to federal employees as well
as ordinary citizens, the dissenters said. One who kills another
human being has the burden of showing the authority by which
the deed was done. In pursuance of what law, they asked, was
Neagle acting when he killed Terry? They professed to be
unable to find the answer in the majority opinion or after analysis of the cases relied on by the majority. Congress had the
exclusive power to enact laws, and the majority holding that
the Attorney General could by order adopt a special or private
law for a particular situation could work the most profound and
baneful havoc on the Constitution and on the institutions which
had developed pursuant to it, they said. Nor had judges the
inherent power unilaterally to order the death of a human being
while granting immunity to the executioner. The right must be
traced to legislative enactment or it did not exist.

"It is a noteworthy fact in our history," said the dissenters,
"that whenever the exigencies of the country, from time to time,
have required the exercise of executive and judicial power for
the enforcement of the supreme authority of the United States
government for the protection of its agencies, it was found
in every instance necessary to invoke the interposition of the
power of the national legislature." So, in 1833, President Jackson
had requested and received a special act to aid in the enforcement of collection of federal revenues in the port of Charleston,
though the revenue law together with all of the President's
traditional powers already existed. How then, the dissenters
asked, could Field, with or without the approval of the Attorney
General, give his bodyguard's action the force of law?

The dissenters also rejected the proposition that the bailiff's
traditional duty to keep order in the court justified the killing.
Even assuming that this general provision empowered the marshal to kill a person under extreme circumstances in court, this
could not be extended to a dining room many miles removed.
"In the first place, the judge is not the court. The person does
not embody the tribunal, nor does the tribunal follow him on
his journeys." Hence, Terry's actions, even if criminal, did not
constitute a contempt of court.

Assuming the facts to be as Neagle and Field related them, said the dissenters, Neagle no doubt had the right to defend Field from attack, but only as any other private citizen had the same right. Field was merely Citizen Field in the incident in question. If Terry had killed Field would that have been a crime against the United States? Obviously not, the dissenters declared, for murder was not a federal crime except on the high seas, in the territories and other specifically limited places. Similarly the killing of Terry was not by authority of any federal law, and the only proper authority to inquire into it was the state court.

The dissent closed with an expression of concern that the majority decision would blur federal-state relationships by placing in doubt the power of local authority to maintain order by "divesting them of what was once regarded as their exclusive jurisdiction over crimes committed within their own territory against their own laws, and depriving a state of its power to maintain its own public order, or to protect the security of society and lives of its own citizens." The dissenters said they had no doubt that "the authorities of the state of California are competent and willing to do justice and that, even if [Neagle] had been indicted and had gone to trial upon this record, God and his country would have given him a good deliverance."

No one would ever know for sure, as Sawyer had taken the precaution of intervening on His behalf.

✓   ✓   ✓

Sarah had attended none of the Neagle hearings, but was required to appear in another department of the federal court while it was in progress. She and Terry were not in San Francisco on the 14th, of course, to answer the criminal charges pending against them, and the judge had rescheduled Sarah's case. The small audience in Judge Hoffman's court was dismayed at Sarah's condition. She appeared to have slept and eaten very little in the week since Terry's death, and had abandoned any concern for her grooming. She spent her whole time in court with her head on her folded arms on the table, sobbing. The case was again postponed, and reporters, who had been unable to learn where she was, followed her from court though she refused to speak to anyone. She was apparently staying at a hotel alone. She would not admit reporters, but could be heard pacing her room and crying most of the night and the following day.

The same day attorneys for the Senator's estate requested one of Judge Sullivan's associates on the Superior Court to dismiss the divorce case, which had now been sent back by the state Supreme Court for retrial. The judge granted Sarah ten days in which to show cause why the dismissal should not be granted.

Chapter XXI FINAL COURT ACTION

HE SUPERIOR COURT at the City Hall heard argument on the motion to dismiss the divorce case while the Neagle hearing was in progress. Attorneys for the Sharon estate argued that as the Senator was now dead there could no longer be any marriage, hence no right to a divorce and no purpose in a retrial of the case. Sarah's attorney, W. T. Baggett, who had been associated with Terry on the last stages of the appeal and now was the sole attorney representing her, argued that the suit was not merely for divorce but would determine Sarah's community property and inheritance rights as the Senator's widow, and that his death could not preclude litigating that issue. After several weeks' deliberation, the court rejected the motion to dismiss the case and set it for trial the following July, 1890.

The appeal Barnes had taken from Judge Sullivan's order for payment of accumulated alimony and court costs lay dormant for some time in the state Supreme Court but was finally decided a few days before the divorce was to be retried.*

Sarah's attorney had pointed out that temporary alimony was intended to provide support for a wife pending the outcome of the trial, and that courts had always held that such an award as it became due was a debt which must be paid regardless of the outcome of the case, even though the court might ultimately conclude that there had been no valid marriage. The alimony order had been based on the Supreme Court decision reducing alimony to five hundred dollars per month. So, he argued, Sarah was only seeking that alimony to which the Supreme Court itself had declared her to be entitled.

---

* *Sharon* v. *Sharon*, 84 Cal. 424 (23 Pac. 1100).

The attorney for the estate conceded the proposition but urged again as on the earlier appeal, that the state courts were required to honor the federal injunction and deny Sarah any relief, even including the accumulated alimony payments.

The question in this "peculiar case" the Court now agreed was which court first obtained jurisdiction of the subject matter? As the Senator had filed his federal action against Sarah in October, 1883, a month before the divorce suit was filed, that case must prevail, the state Supreme Court now declared, regardless of when the respective trials were had or the final decisions rendered. Sarah's attorney rejoined that the federal injunction was against Sarah alone and was not binding on the judges of the state. But the Court held that comity prevented it from "lending itself as an instrument in permitting a contempt of the process" of another court.

The Court thus finally abandoned its previous consistent refusal to countenance the proposition that it had to defer to the federal litigation and held that the federal judgment prohibited any further action. It was the final word the state Court would write on the subject. The Court at the same time reversed the judgment which had been entered against the Senator's sureties on the original appeal, as there was now no debt for them to guarantee.*

Sarah had remained in virtual seclusion throughout the months intervening until the time for the retrial of the divorce case arrived. On that day Baggett again appeared for Sarah and W. F. Herrin now replaced Barnes for the estate, though Barnes attended as a spectator. He and Sarah were the only participants in the original trial who were present now, and the audience was reduced proportionately, being little larger than on any ordinary court day.

Sarah's altered appearance matched the change in the trial proceeding. She had aged greatly in the intervening nine months, and no longer gave any care to her grooming or dress. The trial before Judge Shafter, one of Sullivan's associates, was completed in one day. The estate attorney opened the trial by

---

* *Sharon* v. *Sharon*, 84 Cal. 433 (23 Pac. 1102).

vowing that he would have Sarah held in contempt and jailed by the federal court if she attempted to use the marriage contract in support of her case; and the judge, following the example of the state Supreme Court a few days earlier, yielded to the federal decree and banned use of the marriage contract in the trial. But Sarah could not have offered the contract in evidence had she wanted to. It had been destroyed in a fire at Terry's Fresno ranch the previous year.

Sarah was asked to produce the "Dear Wife" letters, however, and she reacted as she always had, reluctantly drawing them from a musty and battered box and handing the tattered papers over for inspection. Tortuous attempts by Sarah's attorney to elicit testimony to prove the marriage without the written contract consumed the greater part of the day. Sarah seemed to lack the will or the understanding to cooperate. She continually alluded to the contract, and at length all of her testimony was stricken. The transcript of testimony at the first trial was then submitted to the judge with the stipulation that he might consider it as though the testimony was now being produced before him. After taking the case under submission for only a day or two, Judge Shafter ruled that as the case was based entirely on the written contract he was compelled to enter judgment and costs against Sarah and in favor of the Senator's estate, and he did so forthwith.

With that decision ("derision," the *Chronicle* reported, in one of its rare misprints) the last of Sarah's attorneys abandoned the case as hopeless. But not so with Sarah. She spent the next two months trying on her own to get an appeal transcript in order. Finally on the afternoon of the last day permitted by law, she appeared in the County Clerk's office in the City Hall to file the appeal record. She was told that the transcript she had prepared must be compared with the original and certified as correct before it could be transmitted to the Supreme Court. Several clerks were assigned to the seemingly impossible task, Sarah running agitatedly from one to the other, crying, "Hurry, hurry! You must hurry. The time is almost up. I will miss it. Hurry!"

Nineteen minutes before closing time the long transcript was corrected, compared, and certified as accurate. Sarah was about to rush out to file it when she was told that she must first serve a copy on the opposition. Only slightly more distraught than she had been, she unhesitatingly started out from Civic Center to go downtown to Barnes' financial district office. Perspiration streamed from her face and her hair lay damply matted on her forehead in the sweltering heat of the autumn afternoon sun.

Much to the surprise of waiting newsmen and the idly curious who had lingered at the City Hall, she managed to deliver a copy to Barnes and return in a remarkably short time. She got back only fifteen minutes after public offices had closed.

The Sharon case had irretrievably reached its end.

Chapter XXII EPILOGUE

HE Senator had escaped the litigation when it was at its height, and Terry had been removed as it neared its end. Death took the other principal actors in the drama, one by one. Tyler continued to refuse payment to Hogan, but regularly petitioned the state Supreme Court for reinstatement as an attorney. He died in 1895, after a brief illness, unaware that his most recent application had been rejected a few days before. Barnes, Field, Sawyer, Sullivan, Neagle, and the others in due time went to their various rewards, Field after achieving the distinction of serving on the United States Supreme Court longer than any man before or since.

In 1906 even the inanimate players were abruptly brought to an ignominious end as the City Hall and the Grand Hotel, crumbled in the great earthquake, and the Palace was gutted by the flames which followed.

The recorded decisions of the judges who found themselves entangled in the Sharon disputes became woven into the law of the land. They remain today a permanent if tattered heritage of judicial fabric; for a large part of the law is formed on what courts have said when confronted with similar problems on prior occasions.

As precedents, the declarations of these judges have enjoyed varying success. Attorneys have freely cited them on a wide variety of subjects, but judges have not always found them convenient to follow. Some of the decisions, indeed, have been disapproved, "distinguished," or "explained" as often as they have been followed. Some have had the rare distinction of being relied on by opposing sides for contrary propositions. Scruti-

nized and cited hundreds of times over the years, they still give
no evidence of soon falling into disuse.

Two soldiers, for example, at the turn of the century, were
arrested on charges of murder and manslaughter in Pittsburgh,
Pennsylvania, where they had been detailed to prevent thefts
and vandalism at the United States Arsenal. In the process
of apprehending thieves, they shot and killed one, and were
charged with murder in the state court. The United States
Attorney General, relying on Neagle's deliverance, confidently
asked the federal courts to intervene to prevent the trial. The
Supreme Court refused, saying "We ought not to encourage the
interference of the federal court with the regular course of justice in the state court," nor "wrest petitioners from the custody
of state officers in advance of trial in the state courts." The
Neagle case was "extraordinary" and "exceptional," the Court
decided, and rejected it in favor of an earlier decision which
had been urged by Sarah's supporters and which the dissenting
justices had likewise considered controlling. Perhaps one reason
for the apparent inconsistency lay in the fact that Chief Justice
Fuller, one of the Neagle dissenters, was author of this later
opinion.*

Again, shortly before the United States entered World War
II a West Coast labor leader was angered by an anticipated
California court decision. He strongly criticized the expected
decision and predicted extensive labor strife and shipping tie-
ups in West Coast ports. This he voiced in a telegram to the
Secretary of Labor and to the press. The judge whose decision
was criticized held him in contempt. The state Supreme Court
agreed that he was punishable, pointing to Tyler's contempt
punishment for writing the scurrilous letter to the Grand Jury.**
The United States Supreme Court reversed the order, holding
that it violated the constitutional guarantee of freedom of
speech and of the press.*** Justice Frankfurter dissented, declaring that courts had the inherent power to protect themselves against intimidation and that freedom of speech should

---

* *Drury* v. *Lewis*, 200 U.S. 1.
** *Bridges* v. *Superior Court*, 14 Cal. 2d 464.
*** *Bridges* v. *California*, 314 U.S. 252.

not be used as a shield for abuse of the courts. He cited the Terry contempt decision as authority.

President Truman ordered seizure of the nation's steel mills in April 1952 to avert a threatened strike. The mill owners appealed to the Supreme Court to declare the President's action unconstitutional. The Attorney General, on behalf of the President, quoted the provision of the Constitution directing him to "take care that the laws be faithfully executed" and reminded the Court of its interpretation of that clause in the Neagle case. Then the Court had held that the Attorney General was empowered to order Neagle to guard Field and that such order made the subsequent killing lawful. This time the majority of the Court held that Congress had not given the President such power by statute and that the power could not be implied. A concurring opinion declared that the long-standing rule first voiced by Chief Justice Marshall had not been changed by the Neagle case. No executive order could "legalize an act which without those instructions would have been a plain trespass."*

One of the country's worst air collisions occurred at 8:30 a.m. April 21, 1958, involving a commercial airplane with 42 passengers and a military craft. All aboard both planes were killed. The heirs of the victims lived in widely scattered parts of the country, suing separately to recover their losses. After several had succeeded in obtaining judgment against the airline in California, others with cases pending elsewhere petitioned their courts to give them judgment on the ground that the California case had established liability. The airline pointed out that the California judgment, pending appeal, was not final. It cited *Sharon* v. *Hill* on the proposition that a court is not bound by another court's action on the same subject matter until judgment is final. But the Court rejected the argument.**

✓   ✓   ✓

Sarah rivalled the durability of the judicial declarations. She withdrew from public attention after Terry's death, and except for her abortive appeal attempt, she was for a time rarely seen

---

* *Youngstown* v. *Sawyer*, 343 U.S. 579.
** *United States* v. *United Air Lines*, 216 Fed. Sup. 709.

and her actions were little noted. Most of her time was spent alone in Stockton at the Terry home but she occasionally went to San Francisco where, unannounced, she would visit various friends briefly and then restlessly move on.

She was back in the lead articles of the papers sixteen months after the final loss of the divorce case. The headlines on St. Valentine's Day, 1892, read "HOPELESSLY INSANE."

She had begun hearing voices and being directed by spirits, and had arrived in San Francisco a few days earlier by steamer from Stockton, seeking refuge in the home of a friend. A doctor called to examine her reported that she was insane but not dangerous to herself or to others; she was apparently entirely rational in everyday matters.

Reporters permitted to interview her were shocked by the still greater changes which time had wrought. Her disordered hair was streaked with gray, her forehead was wrinkled and her dark-ringed eyes deeply sunken. Only her look of determination still lingered. The family with whom she was staying said that she never slept and she ate very little, spending most of her time sitting with her legs drawn up and a handkerchief pressed to her ear, through which she received messages from another world. Most of her conversations with spirits, which she carried on in disregard of others in the room, concerned children and flowers and other pleasant things — never the events of the past years.

Sarah appeared to be aware that she was ill and repeatedly said that she must get well in order to attend to her lawsuits. She at times even appeared to be amused by her hallucinations, and related that one night at the ranch near Fresno she had been awakened by Terry's voice telling her to meet the midnight train to aid a dear friend who was ill aboard. She said she had protested because of the hour and inconvenience, but had finally submitted to his request. Upon boarding the train she had walked its entire length and the only ill person was a stranger with asthma, she laughed.

The next day's headlines read "SARAH DISAPPEARS" and reported that she had told her attending doctor that morning that she wished fresh air and wanted to take a walk. She had seemed rational so he permitted her to go out alone. She had not returned.

The doctor reported that the only danger was that she had a severe cold which could easily develop into pneumonia but that she had already survived conditions which would kill a dozen people and probably could endure that. He said the cold had been brought on because Sarah, complaining frequently of great heat in her head, would pour any available water over herself, even while fully clothed and would then remain in the same sopping clothing until someone urged her to change. Mammy Pleasant was reported to be supplying Sarah's wardrobe but was tiring of having so many expensive costumes ruined by her eccentricities.

"MRS. TERRY IS FOUND," the following day's headline reported. Sarah had been discovered at Mammy's house, and the *Chronicle* reporter, finding Sarah and Mammy about to start on an evening stroll, walked with them. After a few blocks, Sarah said she was tired and wanted to take a streetcar, but as soon as they boarded she wanted to alight. She walked to the steps of the nearest house and sat down to rest and talk, pleading an attack of nausea.

The reporter was struck by the fact that he was interviewing under such circumstances the woman whose name at one time was familiar to the whole civilized world, and who had had more sensational experiences than perhaps any other woman alive. Sarah answered his questions pleasantly, but nervously and somewhat erratically. She spoke clearly and rationally for a time about her activities in recent days, mentioning by name the many friends she had seen and who had visited her, but then said she had sought sanctuary with Mammy because the other friends with whom she had been staying had been trying to pour electricity on her and she feared she would be put in a trance and buried as dead. But she said, laughing as engagingly as ever, she had foiled the plot by spending all of her time sitting on the marble top of the dresser, "and marble being a non-conductor, their electricity could not touch me."

Asked about her future, she said she was selling everything in Fresno and would move back to San Francisco. She might pursue her long-standing plan to be an actress, or she might adopt spiritualism and give public exhibitions of her medium-istic powers.

Having walked back to Mammy's home, Sarah skipped lightly up the steps. She said that no one need bother about her welfare, and Mammy agreed, saying that Sarah was neither sick nor crazy.

Several nights later, passers-by were startled to see a woman at the corner of Post and Kearny Streets in the heart of San Francisco's business district, heedless of a driving rain, with dripping hat and ulster, wading back and forth in the gutter. Occasionally she would step up onto the curbing, stamp her feet, stare at the muddy swirling water, and then step back in to repeat the performance.

Several people muttered that she ought to be put away, but no one seemed to recognize her as Sarah. She finally became alarmed at the attention she was attracting and walked to a nearby restaurant where she took a table, her clothes still streaming. She had a fifteen cent bowl of soup and then asked the waitress to lend her a dollar with which to pay for it, offering a gold watch with the monogram "S.A.H., 1879" as security.

The waitress, pitying the unknown derelict, made the loan but tried to decline the watch.

"You must take it to oblige me," said Sarah. "I do not wish you to give me money without proper security."

She then attempted to get a room at a small hotel over the restaurant. When the clerk learned her name he left to consult others while Sarah played the piano in the lobby. On his return she was refused a room and no one knew where she spent the night.

The next day she returned to the restaurant to redeem her watch, and permitted an enterprising *Chronicle* reporter, who had stationed himself there, to join her at lunch. At his invitation she read the newspaper accounts of her previous night's activities, laughing occasionally, and asked him if he thought she was crazy.

"No, indeed, Madame, I do not," he replied with sincerity.

"Maybe we're all crazy," Sarah said, smilingly shyly. "I've been married twice and I ought to be able to take care of myself." Two nicely dressed young women waved to her at that moment, and she walked out with them in animated and cheerful conversation.

Sarah's friends were reported to be equally divided on her sanity; many were looking for her, hoping to be able to care for her. She proved elusive, however, and except for what they read in the newspapers, her friends knew nothing of her activities. A reporter happened on her one evening several days later and found her well dressed, looking much better. She was in the company of another woman of equally attractive appearance, with whom she was looking for rooms for the night. But when her identity was learned every hotel refused her. She finally wandered into the Palace. As she passed the entrance to the Grand Court and heard the strains of the orchestra she hesitated, listening a moment, then swayed, and placing her hand to her heart she wheeled about and quickly left.

Several days later a reporter again picked up her trail as she wandered aimlessly through downtown churches and the hotels with which she was familiar, the Baldwin and the Grand, but not the Palace. Finally, as she paused on a bench in Union Square, the reporter tried to talk with her but, saying that some of the newspapers were trying to have her hypnotized, she put a stick to her ear and began communicating with spirits. (Her reference to the newspaper hypnotism was not as irrational as it sounded. One enterprising newspaper had in fact offered to pay her for an interview to be held while she was under hypnosis.)

She was reported to have managed to get a hotel room late one night by the ruse of having another woman register for her; but when she was discovered at seven o'clock the next morning she was ejected on the ground that other guests feared she would set fire to the building. Unwilling to go to her friends but unable to find lodging by herself, Sarah for some time spent her nights wandering in downtown parks, sitting on curbs or on park benches. She generally carried balled up electrical wire or some like burden.

Finally March 9, of that year, 1892, Mammy Pleasant had Sarah arrested on an insanity petition and the last curious co-incidence of the many intersecting convolutions of the Sharon affair was unfolded. When she was taken into court for arraignment, her clothing mud-caked and disheveled, the presiding judge was Levy, one of her earliest attorneys in the divorce trial, who had been appointed to the court while the case was still in progress. Levy set the sanity hearing for the following day and Mammy accompanied Sarah to the Inebriate Asylum, where she was to spend the night.

The next day, the last Sarah would ever appear in court, was of the kind she had grown accustomed to. Over a thousand people were on hand that morning at the Inebriate Asylum to see her off to court. Mammy had provided her with another new dress and she looked very presentable. The chief physician reported that she had eaten both her dinner and breakfast and was in good spirits. He predicted that with renewal of regular habits she would be normal in ninety days, saying that her condition was caused entirely by lack of nourishment and sleep.

The courtroom generally used for sanity hearings was too small to accommodate even a fraction of the crowd that wanted to attend, and court was reconvened in a larger room. A number of witnesses were called to relate Sarah's peculiar behavior in recent weeks, Mammy attempting to whisper her testimony to the judge to avoid upsetting Sarah, who had requested an attorney and was provided one, but examined most of the witnesses herself. The court-appointed physician testified that Sarah was insane. She cross-examined him with great zest. After getting him thoroughly muddled on various dates and events she concluded, "And you think I ought to be sent to an asylum?"

"I do, most assuredly, Mrs. Terry."

"Well, Doctor, don't you think that if you were examined pretty closely, some of these people would believe that you ought to be there?"

Judge Levy did not require the doctor to answer, and cutting off further testimony, adjudged Sarah insane, committing her to the state asylum in Stockton.

On being removed from court Sarah did not seem to be immediately aware of her destination but smiled appreciatively

at the crowd on the sidewalk and in the street, and confided
to one of her guards that "the people" had always liked her. On
the ferry boat crossing the bay she said to a group of startled
fellow passengers, "Gentlemen, I am Mrs. Judge Terry. I am
being abducted. These people are carrying me away to lock me
up somewhere and I appeal to you to release me."

A reporter interviewed her during the trip and she told him,
"Mammy Pleasant did that. She caused my arrest because I had
detectives watching her house one night."

"Oh, no," said the reporter, placatingly, "Mammy is your
good friend; you mustn't feel like that."

"No she isn't," said Sarah. "There was something wrong up
there and I got on to it. I'll tell it to you some day. It will come
out. To keep me from revealing it she is going to have me
locked up." (Sarah in all likelihood did know a number of
things about Mammy that Mammy would prefer not to have
generally known, but that did not change the case for Sarah's
commitment.)

Across the bay, Sarah became excited and had to be put
forcibly on the train for Stockton. Once on board, however, she
was in good spirits, laughing about the effort required to get
her aboard. She amused herself on the trip by engaging her
guards and other passengers in arm wrestling and other feats of
strength. She seemed oblivious as the train passed through
Lathrop, but at Stockton she pretended it was Lathrop and
addressed the crowd which had assembled to meet the train,
speaking at some length about Terry's cowardly slaying.

Given a tour of the asylum and introduction to the staff she
was calm, simply saying, "Are you satisfied? I suppose you are
satisfied now that you have got me in the asylum."

She immediately became the asylum's celebrity, and for a
time received many visitors, both personal friends and people
from public life. As time passed friends died and interest in the
Sharon case waned. Eventually years would pass with no visitors, and her only guests were journalists hoping to find material
and occasional lawyers and law students. She was always polite
but gave them little satisfaction, as she was unwilling — or un-

able — to discuss anything connected with the celebrated litigation.

She was never considered to be a danger to herself or others and was soon given the free use of the grounds, where she could be seen wearing her once beautiful Victorian costumes and large hats. She exhibited anger only once, when the last tattered remnant of her former wardrobe was taken from her to be destroyed many years after her commitment. But she apologized for her unladylike conduct before the day was out.

Her principal entertainment was the monthly party held for the patients. She always presided, in the belief or pretense that the functions were held in her honor, ordering ambrosial French dinners and asking that her carriage be brought at their conclusion; but she was never offended when neither the dinners nor the carriage appeared.

She was liked, even loved, by both staff and patients and was of a generous nature. For a number of years she took pleasure in writing checks for large sums on any handy scrap of paper, giving them to staff and fellow patients, and enjoyed having her checks sent to the hospital laundry to be put at random in the trouser pocket of some lucky male patient.

On most subjects her mind remained clear and she spoke intelligently and amusingly on a wide variety of topics. On the other hand, she occasionally told visitors that she had formerly been Attorney General, or that she was the director of the hospital. But she would then peer at her auditor with her still bright, shrewd eyes and chuckle quietly so that one could never tell whether she was delusional or merely curious to see the reaction the assertions brought.

Having survived all of the other participants in the events of the 1880's, she died in the Stockton Asylum on St. Valentine's Day, February 14, 1937, never having left in the 45 years of her commitment.

The answers to a number of questions died with her. But the litigation which she inspired remains as an enduring if accidental legacy. The law of divorce, contempt of court, grand jury powers, habeas corpus, and federal-state relationships all bear the indelible birthmark peculiar to the progeny of Sarah and the Senator.

Index